Survival

GLOBAL POLITICS AND STRATEGY

Volume 62 Number 2 | April–May 202

T0081363

'The existential nature of the risk to democratic regimes in the medium term, and to all states in the long term, means that climate change, unlike other phenomena on which "war" has been declared, can legitimately be considered a vital issue of national security.'

Anatol Lieven, Climate Change and the State: A Case for Environmental Realism, p. 10.

'Both directly and indirectly, the place of democracy in the making of strategy – through the active participation of the citizen soldier or through the indirect contribution of the enfranchised taxpayer – had been marginalised by the beginning of the twenty-first century.'

Hew Strachan, Strategy and Democracy, p. 68.

'It would make sense to create within the Atlantic Alliance a consultative body, supported by substantial administrative machinery, to scrutinise all aspects of China policy carrying demonstrable implications for the security and defence of NATO's members, jointly and severally.'

François Heisbourg, NATO 4.0: The Atlantic Alliance and the Rise of China, p. 96.

Survival

GLOBAL POLITICS AND STRATEGY

Volume 62 Number 2 | April–May 2020

Contents

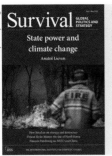

Survival GLOBAL POLITICS AND STRATEGY

State power and climate change

Anatol Lieven

On the cover
A firefighter monitors a bush fire on the outskirts of Bilpin, Australia, on 19 December 2019.

On the web
Visit www.iiss.org/ publications/survival for brief notices on new books on Politics and International Relations, the Middle East, Environment and Resources, and the United States.

***Survival* editors' blog**
For ideas and commentary from *Survival* editors and contributors, visit www.iiss.org/blogs/ survival-blog.

Survival

GLOBAL POLITICS AND STRATEGY

The International Institute for Strategic Studies

2121 K Street, NW | Suite 801 | Washington DC 20037 | USA
Tel +1 202 659 1490   Fax +1 202 659 1499   E-mail survival@iiss.org   Web www.iiss.org

Arundel House | 6 Temple Place | London | WC2R 2PG | UK
Tel +44 (0)20 7379 7676   Fax +44 (0)20 7836 3108   E-mail iiss@iiss.org

14th Floor, GBCorp Tower | Bahrain Financial Harbour | Manama | Kingdom of Bahrain
Tel +973 1718 1155   Fax +973 1710 0155   E-mail iiss-middleeast@iiss.org

9 Raffles Place | #51-01 Republic Plaza | Singapore 048619
Tel +65 6499 0055   Fax +65 6499 0059   E-mail iiss-asia@iiss.org

Survival Online www.tandfonline.com/survival and www.iiss.org/publications/survival

Aims and Scope *Survival* is one of the world's leading forums for analysis and debate of international and strategic affairs. Shaped by its editors to be both timely and forward thinking, the journal encourages writers to challenge conventional wisdom and bring fresh, often controversial, perspectives to bear on the strategic issues of the moment. With a diverse range of authors, *Survival* aims to be scholarly in depth while vivid, well written and policy-relevant in approach. Through commentary, analytical articles, case studies, forums, review essays, reviews and letters to the editor, the journal promotes lively, critical debate on issues of international politics and strategy.

Editor **Dana Allin**
Managing Editor **Jonathan Stevenson**
Associate Editor **Carolyn West**
Assistant Editor **Jessica Watson**
Production and Cartography **John Buck, Kelly Verity**

Contributing Editors

Ian Bremmer	Bill Emmott	Erik Jones	'Funmi Olonisakin	Angela Stent
Rosa Brooks	Mark Fitzpatrick	Jeffrey Lewis	Thomas Rid	Ray Takeyh
David P. Calleo	John A. Gans, Jr	Hanns W. Maull	Teresita C. Schaffer	David C. Unger
Russell Crandall	John L. Harper	Jeffrey Mazo	Steven Simon	Lanxin Xiang
Toby Dodge				

Published for the IISS by
Routledge Journals, an imprint of Taylor & Francis, an Informa business.

About the IISS The IISS, a registered charity with offices in Washington, London, Manama and Singapore, is the world's leading authority on political–military conflict. It is the primary independent source of accurate, objective information on international strategic issues. Publications include *The Military Balance*, an annual reference work on each nation's defence capabilities; *Strategic Survey*, an annual review of world affairs; *Survival*, a bimonthly journal on international affairs; *Strategic Comments*, an online analysis of topical issues in international affairs; and the *Adelphi* series of books on issues of international security.

SUBMISSIONS

To submit an article, authors are advised to follow these guidelines:

- *Survival* articles are around 4,000–10,000 words long including endnotes. A word count should be included with a draft.
- All text, including endnotes, should be double-spaced with wide margins.
- Any tables or artwork should be supplied in separate files, ideally not embedded in the document or linked to text around it.
- All *Survival* articles are expected to include endnote references. These should be complete and include first and last names of authors, titles of articles (even from newspapers), place of publication, publisher, exact publication dates, volume and issue number (if from a journal) and page numbers. Web sources should include complete URLs and DOIs if available.
- A summary of up to 150 words should be included with the article. The summary should state the main argument clearly and concisely, not simply say what the article is about.

- A short author's biography of one or two lines should also be included. This information will appear at the foot of the first page of the article.

Please note that *Survival* has a strict policy of listing multiple authors in alphabetical order.

Submissions should be made by email, in Microsoft Word format, to survival@iiss.org. Alternatively, hard copies may be sent to *Survival*, IISS–US, 2121 K Street NW, Suite 801, Washington, DC 20037, USA.

The editorial review process can take up to three months. *Survival*'s acceptance rate for unsolicited manuscripts is less than 20%. *Survival* does not normally provide referees' comments in the event of rejection. Authors are permitted to submit simultaneously elsewhere so long as this is consistent with the policy of the other publication and the Editors of *Survival* are informed of the dual submission.

Readers are encouraged to comment on articles from the previous issue. Letters should be concise, no longer than 750 words and relate directly to the argument or points made in the original article.

ADVERTISING AND PERMISSIONS

For advertising rates and schedules

USA/Canada: The Advertising Manager, Taylor & Francis Inc., 530 Walnut Street, Suite 850, Philadelphia, PA 19106, USA Tel +1 (800) 354 1420 Fax +1 (215) 207 0050.

UK/Europe/Rest of World: The Advertising Manager, Routledge Journals, Taylor & Francis, 4 Park Square, Milton Park, Abingdon, Oxfordshire OX14 4RN, UK Tel +44 (0) 207 017 6000 Fax +44 (0) 207 017 6336.

SUBSCRIPTIONS

Survival is published bimonthly in February, April, June, August, October and December by Routledge Journals, an imprint of Taylor & Francis, an Informa Business.

Annual Subscription 2020

	UK, RoI	US, Canada Mexico	Europe	Rest of world
Individual	£162	$273	€ 220	$273
Institution (print and online)	£585	$1,023	€ 858	$1,076
Institution (online only)	£497	$869	€ 729	$915

Taylor & Francis has a flexible approach to subscriptions, enabling us to match individual libraries' requirements. This journal is available via a traditional institutional subscription (either print with online access, or online only at a discount) or as part of our libraries, subject collections or archives. For more information on our sales packages please visit http://www.tandfonline.com/page/librarians.

All current institutional subscriptions include online access for any number of concurrent users across a local area network to the currently available backfile and articles posted online ahead of publication.

Subscriptions purchased at the personal rate are strictly for personal, non-commercial use only. The reselling of personal subscriptions is prohibited. Personal subscriptions must be purchased with a personal cheque or credit card. Proof of personal status may be requested.

Dollar rates apply to all subscribers outside Europe. Euro rates apply to all subscribers in Europe, except the UK and the Republic of Ireland where the pound sterling rate applies. If you are unsure which rate applies to you please contact Customer Services in the UK. All subscriptions are payable in advance and all rates include postage. Journals are sent by air to the USA, Canada, Mexico, India, Japan and Australasia. Subscriptions are entered on an annual basis, i.e. January to December. Payment may be made by sterling cheque, dollar cheque, euro cheque, international money order, National Giro or credit cards (Amex, Visa and Mastercard).

Survival (USPS 013095) is published bimonthly (in Feb, Apr, Jun, Aug, Oct and Dec) by Routledge Journals, Taylor & Francis, 4 Park Square, Milton Park, Abingdon, OX14 4RN, United Kingdom.

The US annual subscription price is $1,023. Airfreight and mailing in the USA by agent named WN Shipping USA, 156-15, 146th Avenue, 2nd Floor, Jamaica, NY 11434, USA. Periodicals postage paid at Jamaica NY 11431.

US Postmaster: Send address changes to Survival, C/O Air Business Ltd / 156-15 146th Avenue, Jamaica, New York, NY11434.

Subscription records are maintained at Taylor & Francis Group, 4 Park Square, Milton Park, Abingdon, OX14 4RN, United Kingdom.

ORDERING INFORMATION

Please contact your local Customer Service Department to take out a subscription to the Journal: **USA, Canada:** Taylor & Francis, Inc., 530 Walnut Street, Suite 850, Philadelphia, PA 19106, USA. Tel: +1 800 354 1420; Fax: +1 215 207 0050. **UK/Europe/Rest of World:** T&F Customer Services, Informa UK Ltd, Sheepen Place, Colchester, Essex, CO3 3LP, United Kingdom. Tel: +44 (0) 20 7017 5544; Fax: +44 (0) 20 7017 5198; Email: subscriptions@tandf.co.uk.

Back issues: Taylor & Francis retains a two-year back issue stock of journals. Older volumes are held by our official stockists: Periodicals Service Company, 351 Fairview Ave., Suite 300, Hudson, New York 12534, USA to whom all orders and enquiries should be addressed. *Tel* +1 518 537 4700 *Fax* +1 518 537 5899 *e-mail* psc@periodicals.com *web* http://www.periodicals.com/tandf.html.

The International Institute for Strategic Studies (IISS) and our publisher Taylor & Francis make every effort to ensure the accuracy of all the information (the "Content") contained in our publications. However, the IISS and our publisher Taylor & Francis, our agents, and our licensors make no representations or warranties whatsoever as to the accuracy, completeness, or suitability for any purpose of the Content. Any opinions and views expressed in this publication are the opinions and views of the authors, and are not the views of or endorsed by the IISS and our publisher Taylor & Francis. The accuracy of the Content should not be relied upon and should be independently verified with primary sources of information. The IISS and our publisher Taylor & Francis shall not be liable for any losses, actions, claims, proceedings, demands, costs, expenses, damages, and other liabilities whatsoever or howsoever caused arising directly or indirectly in connection with, in relation to or arising out of the use of the Content. Terms & Conditions of access and use can be found at http://www.tandfonline.com/page/terms-and-conditions.

The issue date is April–May 2020.

The print edition of this journal is printed on ANSI-conforming acid-free paper.

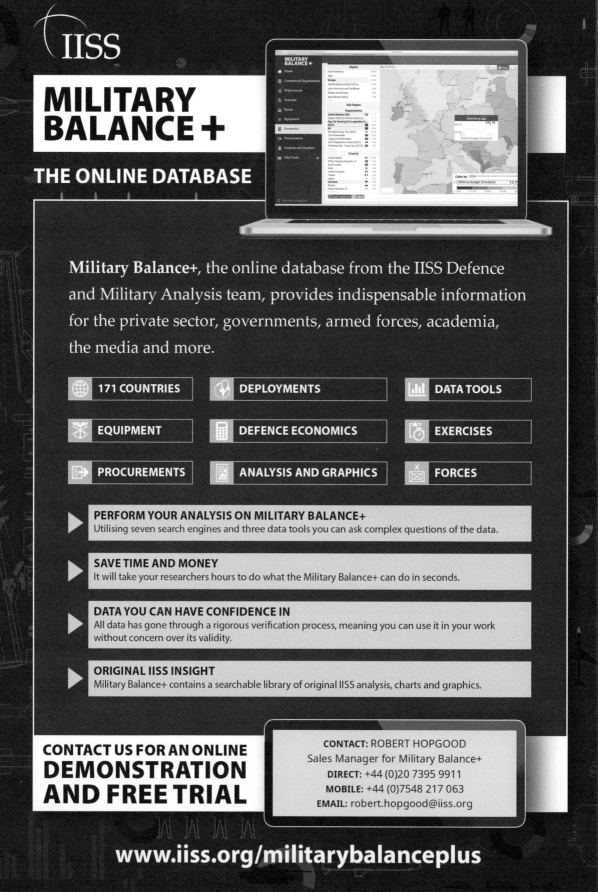

Climate Change and the State: A Case for Environmental Realism

Anatol Lieven

> On the day when the death-roll touched thirty, Dr Rieux read an official telegram which the Prefect had just handed him, remarking, 'So they've got alarmed – at last.' The telegram ran: *Proclaim a state of plague stop Close the town*.
>
> Albert Camus, *The Plague*[1]

In recent years, the internal challenges to Western liberal democracy and the early effects of climate change have both intensified drastically. In early 2020, the impact of the coronavirus outbreak added a harsh reminder of the capacity of epidemic diseases not only to kill human beings but to cause massive economic, social and political disruption.[2]

To shape an appropriate intellectual response to these challenges, security establishments need to prioritise the gravest actual threats to states. Furthermore, proponents of human security (and the environmentalists among them in particular) need to understand the central importance of states, and state legitimacy and strength, to any efforts to limit climate change, to maintain Western democracy, and to defend the lives and well-being of Western citizens.[3]

Anatol Lieven is a professor at Georgetown University in Qatar and a senior fellow of the New America Foundation in Washington DC. His latest book, on which this essay is based, is *Climate Change and the Nation State: The Realist Case* (Allen Lane and Oxford University Press, 2020).

Survival | vol. 62 no. 2 | April–May 2020 | pp. 7–26   DOI 10.1080/00396338.2020.1739945

Climate change as a security threat

Since anything that has the ability to end human lives could potentially be seen as a security threat, the first thing to note about climate change and its associated effects is the number of casualties they are likely to cause. The threats posed by climate change should be divided between the long term (from 2100 CE) and the short to medium term, as much intellectual and political confusion stems from mixing up the two. In the long run, if the rise in global temperatures continues unchecked and leads to runaway climate change, human civilisation itself will be destroyed, except perhaps for a very lucky, very rich and very small minority of humans, or possibly genetically engineered post-humans. The long-term threat is thus existential in the clearest sense of that term.

In the short to medium term, the direct effects of climate change in Western democracies will be more limited, though still acutely unpleasant, as heatwaves and wildfires in California, southern Europe and Australia already demonstrate. The direct effects of heat alone will almost certainly kill far more people than all but the greatest wars. Even before climate change really kicked in, a heatwave in Europe in 2003 killed some 35,000 Europeans, more than the number of French casualties in the eight years of the Algerian War.[4] A Russian heatwave in 2010, compounded with the effects of smoke inhalation from forest fires that same year, killed at least 41,000 people – twice as many as the number of Russians who died during the ten-year Soviet intervention in Afghanistan.[5] The continuous rise in global temperatures over the past 20 years indicates that in many places, heatwaves are going to get far worse and more frequent – not in some distant future, but in the next two decades.[6]

The indirect effects of climate change can also be deadly. Wildfires in Greece in July 2018 killed 102 people, and fires in Australia that started in 2019 had killed more than 30 people by February 2020. The eventual effects of smoke inhalation – for a week in early January, Canberra had the worst air quality in the world[7] – will cause many more deaths. Tropical diseases will spread, possibly reaching epidemic proportions. The coronavirus epidemic of 2020 originating in China, though not itself linked to climate change, is a warning of just how much diseases can harm even highly developed societies.[8]

The economic, social and political effects of the coronavirus on the Chinese economy and governance demonstrate that identifying a security threat is not simply a matter of counting the number of dead. As Richard Ullman has written:

> A threat to national security is an action or a sequence of events that (1) threatens drastically and over a relatively brief period of time to degrade the quality of life for the inhabitants of a state, or (2) threatens significantly to narrow the range of policy choices available to a state or to private, non-governmental entities (persons, groups, corporations) within the state.[9]

In Europe, the most dramatic direct effects of even relatively modest global warming will be seen in the Mediterranean, where the summer is predicted to last for an additional month, heatwaves (with temperatures over 35°C) to be extended by more than a month and rainfall to decrease by up to 20%.[10] The results will include severe damage to the region's agriculture and tourism, the radical transformation of ecosystems towards semi-arid conditions and greatly increased wildfires. Runaway climate change would lead to the complete desertification of the region.

Climate change is bound to increase migration, especially to southern Europe, from badly affected areas in Africa and Asia, though by how much we do not know. Yet migration is helping to undermine the political unity of Western states at a time when such unity is necessary to adopt climate-change policies that will involve sacrifices by national populations.[11] Every opinion poll on the motivations of those who have supported Brexit, Donald Trump or nationalist parties in Western Europe has pointed to anxiety over immigration as a principal factor.[12] With a backlash against migration clearly under way, the only question is how much worse it will get. Moreover, mass migration to the West is likely to coincide with greatly intensified automation of the economy, including the development of some kinds of artificial intelligence. If present patterns continue, many forms of employment, including new ones, are likely to be lower in pay, job security and status than those destroyed by automation. Not just the working classes but sections of the middle classes as well are likely to be badly affected.[13]

For too many unskilled or semi-skilled migrants, poor, insecure jobs are the only ones available. These jobs trap migrants and their descendants in impoverished ghettos, from which bad schools, crime, low property prices and social isolation make it very difficult to escape. At the same time, native-born members of the working classes are competing with migrants for the same low-quality jobs.[14] Thus, climate change will worsen current threats to liberal-democratic legitimacy in the West by amplifying the problems created by economic stagnation, social inequality and above all migration (or, perhaps more accurately, the negative reaction to migration among some citizens). These problems do not pose an existential threat to Western states as such, but they certainly do imperil existing Western political orders.

The existential nature of the risk to democratic regimes in the medium term, and to all states in the long term, means that climate change, unlike other phenomena on which 'war' has been declared, can legitimately be considered a vital issue of national security. Barry Buzan and his colleagues wrote back in 1998:

> The need is to construct a conceptualisation of security that means something more specific than just any threat or problem. Threats and vulnerabilities can arise in many different areas, military and non-military, but to count as security issues they have to meet strictly defined criteria that distinguish them from the normal run of the merely political. They have to be staged as *existential threats* to a referent object by a securitising actor who thereby generates endorsement of emergency measures beyond rules that would otherwise bind.[15]

It is not unheard of for states to securitise their response to natural disasters, both in terms of organising relief efforts and in adopting measures to prevent criminal activity, such as looting. The role of the US Army Corps of Engineers in disaster prevention and relief is a case in point. As the quote from Albert Camus at the start of this essay suggests, disease epidemics have also been treated as a security issue through the proclamation of a state of plague (in effect, a form of martial law) that has allowed the military as well as the police to quarantine cities, and to confine and presumably treat the sick. The plague depicted by Camus may be fictional, but the outbreak of coronavirus in China is all too real, and the Chinese state has effectively imposed martial law in the city of Wuhan, where the outbreak started, to limit people's movements and construct emergency hospitals. So far, the penalty for trying to evade these measures has only been arrest. In the Venetian Republic and elsewhere in the past, rulers ordered guards to kill people attempting to escape from quarantine.[16] Given that the spread of disease is very likely to be a consequence of climate change, Western liberal democracies cannot afford to ignore the prospect that such temptations may arise if they want to remain liberal democracies.

Western security establishments and military chiefs must declare much more strongly and consistently that climate change poses a potentially existential threat to the nations that they are sworn to defend.[17] There are several reasons for this. Firstly, the resources devoted to limiting climate change have so far been grossly inadequate, especially compared to those devoted to military security. Secondly, the sacrifices required from populations will be similar to those needed in times of war. Thirdly, there will be no chance of persuading conservative voters to accept crucial economic changes and sacrifices unless the military can speak authoritatively of an existential threat.[18] This is of particular importance in the United States, where so many Republicans have now adopted climate-change denial as an element of their political culture, and have developed a deep distrust of scientific experts.[19] Only the military retains the cultural prestige among Republican supporters sufficient to convince them that climate change really is a threat to the United States.

On the face of it, Western securitising actors have already spoken. All major Western militaries – even that of the US – have identified climate change as a security threat. But for a statement to be effective, it is not enough just to say it. It needs to be said loudly enough to be heard above the hubbub of other issues. Western security establishments have allowed their inter-mittent statements about climate change to be drowned out by discussion of the traditional threats posed by China and Russia. Not surprisingly, the Western media has followed suit. Concerning NATO's approach to climate change, a RAND Corporation report noted:

> In the case of nuclear weapons, terrorism, and cyber issues, each offers more uncertainty than climate change. However, vast amounts of resources are dedicated to the sponsoring of research, understanding the threat, and the preparations for potential consequences. The contrary is true for the potential security impact of climate change ... The lack of engagement at NATO headquarters on this point is more appropriate for the management of a tolerable or acceptable risk, while the literature suggests that climate change presents risks that likely won't be tolerable or acceptable.[20]

For their part, most climate-change activists have liberal-internationalist or Marxian backgrounds that have given rise to a visceral hostility not only to the 'securitisation' of issues but to nation-states as such. They have addressed their own statements to sympathetic transnational communities, but while these messages have been effective in these circles, it has become miserably apparent that the people to whom they are directed lack both the tools to take effective action and sufficient ability to inspire sacrifices among the wider population.

Security and legitimacy

Securitisation theory, with its emphasis on broadening the concept of security threats to encompass problems without an obvious military component, emerged in the 1990s in response to the apparent collapse of traditional security threats with the end of the Cold War. In recent years, however, Russia's limited recovery and China's rise have supposedly resurrected the old security threats and launched a 'new cold war'. Yet to see the Cold War chiefly in terms of traditional military threats is to radically misunderstand that struggle. It was a cold war, not an incandescent one. The threat of direct military conflict in Europe between the superpower blocs had in fact receded enormously by the mid-1950s.[21] Indeed, it can almost be said that the West had won the Cold War by the late 1940s, with the failure of communist parties to gain power in Western Europe, either by election or revolution, and the resumption of Western European economic growth with the help of the Marshall Plan. After that, it was really a matter – as George

Kennan presciently realised – of containing the communist bloc until it collapsed under the weight of its own failures and oppressions, while the economic and political superiority of Western democracy and social-market capitalism became more and more apparent.[22]

In that sense, the most important battle of the Cold War was fought on the field of state legitimacy. Each side sought to assert and maintain the credibility it derived from victory in the Second World War; to encourage the acceptance of its ideology as superior both at home and further afield; and to demonstrate its success in achieving vital state tasks. Actual war between the superpowers was only likely as the result of miscalculation or accident (as during the Cuban Missile Crisis), rather than deliberate strategy. Of course, the struggle between communism and capitalism became violent outside of Europe, as the Western and communist blocs engaged in proxy conflicts in the developing world.[23] Yet the question of whether Angola or El Salvador would become quasi-capitalist or semi-communist was never of decisive importance; and in these struggles too, the issue of the legitimacy of the state among the population played an important role.

The Soviet Union's communist system derived tremendous legitimacy from its victory in the Second World War, but it was never fully accepted in Eastern Europe and some of the Soviet republics, and its economy ended in utter failure, at least by comparison with the West. Thus, the communist political order was eventually overthrown, and the Soviet Union itself broken up, not because of external invasion or the threat of it, but because of the system's own internal failings and lack of legitimacy. In the West today, only the truly paranoid (or those seeking to protect military budgets) seriously assert the possibility of a Russian invasion of NATO. Western security anxieties concerning Russia (and increasingly China as well) have instead become focused on Moscow's capacity to encourage and manipulate the internal discontent and division within Western democracy, thereby undermining the legitimacy of Western democratic systems.

While the Cold War demonstrates the importance of state legitimacy in determining the fate of regimes, Chinese history shows how ecological factors can play a key part in state weakness and collapse. Situated on the floodplains of two great and unpredictable rivers, China has repeatedly found that the management of water has been central to domestic order and state survival. Even Emperor Yu the Great, one of China's mythical founding emperors, is primarily credited not for law-giving or victory in war, but for the creation of levee and canal systems to irrigate the land and prevent floods and droughts. On repeated occasions, the failure of Chinese authorities to limit the effects of extreme weather events was seen as an indication of a dynasty's loss of the 'Mandate of Heaven' – the ancient Chinese conception of state legitimacy. The result was increased banditry, mass unrest and displacement. Internal rebellion was responsible for the fall of dynasties at least as often as outside invasion, and very often the first led to the second.

In an era of climate change, the legitimacy and security of Western states too will depend on their ability to manage natural disasters and protect populations from their effects. The Netherlands is an example of a society for which defending against the sea has always been just as important as defending against foreign invasion, if not more so, and where the word 'dyke' evokes feelings of security.[24] In the struggle to limit the effects of climate change, including the rise in sea levels that climate change can be expected to produce, every coastal state is gradually becoming like the Netherlands.

In the short to medium term, however, the threat to the West is not of disappearing permanently beneath the waves, but of experiencing a steepening decline in the legitimacy of liberal-democratic political orders due to a variety of factors that climate change is sure to worsen. States need legitimacy at least as much as military or even economic power to raise revenue and maintain order without having to resort to divisive, debilitating, expensive and deeply unpopular applications of force. States and political systems that enjoy legitimacy can survive failures and defeats that would destroy those seen as less legitimate. The varying consequences of the Great Depression for the US and Britain, on the one hand, and Germany and Japan on the other, illustrate the point. Over time, however, no degree of traditional or legal legitimacy will save a state that persistently fails to achieve the vital goals of its population.

Legitimacy in the West

Opinion polls in Western states have revealed a frightening drop in citizens' faith in the legitimacy of the democratic political order since 2008. Surveys in Britain showed that dissatisfaction with democracy reached 61% in 2019, no doubt fuelled by the Brexit shambles. In the US, the proportion of the population dissatisfied with democracy has risen by 34% since the 1990s. For the first time in history, a majority of Americans are unhappy with the democratic system itself.

Confidence in democracy in Europe fell sharply in the 1970s and the 1990s too (to say nothing of the 1920s and 1930s). However, as recent reports by the Bennett Institute for Public Policy at Cambridge University and the *Journal of Democracy* argue, the present decline is considerably more serious, if only because a much higher number of young people are now disillusioned with democracy and willing to consider authoritarian alternatives.[25] The present decline is also of much longer duration, stretching back almost 12 years to the financial recession of 2008, and is more severe within certain European states – notably France and the Mediterranean countries.[26] Faith in the institutions and political processes of the European Union has dropped precipitously in many countries since 2008, crippling efforts at closer union and further expansion.

Unlike the democratic recessions of the 1970s and 1990s, therefore, the prevailing downward trend appears rooted in longer-term causes that seem unlikely to diminish and may well drastically worsen. They include not just prolonged economic stagnation but also new economic patterns whereby even periods of growth provide limited benefits for the majority of the population, and even generally available jobs do not provide the same status or security as in the past. Moreover, anxiety about demographic change seems almost certain to increase as migration continues. Judging by the results of the Syrian refugee crisis, another surge of migrants due to the direct or indirect effects of climate change could plausibly end liberal democracy in several European countries.

In addition, it has become apparent that in some countries different parts of the population hold drastically different views about the cultural and ethnic identity of the nation, and therefore about the basic source of the political order's legitimacy. As a result, the losing side in elections no longer necessarily recognises the moral legitimacy of election results. In the United States, for example, since the 1990s many leaders and members of the Republican Party have not viewed the Democratic presidents as truly legitimate, not because of any electoral malpractice, but because the two men in question failed to correspond to what their Republican detractors see as the fundamental cultural (and in Barack Obama's case, racial) identity of the United States.

Democrats also regard the legitimacy of the Trump administration and George W. Bush's administration before him as undermined by the fact that the curious electoral system established by the US Constitution allowed each to be elected with a smaller share of the popular vote than his Democratic opponent. In the coming years, the considerable electoral advantages enjoyed by the Republican Party – such as the growing mismatch between the distribution of Senate seats and the distribution of the US population – will further sap this legitimacy. Even now, Republicans need not win electoral majorities in order to block legislation and frustrate effective government. In European parliamentary democracies too, it is not necessary for extremist parties to win majorities in order to paralyse democracy; as in Weimar Germany, they only have to win enough parliamentary seats between them to make the creation of a centrist ruling coalition mathematically impossible.

The West may be gradually approaching a situation similar to that of a number of Middle Eastern countries, in which fundamental differences over the identity of the state that cannot be resolved by elections make democracy unworkable. If the legitimacy of the US Constitution is seriously challenged, the very foundations of US democracy will be undermined. No Middle Eastern state has ever doubted that threats to the internal political order were a security issue. Westerners forgot this for a while, because no such threats to Western systems seemed to exist. Now they do.

Realism and climate change

The basic arguments of securitisation theory have been amply confirmed by recent developments. Climate change has evolved from being one of the potential vulnerabilities mentioned by Buzan and his colleagues to *the* central issue for Western states, and indeed for humanity in general. Likewise, migration and the resulting fear-driven identity politics have turned out very much as predicted by the 'Copenhagen School' of Buzan and like-minded scholars, only worse.[27] Yet these ideas continue to meet with immense resistance in international-relations and security-studies circles, both from traditional realists and the various schools linked to liberal internationalism and the Marxian tradition.

Realists such as Stephen Walt are, I believe, correct in their opposition to widening the concept of security so far that it becomes meaningless – for example, by extending it to encompass the impact of illegal narcotics under the unfortunate banner of the 'war on drugs'.[28] However, every variant of realist theory is bound up with the interests, security and power of states and political orders – all of which can be undermined in ways that are not limited to foreign aggression or subversion. The challenge for realists in addressing climate change is therefore not to alter their basic philosophy, or to change their basic premise of the centrality of states, state power and state interests. Instead, they must become more clear-eyed and practical about what constitutes contemporary state interests by acknowledging that states are threatened as much by domestic insecurity as by external attack. History confirms it. In China, as noted, ecological threats and their management have been central to state security and legitimacy. Within the European tradition too, many of the greatest and most intelligent realist practitioners – Cardinal Richelieu, Klemens von Metternich, Pyotr Durnovo – were deeply concerned with threats to the security and legitimacy of their countries' domestic political orders, which was why some of them adopted a very cautious and unaggressive approach to relations with other states. (Whether they were right to respond to domestic threats in the way that they did is another matter.)

Contemporary advocates of this way of thinking have sometimes been accused of drawing some of their ideas from Carl Schmitt, the authoritarian critic of the Weimar system in Germany and (albeit briefly) a Nazi supporter.[29] Perhaps the most sinister and frequently condemned aspect of Schmitt's thought is his insistence on the 'friend–enemy' distinction as central to the self-definition of societies and states, and to domestic and international politics.[30] This topic raises the question of whether the 'enemy' for purposes of defining threats to the state needs to be human. Could climate change and disease possibly play a similar role in consolidating states and societies? This may seem an absurd idea, until one thinks of Beijing's response to the coronavirus outbreak. Schmitt would have approved of it, and in the future Western states will probably also have to adopt similarly martial methods to address disease and the civil disorder ensuing from natural disasters.

Another contribution that realist thought can make to the debate on climate change is the notion of solidarity with future generations. This is an idea that sits uncomfortably in the current zeitgeist, relentlessly focused as it is on the satisfaction of existing consumers. Yet states, and especially nation-states, exist over a long period of time. 'A man knows that he is mortal', wrote Milan Kundera, 'but he takes it for granted that his nation possesses a kind of eternal life'.[31] The central purpose of nationalism is to prolong that life as far as possible into the future. Most realist concerns about the security of states would be completely meaningless if conditions of safety were restricted to existing generations.[32] The fact that previous generations have sacrificed themselves for this purpose creates both the expectation and the obligation that future generations will do so too.[33]

The failures of liberal internationalism

Theorists whose thinking derives from the liberal-internationalist and Marxian traditions (such as those working in critical security studies and emancipatory theory) have greater and more fundamental difficulties than realists in accepting the elevation of climate change and its associated challenges as a national-security threat, because this would require them to qualify or abandon their hostility to existing nations, and to the idea of enduring and powerful collective identities.[34]

These attitudes have had a significant and damaging effect on thinking about action on climate change among environmentalists, since so many of them draw their basic political views from these traditions.[35] Concentrating on global agreements and institutions is not wrong in itself, but it tends to downplay three crucial facts: that whatever international agreements are reached will need to be implemented by states; that states will need to be strong enough to implement them; and that democratic and authoritarian states alike will need to motivate their populations to make the sacrifices required. Furthermore, a desire among many activists to emphasise the dire social consequences of climate change, including greatly increased migration, while simultaneously upholding the traditional liberal-internationalist belief that migration is a good thing, has produced analyses of mass migration that are sometimes self-contradictory to the point of unreason.[36]

It is true that national and ethnic identities, like all collective identities, are not essential or eternal, but change enormously over time; and that national identities are only one form of identity among the many we all possess. But modern history and contemporary experience decisively refute any notion that such identities change quickly, that they can be changed both radically and predictably by elite manipulation, or that they are no more important for politics and political action than any alternative identities. Radical and sudden change in national identities can happen, but usually only in the context of catastrophic transformations such as the French and Russian revolutions or the Second World War, which on the whole we might wish to avoid.[37] Most of the time, the development of national identities tends to be relatively slow and unpredictable, and to carry with it legacies of the past.[38]

Liberal-internationalist and Marxian theoretical approaches are at their core normative or prescriptive (explicitly so in critical security studies and emancipatory theory), and characterised by what Johan Eriksson has called 'instinctive moralism'.[39] Consider, for example, Antonio Franceschet's definition of 'human security':

> Human security is a liberal, cosmopolitan idea that individuals, regardless of their citizenship, location and identity ought to be made secure from a range of fears, threats and deprivations … Human security is made intelligible by the politics of applying law and legalism to global politics. Many of the human security discourses and initiatives to have emerged since the end of the Cold War are shaped, mobilised but also limited and constrained, by this wider problematic of the legal constitution of global politics.[40]

This approach treats human security as a matter of individuals rather than members of societies and citizens of states whose well-being and security depend on the security of their societies as a whole. It ignores the central and inescapable role of states in providing not just physical but social security for their people, and in actually carrying out any agreements made at the international level. In explicitly disregarding the factor of citizenship, it overlooks the duty of care that states owe to their own people, and the solidarity that people feel with their fellow citizens.

Any suggestion that what has been called the 'primacy of the state' is necessarily in opposition to 'human security' and the well-being of individuals is fundamentally false.[41] Of course, prioritising what are presumed to be state interests can have dreadful results, but it is equally true that none of the great advances in collective and individual welfare of the past century – social security and public-health systems among them – could have been achieved without the action of strong states. In the case of limiting climate change, it should be manifestly obvious that only strong and legitimate states will be able to implement changes on the massive scale required. Social and political movements may often play a key role in spurring states to act, but they cannot of themselves either pass or enforce legislation.

In addition, by conceptualising human security in terms of international legal forms, analyses like Franceschet's colossally overestimate the importance of international law, as opposed to national interests, in shaping state actions. By casting human security as a 'liberal, cosmopolitan idea', such thinking alienates both realists and conservative patriots, making it much more difficult to get them to grasp the new and potentially mortal threats to the security and vital interests of their nations. Moreover, the suggestion that an emphasis on states and national identities undermines globalism and global institutions misses the point entirely. Like it or not, the elites of powerful states, backed by burgeoning nationalist sentiment among sizeable portions of their populations, will not in the foreseeable future (if ever) surrender significant economic or legal power to international bodies. As we have seen, even the EU is only a partial exception to this rule. The liberal-internationalist and human-security view of what ought to happen may be noble in itself, but it does not describe what is actually happening, and there is no sign that it will ever happen.

*   *   *

While appeals to international communities of sentiment have succeeded in mobilising useful activist movements, they have so far failed to move solid majorities of voters in key countries to support policies that will require them to make personal sacrifices. It seems clear, therefore, that if the ruling elites of these countries (and, in democratic states, sufficient numbers of voters) are ever to agree to serious and economically painful measures to limit carbon emissions, they will need to be convinced that the direct and indirect effects of climate change pose a serious threat to the security of their states and regimes.

The expansive mode of Western liberal internationalism, insofar as it ever existed, is now well and truly over. The EU will likely survive, but it is highly improbable that its model will spread. If we wish to resist enormous threats and preserve whatever can be preserved of Western liberal democracy, we need to start thinking in terms of state as well as human survival.

Notes

1   Albert Camus (Stuart Gilbert, trans.), *The Plague* (New York: Everyman's Library, 2004), p. 59.

2   This essay is based on the arguments put forward in Anatol Lieven, *Climate Change and the Nation State: The Realist Case* (London and New York: Allen Lane and Oxford University Press, 2020).

3   The strongest arguments for the 'securitisation' of such interests have been made by the so-called 'Copenhagen School' of security studies and international relations. See Barry Buzan and Ole Waever, *Regions and Powers: The Structure of International Security* (Cambridge: Cambridge University Press, 2003); Ole Waever et al. (eds), *Identity, Migration and the New Security*

Agenda in Europe (London: Palgrave Macmillan, 1993); Barry Buzan, *People, States and Fear: An Agenda for European Security Studies in the Post-Cold War Era* (London: ECPR Press, 2007 [1983]); and Jef Huysmans, 'Revisiting Copenhagen: Or, on the Creative Development of a Security Studies Agenda in Europe', *European Journal of International Relations*, vol. 4, no. 4, 1998, pp. 479–505. For an environmentalist critique of the securitisation of environmental issues, see Daniel Deudney, 'The Case Against Linking Environmental Degradation and National Security', *Millennium: Journal of International Studies*, vol. 19, no. 3, 1990, pp. 461–76. It should be noted, however, that Deudney was talking about environmental issues in general, most of which – unlike climate change – do not involve existential threats.

4   Shaoni Bhattacharya, 'The 2003 European Heatwave Caused 35,000 Deaths', *New Scientist*, 10 October 2003, https://www.newscientist.com/article/dn4259-the-2003-european-heatwave-caused-35000-deaths/.

5   'Russia Confirms Deaths Rose by a Quarter in Heatwave', BBC, 6 March 2012, https://www.bbc.com/news/world-europe-11503550.

6   For an assessment of the impact of climate change on heatwaves, see Stefan Rahmstorf and Dim Cornou, 'Increase of Extreme Events in a Warming World', Potsdam Institute for Climate Impact Research, 20 March 2012, http://www.pik-potsdam.de/~stefan/Publications/Nature/rahmstorf_coumou_2011.pdf.

7   See Amy Remeikis, 'Canberra Chokes on World's Worst Air Quality as City All but Shut Down', *Guardian*, 3 January 2020, https://www.theguardian.com/australia-news/2020/jan/03/canberra-chokes-on-worlds-worst-air-quality-as-city-all-but-shut-down.

8   See US Environmental Protection Agency, 'Climate Change Impacts on Human Health', January 2017, https://19january2017snapshot.epa.gov/climate-impacts/climate-impacts-human-health_.html; US Global Change Research Program, 'The Impacts of Climate Change on Human Health in the United States: A Scientific Assessment', 2016, https://health2016.globalchange.gov/; Elizabeth G. Hanna, 'Health Hazards', in John S. Dryzek et al. (eds), *Handbook of Climate Change and Society* (Oxford: Oxford University Press, 2011), pp. 217–31; Paul R. Epstein, 'Climate and Health', *Science*, vol. 285, no. 5,426, July 1999, pp. 347–8; and Jonathan A. Patz et al., 'The Effects of Changing Weather on Public Health', *Annual Review of Public Health*, vol. 21, 2000, pp. 271–307, https://www.annual-reviews.org/abs/doi/10.1146/annurev.publhealth.21.1.271?intcmp=trendmd.

9   Cited in Marc A. Levy, 'Is the Environment a National Security Issue?', *International Security*, vol. 20, no. 2, Fall 1995, pp. 40, 51.

10 Wolfgang Cramer et al., 'Climate Change and Interconnected Risks to Sustainable Development in the Mediterranean', *Nature Climate Change*, 22 October 2018, https://www.nature.com/articles/s41558-018-0299-2; and MedECC (Mediterranean Experts on Climate and Environmental Change), 'Risks Associated to Climate and Environmental Changes in the Mediterranean Region', 2019, https://www.medecc.org/wp-content/uploads/2018/12/MedECC-Booklet_EN_WEB.pdf.

11 For an extended version of this argument, see Lieven, *Climate Change and the Nation State*, chapter 2.

12 See 'Explaining the Brexit Vote', *The Economist*, 16 July 2016; Ispos MORI, 'Concern About Immigration Rises as EU Vote Approaches', 31 July 2016; Richard Wike, Janell Fetterolf and Moira Fagan, 'Europeans Credit EU with Promoting Peace and Prosperity, but Say Brussels Is out of Touch with Its Citizens', Pew Research Center, 19 March 2019, https://www.pewresearch.org/global/2019/03/19/

europeans-credit-eu-with-promoting-
peace-and-prosperity-but-say-
brussels-is-out-of-touch-with-its-
citizens/; Phillip Connor and Jens
Manuel Krogstad, 'Many Worldwide
Oppose More Migration – Both
Out of and Into Their Countries',
Pew Research Center, 10 December
2018, https://www.pewresearch.
org/fact-tank/2018/12/10/many-
worldwide-oppose-more-migration-
both-into-and-out-of-their-countries/;
Pew Research Center, 'Top Voting
Issues in 2016 Election', 7 July
2016, https://www.people-press.
org/2016/07/07/4-top-voting-issues-in-
2016-election/; and 'Exit Polls', CNN,
23 November 2016, https://www.cnn.
com/election/2016/results/exit-polls.

13 See Carl Benedikt Frey and Michael A.
Osborne, 'The Future of Employment:
How Susceptible Are Jobs to
Computerisation?', Oxford Martin
Programme on Technology and
Employment, Oxford University, 2013,
pp. 13, 19, http://www.oxfordmartin.
ox.ac.uk/downloads/academic/future-
of-employment.pdf; P. Beaudry, D.A.
Green and B.M. Sand, 'The Great
Reversal in the Demand for Skill and
Cognitive Tasks', National Bureau of
Economic Research Working Paper
No. 18,901, 2013; Daron Acemoglu and
Pascual Restrepo, 'Robots and Jobs:
Evidence from US Labor Markets',
National Bureau of Economic
Research, Working Paper No. 23,285,
March 2017; Ivan Krastev, After
Europe (Philadelphia, PA: University
of Pennsylvania Press, 2017), p.
24; Michael Chui et al., 'Where
Machines Could Replace Humans and
Where They Can't – Yet', McKinsey

Quarterly, July 2016, https://www.
mckinsey.com/business-functions/
digital-mckinsey/our-insights/
where-machines-could-replace-
humans-and-where-they-cant-yet;
David H. Autor, Frank Levy and
Richard J. Murnane, 'The Skill Content
of Recent Technological Change: An
Empirical Exploration', Quarterly
Journal of Economics, vol. 118, no. 4,
2003, pp. 1,279–333; Branko Milanovic,
Global Inequality: A New Approach for
the Age of Globalization (Cambridge,
MA: Harvard University Press, 2018);
Robert Reich, Saving Capitalism: For the
Many, Not the Few (New York: Vintage,
2016), pp. 203–10; and Ian Bremmer,
Us vs. Them: The Failure of Globalism
(New York: Penguin, 2018), pp. 16–17.
On the threat to jobs in the petroleum
and chemical industries, see Arlie
Russell Hochschildt, Strangers in Their
Own Land (New York: The New Press,
2016), p. 320.

14 See 'Forgotten in the Banlieues:
Young, Diverse and Unemployed',
The Economist, 23 February 2013;
Jonathan Laurence and Justin
Vaisse, 'Understanding Urban Riots
in France', Brookings Institution,
1 December 2006, https://www.
brookings.edu/articles/understanding-
urban-riots-in-france/; and Karina
Piser, 'The Social Ladder Is Broken:
Hope and Despair in the French
Banlieues', Nation, 1 March 2018,
https://www.thenation.com/article/
the-social-ladder-is-broken-hope-
and-despair-in-the-french-banlieues/.
For the tendency of social despair in
France's banlieues to turn some young
people towards Islamist extremism,
see Gilles Kepel, Terror in France: The

Rise of Jihad in the West (Princeton, NJ: Princeton University Press, 2017), pp. 136–9.

15   Barry Buzan, Ole Waever and Jaap de Wilde, *Security: A New Framework for Analysis* (Boulder, CO: Lynne Rienner Publishers, 1998), p. 5, emphasis added. See also Barry Buzan and Ole Waever, *Regions and Powers: The Structure of International Security* (Cambridge: Cambridge University Press, 2003).

16   See Philip Ziegler, *The Black Death* (London: HarperCollins, 2009); and Carlo M. Cipolla, *Fighting the Plague in Seventeenth Century Italy* (Madison, WI: University of Wisconsin Press, 1981).

17   The Copenhagen School coined the term 'speech act' to describe the designation of a problem as a security threat to a 'referent object' (in most cases a state) by an authoritative 'securitising actor', such as a country's political leadership or military establishment. See Ole Waever, 'Securitization and Desecuritization', in Ronnie D. Lipschutz (ed.), *On Security* (New York: Columbia University Press, 1995), pp. 46–86. For an intelligent critique of the concept of the speech act and some examples of its dreadful misuse, see Thierry Balzacq, 'The Three Faces of Securitization: Political Agency, Audience and Context', *European Journal of International Relations*, vol. 11, no. 2, 2005, pp. 171–201.

18   Communication that affirms the sense of self and the basic world views of the intended audience has been shown to create a greater openness to risk information. See Susanne C. Moser and Lisa Dilling,

'Communicating Climate Change: Closing the Science–Action Gap', in Dryzek et al. (eds), *Handbook of Climate Change and Society*, p. 165; Matthew Nisbet, 'Communicating Climate Change: Why Frames Matter to Public Engagement', *Environment*, vol. 51, no. 2, 2009, pp. 12–23; Joseph P. Reser and Graham L. Bradley, 'Fear Appeals in Climate Change Communication', *The Oxford Encyclopedia of Climate Change Communication* (New York: Oxford University Press, 2017), available at https://oxfordre.com/climatescience/page/climate-change-communication/the-oxford-encyclopedia-of-climate-change-communication; Daniel Kahneman, 'Maps of Bounded Rationality: A Perspective on Intuitive Judgement and Choice', Nobel Prize acceptance lecture, 8 December 2002, https://www.nobelprize.org/uploads/2018/06/kahnemann-lecture.pdf; and Jonathan Haidt, *The Righteous Mind: Why Good People Are Divided by Politics and Religion* (New York: Pantheon Books, 2012).

19   For a discussion of the American tradition of distrusting experts, see Richard Hofstadter, *Anti-Intellectualism in American Life* (New York: Vintage, 1966). On the Republican culture of climate-change denial, see Riley E. Dunlap and Aaron M. McCright, 'A Widening Gap: Republican and Democratic Views on Climate Change', *Environment*, vol. 50, no. 5, 2008, pp. 26–35; Nisbet, 'Communicating Climate Change'; and Kari Norgaard, 'Climate Denial', in Dryzek et al. (eds), *Handbook of Climate Change and Society*, pp. 399–413.

20   Tyler H. Lippert, 'NATO, Climate

Change and International Security: A Risk Governance Approach', RAND Corporation, 2016, https://www.rand.org/pubs/rgs_dissertations/RGSD387.html.

21 On the Soviet side, the key moment was Joseph Stalin's decision in 1949 to withdraw support for the communists in the Greek civil war. On the US side, it was Dwight Eisenhower's rejection in 1953 of Republican pressure for a 'rollback' of Soviet power in Central Europe.

22 George Kennan predicted in a 1948 lecture at the Pentagon: 'if economic recovery could be brought about and public confidence restored in western Europe – if western Europe, in other words, could be made the home of a vigorous, prosperous and forward-looking civilization – the Communist regime in eastern Europe … would never be able to stand the comparison, and the spectacle of a happier and more successful life just across the fence … would be bound in the end to have a disintegrating and eroding effect on the Communist world'. See Dana H. Allin, *Cold War Illusions: America, Europe and Soviet Power, 1969–1989* (New York: St. Martin's Press, 1994), p. 13.

23 It is interesting to note that of the three Cold War conflicts in which the armies of one or the other superpower became directly involved, only Korea can be described as wise or successful. The wars in Vietnam and Afghanistan were tragically unnecessary disasters for the US and the Soviet Union, respectively.

24 This is a key example cited by the Copenhagen School. See, for instance, Buzan, Waever and Wilde, *Security: A New Framework for Analysis*, pp. 27–8.

25 Roberto Stefano Foa et al., 'The Global Satisfaction with Democracy Report 2020', Bennett Institute for Public Policy, University of Cambridge, January 2020, https://www.bennettinstitute.cam.ac.uk/media/uploads/files/DemocracyReport2020.pdf; Sean Coughlan, 'Dissatisfaction with Democracy "At Record High"', BBC, 29 January 2020, https://www.bbc.com/news/education-51281722; Richard Wike, Laura Silver and Alexandra Castillo, 'Many Across the World Are Dissatisfied with How Democracy Is Working', Pew Research Center, 29 April 2019, https://www.pewresearch.org/global/2019/04/29/many-across-the-globe-are-dissatisfied-with-how-democracy-is-working/; and Roberto Stefan Foa and Yascha Mounk, 'The Danger of Deconsolidation', *Journal of Democracy*, vol. 27, no. 3, July 2016, https://www.journalofdemocracy.org/wp-content/uploads/2016/07/FoaMounk-27-3.pdf.

26 Poland and Hungary have largely reverted to old patterns of authoritarian nationalism that were masked – but not eliminated – during the EU accession process.

27 See Waever et al. (eds), *Identity, Migration and the New Security Agenda in Europe*; and Buzan, *People, States and Fear*.

28 See Stephen M. Walt, 'The Renaissance of Security Studies', *International Studies Quarterly*, vol. 35, no. 2, June 1991, pp. 211–39.

29 For an analysis of the influence of Schmitt on the Copenhagen School, see Michael C. Williams, 'Words, Images, Enemies: Securitization and

International Politics', *International Studies Quarterly*, no. 47, 2003, pp. 511–31.

30 Carl Schmitt (George Schwab, trans.), *The Concept of the Political* (Chicago, IL: University of Chicago Press, 2007), pp. 27 ff.

31 Milan Kundera, *The Book of Laughter and Forgetting* (London: Penguin, 1980), p. 229.

32 For an extended version of this argument, see Lieven, *Climate Change and the Nation State*, pp. 63–90.

33 See Richard Weaver, 'The Problem of Tradition', in Russell Kirk, *A Program for Conservatives* (Washington DC: Regnery, 1956); Richard B. Howarth, 'Intergenerational Justice', in Dryzek et al. (eds), *Handbook of Climate Change and Society*, pp. 338–54; Yael Tamir, 'Pro Patria Mori! Death and the State', in Robert McKim and Jeff McMahan (eds), *The Morality of Nationalism* (New York: Oxford University Press, 1997), pp. 227–44; and Roger Scruton, *Green Philosophy: How to Think Seriously About the Planet* (New York: Atlantic Books, 2013), pp. 91–2.

34 For an introduction to critical security theory and emancipatory theory in security studies, see Keith Krause and Michael C. Williams, *Critical Security Studies: Concepts and Cases* (London: UCL Press, 1997); Bill McSweeney, *Security, Identity and Interests: A Sociology of International Relations* (Cambridge: Cambridge University Press, 1999); and Ken Booth, 'Security

and Emancipation', *Review of International Studies*, vol. 17, no. 4, 1991, pp. 313–27.

35 See Paul G. Harris, *What's Wrong with Climate Politics and How to Fix It* (Cambridge: Polity Press, 2013), pp. 33–63; Gregory White, *Climate Change and Migration* (New York: Oxford University Press, 2011); and Naomi Klein, *This Changes Everything: Capitalism Versus the Climate* (New York: Simon & Schuster, 2014).

36 See, for example, Christian Parenti, *Tropic of Chaos: Climate Change and the New Geography of Violence* (New York: Nation Books, 2011), pp. 179–224.

37 For a counter-argument, see Andrew Moravcsik, 'Is Something Rotten in the State of Denmark? Constructivism and European Integration', *Journal of European Public Policy*, vol. 6, no. 4, 1999, pp. 669–81.

38 For an example of this approach, see Bill McSweeney, 'Identity and Security: Barry Buzan and the Copenhagen School', *Review of International Studies*, vol. 22, no. 1, 1996, pp. 81–93.

39 Johan Eriksson, 'Observers or Advocates? On the Political Role of Security Analysts', *Cooperation and Conflict*, vol. 34, no. 3, 1999, pp. 311–30.

40 Antonio Franceschet, 'Global Legalism and Human Security', in Sandra J. Maclean et al. (eds), *A Decade of Human Security* (Aldershot: Ashgate Publishing, 2006), p. 31.

41 See McSweeney, 'Identity and Security'.

Trump's Policies and the Sino-Russian Entente

Alexander Lukin and Anatoly Torkunov

For many years, US geopolitical thinking focused primarily on the danger that would arise if an anti-US alliance, coalition of powers or single anti-US state were to gain dominance on the Eurasian continent. This idea has its roots in the writings of two pioneers of geopolitics, Halford Mackinder and Nicholas Spykman.[1] They attached great strategic importance to the central part of the continent (the 'Heartland') that Russia had historically dominated and argued for the need to contain Russian influence. In their view, only military and political expansion by a major continental power could unify Eurasia. That would spell the defeat of the West and, effectively, world domination by that conquering power. According to Mackinder's famous formula, 'who rules the Heartland commands the World Island; and Who rules the World Island commands the World'.[2]

Influenced by this line of thought, the next generation of American strategists sought to ensure that no single power or alliance controlled the Eurasian continent. At the same time, practical geopolitical interests usually held sway over ideology. Despite his right-leaning, anti-communist convictions, US president Richard Nixon followed the recommendation of Henry Kissinger, his national security advisor and secretary of state, in improving relations with communist China. Similarly, US president Jimmy Carter,

Alexander Lukin is director of the Center for East Asian and Shanghai Cooperation Organization Studies at the Moscow State Institute of International Relations (MGIMO-University). **Anatoly Torkunov** is president of MGIMO-University and a full member of the Russian Academy of Sciences.

Survival | vol. 62 no. 2 | April–May 2020 | pp. 27–36   DOI 10.1080/00396338.2020.1739946

a champion of human rights, followed the advice of his national security advisor, Zbigniew Brzezinski, in establishing diplomatic relations with Beijing, which had a worse human-rights record than Moscow. Geopolitical considerations demanded that the weaker communist state be torn away from its stronger ally to prevent their hegemony in Eurasia.

More recent US and Western strategic thinking on Eurasia incorporated the same geopolitical tenets. Well after the break-up of the Soviet Union, Brzezinski wrote:

> Potentially, the most dangerous scenario would be a grand coalition of China, Russia, and perhaps Iran, an 'anti-hegemonic' coalition united not by ideology but by complementary grievances. It would be reminiscent in scale and scope of the challenge once posed by the Sino-Soviet bloc, though this time China would likely be the leader and Russia the follower. Averting this contingency, however remote it may be, will require a display of US geostrategic skill on the western, eastern, and southern perimeters of Eurasia simultaneously.[3]

Brzezinski noted that 'America's global primacy is directly dependent on how long and how effectively its preponderance on the Eurasian continent is sustained'.[4] At the same time, US strategists advocated restricting Russia's – or, for that matter, any other power's – development in the region. Kissinger wrote:

> The domination by a single power of either of Eurasia's two principal spheres – Europe and Asia – remains a good definition of strategic danger for America. Cold War or no Cold War. For such a grouping would have the capacity to outstrip America economically and, in the end, militarily.[5]

The danger to the US was not a particular political regime, but simply all major, independent and influential states as such. At the same time, Western strategists saw the collapse of the Soviet Union as a triumph of their ideology, presenting a unique opportunity for the US itself to consolidate hegemony in Eurasia. Precautions and geopolitical nuances no longer seemed necessary: why worry about the reaction of Russia, China and other countries if the 'liberal world order' had won and all countries would soon be lining up in orderly rows to march towards freedom, democracy and the market economy?

In the event, the collapse of the Soviet Union did not stop the non-Western centres of power from gaining strength – as experts back in the 1970s and 1980s had predicted would happen – and a multipolar world from emerging. The reluctance of the US to accept this process led these non-Western powers to establish a counterweight to the United States by forming their own organisations and groups. Two especially significant ones are the Shanghai Cooperation Organisation (SCO) and the grouping of Brazil, Russia, India, China and South Africa (known as the BRICS). The main consequence of Washington's policy, however, has been to accelerate what had been only a gradual rapprochement between Russia, which was re-establishing its power base, and China, which was already growing rapidly. That relationship has developed into a deep and close strategic partnership, deemed an 'entente' by Dmitri Trenin – that is, 'a basic agreement about the fundamentals of world order supported by a strong body of common interest'.[6]

Trump's dispensation

With Donald Trump in the White House, the policy of promoting or imposing liberal democracy on other countries came to an end. But the United States still aimed to assert a dominating ideology, with 'America First' replacing liberalism. This new framework differs little in substance from the previous one. The objective remains for America to build a world order that benefits primarily the US. According to the Trumpist ideologues, previous US administrations failed to achieve this goal because the US had ceased to lead the process. The current priority, therefore, is to regain that leadership.

The difference between this and more realist approaches to geopolitics is that it takes insufficient account of the constraints of the world system. Trump and his lieutenants appear to believe that the US is practically all-powerful and that they can achieve their aims not through engaging with major non-Western states as their predecessors had done – an approach they consider to have been weak and unsuccessful – but through direct pressure. But that course is likely to lead to the consolidation of the non-Western world, and in particular to Russian and Chinese cooperation in Eurasia. This is especially evident in Trump's policy in the Asia-Pacific, a region that his administration has made a priority.

During his election campaign and soon after taking office, Trump stated that the situation in the Asia-Pacific region did not serve key US interests and blamed the previous administration for having committed numerous blunders that enabled China to strengthen its presence there at the expense of the US. He also directed his ire against Japan and South Korea – Washington's traditional allies – for contributing too little towards the cost of security in Asia and for their 'egotistical policies' concerning economic ties with the US. The new administration established three primary objectives in the region: maintaining and strengthening US leadership, 'containing' a rapidly growing China that had managed to mount a significant challenge to the US over the course of the previous decade, and uniting and mobilising US allies behind Washington's policies. To accomplish these objectives, Washington adopted the concept of the Indo-Pacific Region (IPR) – which stretches from the west coast of the United States to the west coast of India – as its main geopolitical frame of reference.[7]

The US strategy is clearly aimed at checking a rapidly rising China and its Belt and Road Initiative, by which Beijing allegedly 'seeks Indo-Pacific regional hegemony in the near-term and, ultimately global pre-eminence in the long-term', and describes Russia as a 'revitalized malign actor'.[8] The strategy contemplates a 'quadrilateral security dialogue' among the US, Japan, Australia and India – the Quad – which will manage Asian affairs under Washington's leadership. More particularly, Washington wants to increase the role and contribution of its regional allies in implementing US strategy. The Trump administration has encouraged the growth of Japanese nationalism under Prime Minister Shinzo Abe and Japan's inclination to play a more independent security role in the region, despite China's traditional enmity towards Japan and its perception that Tokyo has failed to adequately acknowledge its war crimes. The US still considers South Korea its most important stronghold in Northeast Asia, and deployed six US

Terminal High Altitude Area Defense (THAAD) anti-missile batteries there in autumn 2017. These American moves have increased China's concerns and spurred its militarisation.

Finally, the Trump administration has engineered a major shift in Washington's economic policy in the Asia-Pacific. Levelling serious complaints about the allegedly unfair nature of their economic ties with the US, it has set out to revise economic relations with Washington's main partners in Asia, China in particular. What especially aggravates Washington is Beijing's unabashed intention to become a leading technological power, with its Made in China 2025 programme focused on key sectors in which the US currently holds an undisputed advantage.[9] While temporary agreements such as the initial trade deal between the US and China reached in December 2019 may be achieved in the future, the general geopolitical rivalry is likely to continue and even intensify since all political parties in the United States agree that a Chinese threat to US dominance is growing.

Chinese and Russian reactions

Moscow and Beijing are not happy about the bloc-like character of the IPR concept and its exclusion of both Russia and China. Beijing has been outwardly dismissive. Speaking in March 2018, Chinese Foreign Minister Wang Yi said that the IPR concept and similar ideas were 'like the sea foam in the Pacific or Indian Ocean: they may get some attention, but soon will dissipate'. He also expressed the hope that the Quad format would not be directed against other countries. 'Nowadays', said Wang, 'stoking a new Cold War is out of sync with the times and inciting bloc confrontation will find no market'.[10] Chinese academics were less coy. According to Qu Caiyun of the Chinese Academy of Social Sciences, the Quad 'is a competitive and strategic game aimed at pursuing multiple goals of the participating states and with a common goal of containing China'.[11]

Russia took an even harsher position. Speaking at the International Valdai Club conference in Vietnam in February 2019, Russian Foreign Minister Sergei Lavrov said that the IPR was an 'artificially imposed construct' with 'the far-reaching context of containing China. This is a clear attempt to get India involved in military–political and naval processes.

This concept undermines the ASEAN-centricity of the formats that have been created in that region ... So, we prefer to call it the Asia-Pacific Region.'[12] Russia believes that the US conceptualisation of an Indo-Pacific bloc might not only take on an anti-Chinese character, but also eventually extend to eastern and southern Eurasia, and undermine Russia's plans for cooperation in that region.

If the Trump administration's geopolitical concept has only increased China's and Russia's incentives to forge a rapprochement, the US reaction to China's growing military strength in the Asia-Pacific has intensified them. The most recent official US national-security documents identify China as the main threat to US interests in the region. Chinese leaders, who had offered to pursue constructive but equal relations with the US as part of a 'New Model of Great Power Relations', are now instead preparing for a protracted confrontation they have labelled the 'New Long March' – a reference to the Red Armies' series of gruelling strategic retreats during the Chinese Communist campaign against the Kuomintang in the 1930s that required citizens to endure deprivations and make sacrifices for the sake of future victory.[13]

Moreover, Beijing is rekindling military cooperation with Moscow. In 2014, China became the first foreign country to purchase Russia's Almaz Antey S-400 (SA-21 *Growler*) medium-to-long-range surface-to-air missile system. The following year, Russia sold China 24 Sukhoi Su-35 *Flanker* M fighter jets. The two countries have conducted a series of joint naval manoeuvres, for the most part modest, in the Mediterranean in 2015, the South China Sea in 2016 and the Baltic in 2017, as well as a small naval exercise also involving Iran in the north Indian Ocean and the Gulf of Oman at the end of 2019. In July of that year, Russia and China carried out a symbolic joint air patrol in the Asia-Pacific, prompting warning shots from South Korean jets and a protest from Japan. In October 2019, Russian President Vladimir Putin announced that Russia was assisting China in creating an integrated missile-attack warning system.

Both China and Russia have an interest in a peaceful resolution of the North Korean nuclear problem because both countries border North Korea and any war there – particularly a nuclear conflict – would inevitably create serious problems for their territories and populations. In addition, North Korea is their long-time partner and China's only official ally. For Russia, peace on the Korean Peninsula would open up significant opportunities for, among other things, developing its far-eastern region. Russia could, for example, build trans-Korean rail and road routes connecting the two countries with Russia, lay oil and gas pipelines to South Korea, or carry forward a trilateral transport and trans-shipment hub project at the mouth of the Tumen River. In this connection, Trump's inability to reach agreements with North Korea based on the principle of gradualness has only served to stiffen the positions of Russia and China.

Washington's economic pressure on its partners in the region in order to win economic concessions from them and its trade war against China have only caused a backlash from Beijing. The Chinese leadership has concluded that it should conduct trade negotiations with the US in a constructive manner, and even be prepared to make certain concessions and compromises. But it has drawn a red line in front of anything it considers an impingement on state sovereignty. For Beijing, Trump's demands for fundamental changes in Chinese legislation, for effectively placing the work of Chinese companies under outside control and for creating a body that would monitor compliance with agreements cross that line, recalling the time when China was a quasi-colony and foreigners controlled its customs operations. The difficulty encountered in reaching an agreement with Washington has prompted Beijing to restructure its foreign policy to make it less dependent on the US.

Beyond that, it has increased China's interest in developing deeper economic cooperation with Russia. Sino-Russian trade volume grew from about $70 billion in 2016 to $110bn in 2019, with Russia's exports exceeding imports by more than $10bn. China is becoming interested not only in Russian raw materials but also in agricultural products, foodstuffs, manufacturing and some information technologies. Interconnectivity has also seen serious improvements in the form of new pipelines, bridges and motorways, and upgraded and expanded railroads.

*　　*　　*

Washington's Asia-Pacific policy assumes that the US is strong and can cope with its problems and opponents, pressuring all of them simultaneously. This assumption is likely to hold for countries such as Vietnam, Australia and New Zealand, which share America's geopolitical concerns about China. And Trump administration policy also may see qualified success with allies such as Japan and South Korea, which have fraught relationships with China, although it could also alienate those countries and prompt them to pursue a more independent course over the long term. The main geopolitical consequence of US policy, however, is that it drives Moscow and Beijing closer together. China and Russia, notably during the latter's Soviet incarnation, have had conflicts that remain potential sources of tension. However, the two countries share an increasingly similar outlook for global development and the need to join forces to create a Eurasian order independent of the US. By shutting China out of the Asia-Pacific on all fronts, Washington leaves Beijing no choice but to seek partners on an anti-US basis, just as shutting Russia out of Europe leaves Moscow with no other choice. As a result, efforts by China and by Russia – which less than a decade ago contemplated a greater Europe 'stretching from Lisbon to Vladivostok' and 'a new model of great power relations' – are now aimed at creating a comprehensive Eurasian partnership.

The countries have affirmed their support of this approach in several official Russian–Chinese documents. Russian strategists developed the concept of a 'Greater Eurasia' in 2015 after they concluded that the deterioration in relations with the West over the Ukrainian crisis was irreversible.[14] Putin incorporated the idea into his speech and interview at the St. Petersburg International Economic Forum in June 2016. He suggested that the Eurasian Economic Union (EAEU), promoted by Russia and Kazakhstan, could anchor an emergent area of greater integration, mooting 'prospects for a more extensive Eurasian partnership involving the EAEU and countries with which we already have close partnerships – China, India, Pakistan and Iran – and certainly our CIS partners, and other interested countries and associations'.[15] The geography of this partnership almost completely matches the geography of the 'anti-hegemonic alliance' whose creation Brzezinski had feared.

The Russian–Chinese declaration signed by the two leaders during Putin's visit to China in late June 2016 incorporated Putin's formulation. That document stressed the paramount importance of linking the formation of the EAEU with the realisation of China's Belt and Road Initiative. It also called for a 'comprehensive Eurasian partnership based on the principles of openness, transparency, and mutual interests, and including the possible involvement of EAEU, SCO, and ASEAN member countries'.[16] In June 2018, during Putin's visit to China, Chinese Minister of Commerce Zhong Shan and Russian Minister of Economic Development Maxim Oreshkin signed the Joint Declaration of the Joint Feasible Studies on Completing Eurasian Economic Partnership Agreement.[17]

As Putin said in his speech before the Second Belt and Road Forum in Beijing in April 2019, a Eurasian partnership would 'integrate integration frameworks, and therefore … promote a closer alignment of various bilateral and multilateral integration processes that are currently underway in Eurasia – particularly the Chinese Belt and Road Initiative'.[18] Thus, the Trump administration's policy in the Asia-Pacific has effectively stimulated the very eventuality that several generations of US strategists had feared – namely, Washington's loss of control over Eurasia resulting from the deepening rapprochement between the two major Eurasian powers. It remains to be seen whether Washington will be able to cope with it.

Acknowledgements

Alexander Lukin's research for this article was funded by MGIMO-University (Project Number 1921-01-04).

Notes

1   H.J. Mackinder, 'The Geographical Pivot of History', *Geographical Journal*, vol. 23, no. 4, April 1904, pp. 421–37; and Nicholas J. Spykman, *America's Strategy in World Politics: The United States and the Balance of Power* (New York: Harcourt: Brace and Company, 1942).

2   H.J. Mackinder, *Democratic Ideals and Reality: A Study in the Politics of Reconstruction* (London: Constable and Company Ltd., 1919), p. 150.

3   Zbigniew Brzezinski, *The Grand Chessboard: American Primacy and Its Geostrategic Imperatives* (New York: Basic Books, 1997), p. 54.

4   *Ibid.*, p. 27.

5   Henry Kissinger, *Diplomacy* (New York: Simon & Schuster, 1994), p. 813.

6   Dmitri Trenin, *From Greater Europe to Greater Asia: The Sino-Russian Entente* (Moscow: Carnegie Moscow Center, 2015), https://carnegieendowment. org/files/CP_Trenin_To_Asia_ WEB_2015Eng.pdf.

7   US Department of Defense, 'Indo-Pacific Strategy Report: Preparedness, Partnerships, and Promoting a Networked Region', 1 June 2019, https://media.defense. gov/2019/Jul/01/2002152311/-1/-1/1/ DEPARTMENT-OF-DEFENSE-INDO-PACIFIC-STRATEGY-REPORT-2019. PDF.

8   *Ibid.*, pp. 8, 11.

9   See Alexander Lukin, 'The US–China Trade War and China's Strategic Future', *Survival*, vol. 61, no. 1, February–March 2019, p. 26.

10 Ministry of the Foreign Affairs of the People's Republic of China, 'Foreign Minister Wang Yi Meets the Press', 9 March 2018, https://www.fmprc.gov.cn/ mfa_eng/zxxx_662805/t1540928.shtml.

11 Qu Caiyun, 'Jiezhe "Ri-Mei-Ao-Yin" zhanlue hezuode juxianxing' [Analysis on the Limits of Japan–US–Australia–India Strategic Cooperation], *Nanhai wenti yajiu*, no. 1, March 2018, pp. 32–45.

12 Ministry of Foreign Affairs of the Russian Federation, 'Foreign Minister Sergey Lavrov's Remarks and Answers to Media Questions During the Russian–Vietnamese Conference of the Valdai International Discussion Club, Ho Chi Minh City', 25 February 2019, https://www.mid.ru/en/foreign_ policy/news/-/asset_publisher/ cKNonkJE02Bw/content/id/3541050.

13 Zhou Xin, 'Xi Jinping Calls For "New Long March" in Dramatic Sign that China is Preparing for Protracted Trade War', *South China Morning Post*, 25 May 2019, https://www.scmp.com/economy/ china-economy/article/3011186/ xi-jinping-calls-new-long-march-dramatic-sign-china-preparing.

14 See Trenin, *From Greater Europe to Greater Asia*.

15 President of Russia, 'Plenary Session of St Petersburg International Economic Forum', 17 June 2016, http://en.kremlin.ru/events/president/ news/52178.

16 President of Russia, 'Sovmestnoe zayavlenie Rossiyskoy Federatsii i Kitayskoy Narodnoy Respubliki' [Joint Statement of the Russian Federation and the People's Republic of China], 25 June 2016, http://www. kremlin.ru/supplement/5100.

17 Ministry of Commerce of the People's Republic of China, 'China and Russia Sign the Joint Declaration of the Joint Feasible Studies on Completing Eurasian Economic Partnership Agreement', 9 June 2018, http://english.mofcom.gov.cn/ article/newsrelease/significantnews/ 201806/20180602754961.shtml.

18 President of Russia, 'Belt and Road Forum for International Cooperation', 26 April 2019, http://en.kremlin.ru/ events/president/news/60378.

Reconsidering Spheres of Influence

Evan R. Sankey

Spheres of influence have become a great taboo of American foreign policy. A great power's assertion of exclusive rights or veto powers over its weaker neighbours offends America's professed commitment to the norms of national self-determination and sovereign equality. America's foreign-policy elite bolsters this idealistic judgement with a strategic one: that spheres of influence breed international instability and that their re-emergence would herald a return to the great-power conflicts of the first half of the twentieth century. Reflecting this view, Robert Kagan argues that 'if the United States wants to maintain a benevolent world order, it must not permit spheres of influence to serve as a pretext for aggression'.[1] Since the end of the Cold War, America has pursued a policy of preventing the emergence of rival spheres of influence as a means of transcending the power politics of the past.

The strategic argument against spheres of influence and the corollary policy of preventing them from taking root, however, rest on the dubious assumptions that doing so is stabilising and even possible.

The logic of spheres of influence

Spheres of influence reflect structural asymmetries of political interest and military advantage. Great powers have extraterritorial interests and, perhaps, the means to secure them.[2] A sphere of influence is a geographic area within which a great power enforces limits on the policy autonomy of

Evan R. Sankey is a research analyst at the Johns Hopkins University Paul H. Nitze School of Advanced International Studies.

Survival | vol. 62 no. 2 | April–May 2020 | pp. 37–47   DOI 10.1080/00396338.2020.1739947

weaker states in order to make those states friendly towards it, or at least neutral with respect to rival powers.[3] Whether great powers seek extraterritorial privileges primarily out of insecurity, national pride or economic greed, they are likely to prioritise them above many other interests.

A policy of preventing spheres of influence also runs up against a hard truth: the United States' specific national-security interests in the backyards of rival great powers are usually relatively weak. Russia's actions in Ukraine and China's behaviour in the South China Sea prove their willingness to take risks and concentrate resources to make their immediate neighbourhoods congenial to their interests. Despite America's advantage in raw national power, it has repeatedly demonstrated that it lacks the patience and risk tolerance to prevent determined adversaries from making local gains, especially given its commitments elsewhere in the world.

Compounding the asymmetry of political stakes are the geographic and technological advantages of Russia's and China's military postures. It is inherently easy for them to deploy concentrated military forces close to their borders where they benefit from close logistics support, deep knowledge of local geography and resilient homeland-based sensor coverage.[4] By contrast, the US must deploy across great distances. It maintains an impressive expeditionary military force and a global basing and logistics network to meet this challenge, but these capabilities are expensive, vulnerable and dispersed.

China and Russia cannot directly match US expeditionary assets such as aircraft carriers, but their arsenals of cheap sensor-based weapons such as anti-ship missiles, integrated air-defence systems and quiet diesel-electric submarines could impose heavy costs on US forces approaching their borders during a conflict. The RAND Corporation estimates that the average US expeditionary capability is 50 times more expensive than the asymmetric capability that could disable or destroy it.[5] Military trends and geography therefore favour the ability of powerful countries to generate zones of military advantage adjacent to their homelands.[6] These zones fortify their spheres of influence against external interference.

American presidents sometimes appreciate the inevitability of rivals' local military advantages. Barack Obama, for example, refused to supply lethal weapons to the Ukrainian government out of concern that Russia could easily out-escalate the US.[7] But, under freedom-of-navigation principles observed for decades, the Department of Defense generally insists that US forces 'fly, sail and operate wherever international law allows', and has initiated a 'Third Offset Strategy' to develop new stealth, robotic and sensor-fusion capabilities to preserve freedom of operation in contested zones.[8] In the long run, this approach is likely to prove quixotic, as the cost of fielding these frontier technologies far exceeds the cost of the Chinese and Russian capabilities they are designed to overcome. Moreover, impending US–China GDP parity means that 'outspend them forever' strategies are probably unsustainable.[9] Given escalating military costs and the lack of political appetite to support them, an American effort to prevent spheres of influence looms as an exercise in strategic futility.

The instability of prevention

The most articulate opponents of spheres of influence argue that they have contested boundaries which are 'prone to great power conflict' and that prevention enhances international stability.[10] But the policy of universal deterrence believed necessary to forestall the emergence of spheres of influence is also subject to great-power tension and instability. Russia and China are alarmed by America's efforts to cultivate strong relationships with their neighbours. Russia partially dismembered Ukraine when America and the European Union tried to draw it towards the West. China's leaders regard America's ongoing defence relationship with Taiwan as a threat to the 'One China' principle, a paramount national-security interest. They have repeatedly made clear that use of force is on the table.

Additionally, Russian and Chinese policymakers resent America's efforts to maintain military primacy, especially because it requires the presence of US military forces on their frontiers. America perceives itself as a peacekeeper, but it does not get to decide the perceptions of its rivals. The latter view these deployments as a potential threat and challenge them on a semi-regular basis. Close encounters between American and Chinese vessels in the South China Sea, Russian aircraft buzzing American ships in the Black Sea, the 2001 collision between an American spy plane and a Chinese interceptor: each of these incidents carried the potential for miscalculation, accident and escalation. The US military continues to dominate the global air and maritime commons, but it would struggle in a conflict on the doorstep of another great power. Russia's and China's local access to reinforcements, sensor coverage and land-based precision weapons will increasingly put America's expeditionary forces at a severe disadvantage.

Nuclear weapons compound the problem. Russia and China could risk nuclear escalation to secure geographically proximate interests, and could issue credible nuclear threats if the US began to prevail in a conventional fight. US decision-makers struggling to win a conventional war could also be tempted to strike sensors and missile batteries inside the borders of Russia or China that are integral to their nuclear command-and-control systems.[11] Chinese officials, in particular, might interpret such strikes as an American attempt to eliminate their relatively small nuclear arsenal and conclude that they must use their weapons before they lose them.

The US foreign-policy establishment is not blind to these emerging military quandaries. The National Defense Strategy Commission's recent assessment of the 2018 National Defense Strategy, for example, admits that 'regional military balances have deteriorated' and that America 'might struggle to win, or perhaps lose, a war against China or Russia'.[12] The commission's report recommends boosting defence spending to reinforce deterrence, but neglects the question of whether America should fight risky wars on great-power frontiers in the first place.

Spheres of influence as stabilisers

Conceptually, spheres of influence are security-enhancing because they serve as buffers to secure vital interests, those for which a great power would risk war. They are stability-enhancing when rivals recognise them as a means of signalling respect for vital interests. The US has historically benefited from these security- and stability-enhancing effects.

Beginning with the Monroe Doctrine in 1823, America claimed a sphere of influence in order to prevent the expansion of European, especially British, colonial interests in the New World. It took until the late nineteenth century for the US to develop the means of enforcing this claim, but since then the western hemisphere has been kept largely free of great-power conflict. The Cold War superpowers were mostly respectful of each other's European spheres of influence because their respective security needs were satisfied and intervention risked provoking a costly military response, and potentially nuclear annihilation.

Liberal interventionists such as Robert Kagan are correct that other historical spheres of influence did not lead to stability. The Russo-Japanese War of 1904–05 was a successful Japanese military challenge to Russian primacy in Korea and Manchuria. In 1914, competing Russian and Austro-Hungarian spheres of influence in the Balkans sparked a military crisis that led to the outbreak of the First World War. Japan's pursuit of an ever-expanding Asian sphere of influence in the 1930s led it into unwinnable wars with China and the United States. But the uneven historical record of spheres of influence does not discredit the entire concept.

A stable sphere of influence is a product of five factors. Firstly, it requires relatively clear boundaries. The Monroe Doctrine explicitly covered North and South America and the Caribbean, and the Yalta and Potsdam conferences laid out tentative superpower understandings on the post-war division of Europe. Secondly, the state asserting a sphere of influence must command the military means to enforce claimed extraterritorial privileges and deter outside interference. The US Navy's 'big stick', for example, was crucial to settlements favourable to the United States in the Venezuela crises of 1895 and 1902–03. Thirdly, influenced states should be largely, if grudgingly, acquiescent. Latin American countries, while sometimes truculent, have never mounted a serious challenge to America's hemispheric primacy. Fourthly, the asserted sphere ideally should not compromise other great powers' perceived vital interests. Both US hegemony in the western hemisphere and the Cold War alignments of Europe qualify on this score: European powers' colonial interests paled next to their continental concerns, and for both Russia and the West survival trumped rollback – even if crises in Berlin and Cuba stress-tested that proposition early on. Fifthly, for a sphere of influence to be stable, other great powers ought to at least tacitly recognise it. For instance, the League of Nations Covenant acknowledged US hegemony in the western hemisphere, and American and Soviet actions in the Cold War amounted to mutual recognition of their respective European spheres.

Destabilising spheres of influence lacked some or all of these five traits. Japan started the Russo-Japanese War because its leaders regarded the Korean Peninsula as a vital interest and Russia refused to recognise it as part of a Japanese sphere. The Austro-Hungarian and Russian spheres in the Balkans were unstable because each power perceived the other's area as implicating its vital interests. Japan's Greater East Asia Co-Prosperity Sphere proved unstable because Japan failed to secure the acquiescence of China and because America came to view it as a threat to its vital interests in Asia.

The upshot is that great powers with compatible interests can express and consolidate that compatibility by establishing spheres of influence. But those with incompatible interests cannot stabilise their relationships by imposing spheres of influence. In light of the complexity of the current strategic environment, however, it can be difficult to determine whether recognising a given sphere of influence would make the international system more or less stable. In general, however, the revolution in sensor-based precision weapons and the logic of nuclear deterrence are causes for relief. These systems are likely to inhibit the contestation of contemporary spheres of influence by making it relatively easy for great powers to defend their spheres against outside military intervention. At the same time, they will frustrate ambitious powers' attempts to expand their spheres of influence far from home.

Nuclear weapons remain a key stabilising constraint. Whether the rationale for an outside intervention is moral, legal or strategic, it is unlikely to be worth the risk of nuclear destruction. Nuclear weapons also condition how vital interests are defined. If little is worth the risk of nuclear war, great powers may learn to rein in their ambitions. As an analytical matter, the nuclear revolution means that the relative stability of the Cold War, rather than the First World War, is the most appropriate case study for developing accurate expectations about how a spheres-of-influence system would operate today.

America's sphere of influence expanded after the Cold War under the rules-based international order even as nuclear weapons remained deployed around the world. Yet the United States' most important post-Cold War initiatives have been frustrated and checked. NATO expansion poisoned US–Russia relations and set the stage for sobering crises in Georgia and Ukraine. The wars in Afghanistan and Iraq became costly fiascos rather than democratising triumphs. American influence did not markedly expand in post-Cold War Asia. Even at its moment of maximum potency, the United States' aggrandisement was subject to geopolitical limits. These limits would be even more pronounced in a multipolar world of spheres of influence.

Spheres of restraint: a liberal solution

American ambivalence about spheres of influence reflects a tension between competing concepts of US national interest: a universal version that seeks to enforce a liberal world order and a more particular version that focuses on securing the homeland vis-à-vis the other great powers.

The universalist hope is that a liberal peace will eliminate the rationale for spheres of influence, or that America's military preponderance will allow it to eliminate them by the threat of military force. Hal Brands and Charles Edel argue that universalist hostility to spheres of influence constitutes the baseline of American foreign policy. They dismiss the Monroe Doctrine and America's de facto recognition of the Soviet sphere as 'concessions to expediency'.[13] But this concedes the key point: when the geopolitical going gets tough, even the US will recognise limits on its power and adjust its ambitions.

From the particularist perspective, America is not powerful enough to deny spheres of influence to other great powers. To avoid confrontations and nuclear risk-taking, the particularist would recognise rival spheres and seek reciprocal recognition of America's vital interests in the western hemisphere. Since recognition is the *sine qua non* of stability, only the particular version of America's interests can sustain stable spheres of influence. This version is likely to become more attractive to US policymakers as the economic and security costs of prevention rise.

Since America would be loath to shed its concern for the norms of sovereign equality and non-intervention, it will have to reconcile them with the illiberalism of spheres of influence. For this purpose, it can avail itself of spheres' relatively liberal cousin: neutrality. The Cold War neutrality of Finland and Austria enabled them to stay on good terms with the superpowers by avoiding overt alignment with either. They were able to preserve Western-orientated domestic institutions, but were obliged to adopt restrained national-security policies to accommodate Soviet interests.[14] The superpowers' restraint allowed the two countries' neutrality to flourish: neither superpower insisted on Austria's or Finland's overt alignment because each feared a destabilising response by the other. This enforced neutrality yielded 'spheres of restraint' in which the United States and the Soviet Union permitted non-alignment in lieu of courting great-power instability.

Unlike spheres of influence, spheres of restraint can secure great-power interests without violating the sovereignty of weaker countries. If such countries are convinced that their domestic institutions will not be subject to great-power domination, they may be more willing to acquiesce to geopolitical neutrality. In that respect, spheres of restraint could be more liberal as well as more stable.

Spheres of restraint can secure great-power interests

Before events force its hand, the US should use its considerable diplomatic clout to negotiate similar spheres of restraint at the frontiers of Russia and China. By its acceptance of the One China principle, the US already recognises Taiwan as a Chinese sphere. This is effectively a sphere of restraint in that Taiwan retains its liberal institutions and maintains a restrained national-security posture. Not only have China and America so far refrained from attempting to dominate Taiwan, they have actively collaborated to prevent it from declaring independence.[15] Neither, however, exercises as much restraint as the Cold War superpowers did vis-à-vis Finland and Austria. China continues to regard Taiwan as a target for conquest, and America continues to sell it arms and extend a unilateral security guarantee. Lyle Goldstein has described this situation as a potential 'Cuban Missile Crisis in reverse', with the tables turned against the United States.[16] In order to build a more sustainable sphere of restraint, the US could seek a reunification deal whereby China renounces the use of force, the US–Taiwan security relationship ends and China credibly guarantees non-interference with Taiwan's liberal institutions. Perhaps no such deal is possible, but the

US should initiate a diplomatic process to find out and make it a major priority of US–China relations.

The Korean Peninsula, where China's political interests and local military advantages are also overwhelming, might be another promising sphere of restraint. Under present circumstances, China would insist on troop withdrawals and the end of the US–South Korea alliance as a prerequisite for any peaceful-reunification deal. Washington and Seoul could make the path to reunification less contentious by taking the initiative to make South Korea neutral, which would induce Beijing to remove the threat of a veto over a potential reunification deal. As part of the same bargain, the United States and South Korea could ask China to reduce its support for North Korea and actively back a reunification programme under which South Korea would absorb the North.

US unwillingness to accept great powers' claims to special privileges in their respective neighbourhoods forecloses opportunities to negotiate sphere-of-restraint settlements that might be able to enshrine those privileges in a peaceful and orderly manner. The Russian intervention in Ukraine arguably reflected US short-sightedness along these lines. A US–EU attempt to bind Ukraine to the West undermined the political cohesion of Ukraine and provoked a Russian military intervention. Before 2013, there may have been an opportunity for great-power restraint to preserve the integrity of Ukraine, but today there is little hope of its recovering Crimea or eliminating Russia's influence in the east. Now Washington has to accept these realities as fait accomplis. But the US and the EU should still seek to establish a sphere of restraint over what is left of Ukraine by making clear that it will never be a NATO or an EU member, and by discouraging further Russian aggression with economic sanctions.

More broadly, an inflexible US policy of preventing spheres of influence increases the likelihood of military crises on great-power frontiers. And the relative erosion of America's military power-projection capabilities increases the likelihood that such crises will end badly for the United States and compromise the territorial integrity of small front-line countries.

*   *   *

America's post-Cold War 'unipolar moment' obscured the reality that spheres of influence are inherent to international politics. America's modern crusade against them is a futile, risky and destabilising business. Fixtures of American diplomacy in the nineteenth and twentieth centuries, spheres of influence can be tools of coexistence. Peer competition will force US policy-makers to extend at least de facto recognition to rival spheres. But it matters how this happens. Anticipatory negotiation of spheres of restraint could enable spheres of influence to accommodate the interests of both great and small powers, including those of the United States. In the future, there may not be a choice.

Acknowledgements

I am grateful to Alicia Campi, Christopher Preble, Rachel Xian and an anonymous reviewer for reading and commenting on earlier drafts of this article. Thanks also to William Ruger for allowing me to present a draft to the Charles Koch Institute's foreign-policy reading group.

Notes

1   Robert Kagan, 'The United States Must Resist a Return to Spheres of Interest in the International System', Brookings Institution, 19 February 2015, https://www.brookings.edu/blog/order-from-chaos/2015/02/19/the-united-states-must-resist-a-return-to-spheres-of-interest-in-the-international-system/.

2   I adopt John Mearsheimer's definition of 'great power' as a state with 'sufficient military assets to put up a serious fight in an all-out conventional war against the most powerful state in the world' and 'a nuclear deterrent that can survive a nuclear strike against it'. John J. Mearsheimer, *The Tragedy of Great Power Politics* (New York: W.W. Norton & Co., 2001), p. 5.

3   See Paul Keal, 'Contemporary Understanding About Spheres of Influence', *Review of International Studies*, vol. 9, no. 3, July 1983, p. 156.

4   See Lyle J. Goldstein, 'China's Logistics Modernization Is Changing the Pacific Military Balance', *National Interest*, 17 February 2019, https://nationalinterest.org/feature/chinas-logistics-modernization-changing-pacific-military-balance-44612.

5   Terrence K. Kelly, David C. Gompert and Duncan Long, *Smarter Power, Stronger Partners, Volume I: Exploiting U.S. Advantages to Prevent Aggression* (Santa Monica, CA: RAND Corporation, 2016), pp. 90–1, https://www.rand.org/pubs/research_reports/RR1359.html.

6   See Barry R. Posen, 'Command of the Commons: The Military Foundation of U.S. Hegemony', *International Security*, vol. 28, no. 1, Summer 2003, pp. 5–46.

7   See Jennifer Steinhauer and David M. Herszenhorn, 'Defying Obama, Many in Congress Press to Arm Ukraine', *New York Times*, 11 June 2015, https://www.nytimes.com/2015/06/12/world/europe/defying-obama-many-in-congress-press-to-arm-ukraine.html.

8   See, for example, Patrick M. Cronin, 'Power and Order in the South China Sea', Center for a New American Security, 10 November 2016, https://www.cnas.org/publications/reports/power-and-order-in-the-south-china-sea.

9   Stephen Sestanovich, *Maximalist: America in the World from Truman to Obama* (New York: Alfred A. Knopf, 2014), pp. 221–42.

10 Hal Brands and Charles Edel, 'The Disharmony of the Spheres: The U.S. Will Endanger Itself if It Accedes to Russian and Chinese Efforts to Change the International System to Their Liking', *Commentary*, 14 December 2017, https://www.commentarymagazine.com/articles/the-disharmony-of-the-spheres/. See also Kagan, 'The United States Must Resist a Return to Spheres of Interest in the International System'; Thomas J. Wright, *All Measures Short of War: The Contest for the Twenty-first Century and the Future of American Power* (New Haven, CT: Yale University Press, 2017), p. 184.

11 See James M. Acton, 'Escalation Through Entanglement: How the Vulnerability of Command-and-control Systems Raises the Risks of an Inadvertent Nuclear War', *International Security*, vol. 43, no. 1, Summer 2018, pp. 56–99.

12 National Defense Strategy Commission, 'Providing for the Common Defense: The Assessments and Recommendations of the National Defense Strategy Commission', 13 November 2018, https://www.usip.org/publications/2018/11/providing-common-defense.

13 Brands and Edel, 'The Disharmony of the Spheres'.

14 See Hans Mouritzen, 'Small States and Finlandisation in the Age of Trump', *Survival*, vol. 59, no. 2, April–May 2017, pp. 67–84; and Erwin A. Schmidl, 'Lukewarm Neutrality in a Cold War? The Case of Austria', *Journal of Cold War Studies*, vol. 18, no. 4, Fall 2016, pp. 36–50.

15 See Brian Knowlton, 'Bush Warns Taiwan to Keep Status Quo; China Welcomes U.S. Stance', *New York Times*, 10 December 2003, https://www.nytimes.com/2003/12/10/news/bush-warns-taiwan-to-keep-status-quo-china-welcomes-us-stance.html.

16 Lyle J. Goldstein, 'Storm Clouds Are Gathering over the Taiwan Strait', *National Interest*, 18 July 2018, https://nationalinterest.org/feature/storm-clouds-are-gathering-over-taiwan-strait-26146.

Noteworthy

Impeachment and acquittal

'No matter how close you are to this president, do you think for a moment that if he felt it was in his interest he wouldn't ask *you* to be investigated? … If somewhere deep down below you realise that he would, you cannot leave a man like that in office when he has violated the Constitution.'

> *Adam Schiff, lead impeachment manager in the US House of Representatives, presents his opening argument in the Senate trial of US President Donald Trump on 24 January 2020.[1]*

'Washington Democrats think President Donald Trump committed a high crime or misdemeanour the moment he defeated Hillary Clinton. That is the original sin of this presidency: that he won and they lost.'

> *Senator Mitch McConnell speaks on 4 February.[2]*

'The people will judge us for how well and faithfully we fulfil our duty. The grave question the Constitution tasked senators to answer is whether the president committed an act so extreme and egregious that it rises to the level of a high crime and misdemeanour. Yes, he did.
The president asked a foreign government to investigate his political rival. The president withheld vital military funds from that government to press it to do so. The president delayed funds for an American ally at war with Russian invaders. The president's purpose was personal and political. Accordingly, the president is guilty of an appalling abuse of public trust.
What he did was not perfect. No, it was a flagrant assault on our electoral rights, our national security and our fundamental values. Corrupting an election to keep oneself in office is perhaps the most abusive and destructive violation of one's oath of office that I can imagine. […]
My promise before God to apply impartial justice required that I put my personal feelings and political biases aside. Were I to ignore the evidence that has been presented and disregard what I believe my oath and the Constitution demands of me for the sake of a partisan end, it would, I fear, expose my character to history's rebuke and the censure of my own conscience.
  I'm aware that there are people in my party and in my state who will strenuously disapprove of my decision, and in some quarters I will be vehemently denounced. I'm sure to hear abuse from the president and his supporters. Does anyone seriously believe that I would consent to these consequences other than from an inescapable conviction that my oath before God demanded it of me?'

> *Republican Senator Mitt Romney explains his decision to vote to convict President Trump of abuse of power on 5 February.[3]*

'It is, therefore, ordered and adjudged that the said Donald John Trump be, and he is hereby, acquitted of the charges in said articles.'

> *US Chief Justice John G. Roberts, Jr, announces a not-guilty verdict in President Trump's impeachment trial after a majority of senators acquitted him on the charges of abuse of power and obstruction of Congress in a vote on 5 February 2020.[4]*

DOI 10.1080/00396338.2020.1739948

Viral

'Low Ratings Fake News MSDNC (Comcast) & @CNN are doing everything possible to make the Caronavirus [sic] look as bad as possible, including panicking markets, if possible. Likewise their incompetent Do Nothing Democrat comrades are all talk, no action. USA in great shape!'

President Trump tweets on 26 February 2020 on the global spread of the viral disease COVID-19, also known as coronavirus, which was first detected in China in December 2019.[5]

'As a precaution we are advising to distribute the Eucharist preferably into the hands of the faithful, and to avoid the physical contact from a peaceful handshake.'

Religious authorities in Sicily, Italy, recommend changes to the way that Mass is celebrated in Roman Catholic churches as a means of avoiding the spread of coronavirus.[6]

'The kingdom's government has decided to [suspend] entry to the kingdom for the purpose of *umrah* [pilgrimage] and visit to the prophet's mosque temporarily.'

The government of Saudi Arabia announces a ban on foreign pilgrims entering the country.[7]

'One thing becoming clear is we just can't predict the spread of this and how bad it can be. But it's not difficult to get to something similar to the 2008 [financial] crisis with a pandemic situation. Of course, we hope it won't get that bad.'

Jennifer McKeown of Capital Economics comments on the potential consequences of coronavirus for the global economy.[8]

'WHO has already declared a public health emergency of international concern – our highest level of alarm.
[…]
For the moment, we are not witnessing sustained and intensive community transmission of this virus, and we are not witnessing large-scale severe disease or death.
[…]
Do not mistake me: I am not downplaying the seriousness of the situation, or the potential for this to become a pandemic, because it has that potential. Every scenario is still on the table.'

Tedros Adhanom, director-general of the World Health Organization (WHO), speaks on 26 February 2020.[9]

'Seriously people – STOP BUYING MASKS! They are NOT effective in preventing general public from catching #Coronavirus, but if healthcare providers can't get them to care for sick patients, it puts them and our communities at risk!'

The US Surgeon General Jerome Adams tweets on 29 February 2020.[10]

Sources

1 Nicholas Fandos, 'Branding Trump a Danger, Democrats Cap the Case for His Removal', *New York Times*, 24 January 2020, https://www.nytimes.com/2020/01/24/us/politics/democrats-impeachment-trial.html?action=click&module=Top%20Stories&pgtype=Homepage.

2 Patricia Mazzei and Catie Edmondson, 'Susan Collins Announces She Will Vote to Acquit Trump, Calling Conduct "Wrong"', *New York Times*, 4 February 2020, https://www.nytimes.com/2020/02/04/us/politics/senate-impeachment-vote.html.

3 'Full Transcript: Mitt Romney's Speech Announcing Vote to Convict Trump', *New York Times*, 5 February 2020, https://www.nytimes.com/2020/02/05/us/politics/mitt-romney-impeachment-speech-transcript.html.

4 Nicholas Fandos, 'Trump Acquitted of Two Impeachment Charges in Near Party-line Vote', *New York Times*, 5 February 2020, https://www.nytimes.com/2020/02/05/us/politics/trump-acquitted-impeachment.html?action=click&module=Spotlight&pgtype=Homepage.

5 Donald J. Trump (@realDonaldTrump), tweet, 26 February 2020, https://twitter.com/realDonaldTrump/status/1232652371832004608.

6 Lorenzo Tondo, 'Italy's Priests Told to Take Steps at Mass to Counter Coronavirus', *Guardian*, 27 February 2020, https://www.theguardian.com/world/2020/feb/27/italy-priests-told-take-steps-mass-counter-coronavirus.

7 Sam Jones and Martin Farrer, 'Saudi Arabia Bans Foreign Pilgrims as Japan Plans to Close Schools', *Guardian*, 27 February 2020, https://www.theguardian.com/world/2020/feb/27/saudia-arabia-bans-foreign-pilgrims-as-coronavirus-hits-region.

8 Rob Davies, Richard Partington and Graeme Wearden, 'Coronavirus Fears Trigger Biggest One-day Fall on US Stock Market', *Guardian*, 27 February 2020, https://www.theguardian.com/business/2020/feb/27/coronavirus-could-trigger-damage-on-scale-of-2008-financial-crisis-covid-19.

9 World Health Organization, 'WHO Director-General's Opening Remarks at the Mission Briefing on COVID-19 – 26 February 2020', 26 February 2020, https://www.who.int/dg/speeches/detail/who-director-general-s-opening-remarks-at-the-mission-briefing-on-covid-19---26-february-2020.

10 Jerome M. Adams (@Surgeon_General), tweet, 29 February 2020, https://twitter.com/Surgeon_General/status/1233725785283932160.

Strategy and Democracy

Hew Strachan

On 18 June 2012, a group of academics and think-tank experts from NATO member states went to Kabul University to meet a class of politics students.[1] The visitors had imagined that it would be an opportunity to discuss the upcoming presidential election, due in 2014. Hamid Karzai was not eligible to run again, and the proliferation of parties in Afghanistan made it even more important to identify who the principal candidates might be. However, like many Afghans, the students felt there was still plenty of time to sort out the issue. More pressing for them was their security. The schedule for NATO's withdrawal from active combat operations, also due to be completed in 2014, had been set. Understandably, the students wanted to know what NATO was going to do after 2014.

One particularly outraged student referred to president Barack Obama's visit to Kabul just over six weeks previously. On 1 May 2012, Obama had met Karzai to sign the 'Enduring Strategic Partnership Agreement between the Islamic Republic of Afghanistan and the United States of America'. The agreement included arrangements for a long-term security commitment, and for the possibility of US forces remaining in Afghanistan after 2014 'for the purposes of training Afghan Forces and targeting the remnants of al-Qaeda'.[2] The deal had been trumpeted on Afghan television by both Obama and Karzai. However, this was not what agitated the student. In the early hours of the following morning, at 4.01 Afghan time, he had again seen

Sir Hew Strachan is Wardlaw Professor of International Relations at the University of St Andrews and Emeritus Fellow of All Souls College, Oxford.

Survival | vol. 62 no. 2 | April–May 2020 | pp. 51–82   DOI 10.1080/00396338.2020.1739949

Obama on television, on this occasion addressing an American audience from the US base at Bagram. The president told the United States that 'our troops will be coming home'.[3]

In 2005, General Sir Rupert Smith characterised today's wars as 'wars among the people'.[4] He was reflecting on his own experiences in Northern Ireland and Bosnia, but what he wrote captured the emerging concerns of American and British soldiers in Iraq and Afghanistan. They were engaged, much like the armies in past counter-insurgency campaigns, in securing the loyalty of the local people. For Smith, 'wars among the people' characterised the operating environment in which armies have often, and not only recently, found themselves. But what does 'war among the people' mean in the context of national strategy? In seeking to answer that question, this article is less concerned with the loyalties of peoples caught in the crossfires of combat zones, and more with the role of peoples in mature democracies in the shaping of the decisions to intervene in fragile states.

Mixed messages

These are not separate issues. In May 2012, Obama gave one message to the people of Afghanistan and another to the people of the United States. Although both statements could be reconciled, outwardly they contradicted each other. He told each community what he thought it wanted to hear, but in the process he caused confusion and dismay. He was not the only leader of a democratic state to use public statements to send mixed messages. Britain's prime minister, David Cameron, said in 2010 that the country would end its war in Afghanistan by 2015, and went on to explain that he had set a clear withdrawal date because the British people expected it and were right to do so.[5] He said nothing about the objectives of the UK government within Afghanistan, what a desirable outcome might look like for that country, or what the political consequences of the timing might be for the Afghan people.

Both the president of the United States and the prime minister of the United Kingdom were effectively treating their own electorates as partners in their decision-making processes – a much more significant development in strategy-making than 'waging war among the people'. In the latter scenario the people are treated as the passive objects of influence; in the former, they become active participants in the formation of policy. As Obama's mixed messages on 1 May 2012 showed, however, the people in the theatre of war and the people at home are not so easily separated, especially in a world where reporting is interconnected and no longer easily managed by governments or exclusively handled by professional journalists. Today, the message given in the theatre of operations cannot in practice diverge from that given at home without running the risk of inconsistency at best and direct self-contradiction at worst.

Both Obama and Cameron chose deadlines for the withdrawal of troops from Afghanistan which bore less relationship to the possible situation in Afghanistan than to the electoral cycles in their own countries. Their objectives were defined not so much in terms of identifiable objectives within Afghanistan and more in terms of what have come to be called 'exit strategies'. Exits are not strategies. Exits are means, or possibly more accurately ways, but they are not ends. By admitting the role of democracy in strategy, the leaders of democratic states have put themselves between a rock and a hard place. In order to explain to their nations why their armed forces are engaged in faraway places of which their peoples know little, they use the vocabulary of mass mobilisation borrowed from the Second World War. They are ready to let these wars be called 'wars of choice', but they employ phrases borrowed from 'existential' conflict, which suggest they are 'wars of necessity'. George W. Bush compared the 9/11 attacks with Pearl Harbor, and Tony Blair cited the appeasement of Adolf Hitler when calling for action against Saddam Hussein.[6] Obama was much more circumspect in his choice of words than his predecessor. By then, many Americans were becoming war weary, and Obama may therefore have felt that he was responding to the wishes of the American people. But this also created challenges. The consequence of Obama's more measured approach was that he earned a reputation for indecision, for lack of clarity, and for a failure to provide the strategic leadership required not just by the United States but also by NATO and the West as a whole.

Britons too had become doubtful of the value of intervention by 2009–10. However, unlike Obama, Cameron continued to use the language of Bush and Blair. Three times in his tenure as prime minister Cameron spoke of an existential conflict, of a generational war and of direct threats to the British way of life: in 2011 over Libya; in January 2013 after an al-Qaeda attack on a BP gas installation in Algeria; and in June 2015 after an Islamic State-inspired attack on British citizens in Sousse, Tunisia.[7] As in Obama's case, his words created strategic uncertainty, albeit for different reasons. They exposed a gap between his rhetoric and his intent. He used big words, but did less: during his premiership, British society, although apparently engaged in multiple wars simultaneously, continued to look and behave as though it was at peace. Its domestic circumstances were characterised by levels of security which contradicted Cameron's calls to arms. His audience knew that Britain was not in the dire straits of summer 1940, and they also knew that their lives were much safer than was the case for inhabitants of many other parts of the contemporary world. The effect of democracy on strategic decision-making seems to encourage many national leaders to over-promise and under-deliver, or to over-dramatise and under-perform, when they should be under-promising and over-delivering. If substance matched rhetoric, Britain would have done much more than commit 2% of its GDP to defence in the Cameron years.

There is a conundrum here. Democratic leaders are under pressure to exaggerate the threat precisely because their electorates don't feel threatened, and yet the more they do so the less convinced their publics seem to be. Gordon Brown, when prime minister, explained the war in Afghanistan in terms which related to domestic security. He said British troops were fighting, killing and dying in Helmand to keep the streets of Britain safe.[8] The public was not convinced – and nor were many of the soldiers who were deployed to Afghanistan to protect them.

Peace, not war

Democracy has so associated itself with material and personal security, with the functioning of liberal capitalism, that it has divorced itself from war. The identity of the nation-state itself has been weakened, on the one hand by its reliance for security on supranational organisations such as the United Nations, NATO and the European Union, and on the other by its transfer of what used to be state functions to private companies and multinational corporations. This process applies even within defence, with the growth of private military companies. Democracy has, furthermore, become associated with peace, not war. That was Woodrow Wilson's vision in 1917: he believed that democratic states could create a peaceful world order, and, for all the failure of the Versailles settlement of 1919, that ambition has not only survived but grown.[9] Democracies are characterised as risk- and casualty-averse, and they are seen as reluctant to be taxed in order to fund national, as opposed to medical or social, security.

Many of these hypotheses are exactly that, but they have achieved an authority almost independent of contingency in the form of democratic-peace theory. In 1989, Jack Levy wrote that 'the absence of war between democracies comes as close as anything we have to an empirical law in international relations'.[10] True believers in democratic-peace theory argue that democracies do not go to war with one another, and see this as a direct consequence of the character of democracy itself. Of course, democratic-peace theory does not rule out democracies going to war with non-democracies, but that in itself raises the question of what is a democracy and what is not. At the outbreak of the First World War in 1914, Britain had the lowest level of male suffrage of any belligerent except Hungary. About 60% of British men had the vote; in Germany every male was able to vote. And yet Britain portrayed its war as one for democracy, an image that the Entente powers burnished, and that the United States endorsed after it entered the conflict in 1917. The demarcation line that separates democratic from non-democratic government is more blurred than theory suggests. Even states that political scientists might classify as non-democracies are not necessarily states that lack mass participation in their political life: a point true not just of Wilhelmine Germany in the First World War but also of Nazi Germany in the Second. Neither of those German governments is conventionally described as a democracy, but both enjoyed periods of genuinely popular support. One man's political populism can be another man's democracy.

The assumption that populism is not democracy is a product of the master narrative of liberalism, an inheritor of the Whig view of history. Wilson's conviction, that liberal democracy would produce not just domestic but also international harmony, was a belief which many of the wars of the last century were in part fought to prove, albeit with variable results. Its logical corollary is that democracies struggle to reconcile themselves to war and are therefore slow to undertake it. An inherent tension therefore exists between the two principal words in the title of this article, strategy and democracy. Historically, this is absurd: from classical Athens to modern America, democracies have waged war, and done so through a participatory decision-making process. Much of Thucydides's *History of the Peloponnesian War* is concerned with exactly this problem – the difficulties faced by Athens as a democracy in waging war coherently and consistently. However, for modern historians the story of democracy's engagement with strategy begins not with Thucydides but with the eighteenth-century Enlightenment. Indeed, the concept of strategy itself can be seen as a product of the Enlightenment.[11]

The idea of the democratic peace, after all, takes its argument from Immanuel Kant's essay on 'Perpetual Peace'. Kant contended that republics would enjoy peace with other republics. He did so in 1795, when Europe was still exploring the foothills of a series of wars which would last another 20 years, and which were driven by the French republic fighting – or so it claimed – for liberty, equality and fraternity, against a league of absolute monarchies. Despite the horrors which the wars of the French Revolution brought to Europe, most revolutionaries, at least in 1795, would not have disagreed with Kant. The reason that France found itself at war, they believed, was not its fault but the responsibility of autocracies and absolute monarchies that failed to recognise the need to democratise by giving power to the people. They were waging war to spread republicanism, which in turn would foster perpetual peace; this was 'a war to end all wars', to use a phrase from the next major European war fought a century later.[12]

Democracy and mobilisation

Running against this narrative was a powerful alternative: the notion that democratisation was a tool for national mobilisation in time of war. A French officer, the aristocratic and enlightened Comte de Guibert, first published his 'Essai général de tactique' anonymously in 1770, but it appeared under his own name in 1772 and in an English translation in 1781. Most of those who quote Guibert do so by citing the following passage:

Let us suppose in Europe, there was to spring up a vigorous people, with genius, with power, and a happy form of government; a set of people that to strict virtue, and a national soldiery, joined a fixed plan of aggrandizement, who never lost sight of that system, who, knowing how to carry on a war with little expence, and so subsist by their conquests, was not reduced to the necessity of laying down their arms by the calculations of financiers.

Guibert argued that, for France, the first step to a successful exterior policy was domestic reform: 'Politics are naturally divided into parts, INTERIOR and EXTERIOR Politics. The first is as a basis for the second.' 'Interior Politics,' he went on,

having thus prepared a state, with what facility external Politics can resolve upon the system of her own interests in opposition to her foreign ones, by the raising of a respectable military power! How easy it is to have armies invincible, in a state where its subjects are citizens, where they cherish and revere government, where they are fond of glory, where they are not intimidated at the idea of toiling for the general good!

Guibert dedicated his book 'to my Country', not to his king, to whom as an army officer he owed allegiance. His idea of France included the monarch, the country's 'father', but it also embraced its ministers or administrators, and its people or 'children'. He looked forward to the day when all France would be united. 'May the Ruler and his Subjects, the high and low degrees of the community, with one accord, feel themselves honoured with the title of Citizens', he wrote.[13]

Guibert died on 6 May 1790. The French Revolution had yet to reach its apogee in the Terror, nor had the transformation of the French state yet revolutionised the structure of the French army. By 1795, both developments were obvious. Revolutionary France regarded those who opposed the logic of its own position, its conflation of the revolution with universal principles, as enemies caught in the vice of political backwardness. In the Vendée, Catholic, counter-revolutionary peasants were treated not as naive and ill educated, but as political actors conspiring against the revolution and its government. About a quarter of a million men, women and children, or 25% of the population of the Vendée, were exterminated by the revolutionary armies in 1793–94.[14] Those armies were themselves politicised: their soldiers were now, in conformity with Guibert's hopes, citizens.[15] Democratisation became the agent, not of moderation in war, but of its intensification. Captain Dupuy wrote to his sister from the Vendée in January 1794:

> Wherever we go we are bearing fire and death. Age, sex, nothing is being respected. Yesterday, one of our detachments burned a village. One volunteer killed three women with his own hands. It is atrocious, but the safety of the Republic demands it imperatively.[16]

One reason for Dupuy's sense of urgency related to the fact that revolutionary France faced an external threat as well as an internal war: while it was dealing with counter-revolution in the Vendée, it was also fighting the War of the First Coalition against Britain, Austria and Prussia. If the enemy within was not eradicated, he could facilitate the enemy without. So republicanism and revolutionary fervour fused with nationalism and patriotism.

In 1797, Gerhard von Scharnhorst, a Hanoverian by birth, who had served with the Prussian army in the War of the First Coalition, published his general reflections on the armies in the French revolutionary wars. He asked why those of France had fared as well as they had, given that they had purged most of their officers and overthrown their disciplinary systems. His answer was that the French army had been transformed by the revolution, by the political impetus given to its army as a result, and by the identification of the army with the nation. For Scharnhorst, as for other military reformers in the following decade, citizenship created soldiers with a stake in the nation, who were readier to fight and die because they had rights, than were the soldiers of pre-1789 autocracies.[17]

Prussia took no part in the wars with France between 1795 and the Jena campaign in 1806. Smashed by Napoleon in that year, it agreed humiliating terms at Tilsit in December 1807, and again stayed clear of war until 1812. Those Prussians who saw Napoleon as a tyrant looked enviously to

Spain and Italy for evidence of effective popular resistance to French rule, waged by guerrillas and stoked by national sentiment. Scharnhorst was one of them, as were August von Gneisenau and Scharnhorst's protégé, Carl von Clausewitz. From 1809, Gneisenau and Clausewitz plotted a national insurgency against French occupation in defiance of the more complaisant attitude of their king, Friedrich Wilhelm III. When the king agreed to Napoleon's demand that Prussia supply a contingent for his invasion of Russia, all three were disgusted. In February 1812, Clausewitz sent a long, three-part memorandum to Gneisenau, in which he called on the German nation to wage a war of national liberation. The entire population should be mobilised, be ready to use terror and prepare itself to die rather than admit defeat, he said. He specifically quoted Guibert, albeit without acknowledgement, calling for 'a people, with genius, with power, and a happy form of government'.[18]

This was the same Clausewitz who, when he came to write Book VIII, Chapter 3 of *On War*, identified the French Revolution as having put the state's mobilisation for war on a new and unprecedented level.

> Suddenly war again [as in ancient Rome] became the business of the people – a people of thirty millions, all of whom considered themselves to be citizens ... The people became a participant in war; instead of governments and armies as heretofore, the full weight of the nation was thrown into the balance.[19]

The question for Clausewitz was whether this would be the pattern for the future:

> From now on, will every war in Europe be waged with the full resources of the state, and therefore have to be fought only over major issues that affect the people? Or shall we again see a gradual separation taking place between government and people?[20]

Clausewitz was clear about the 'enormous contribution the heart and temper of the nation can make to the sum total of its politics, war potential and fighting strength'.[21]

In Book I of *On War*, Clausewitz described war as being made up of three parts: passion, the play of probability and chance, and reason. He then associated each of these qualities, the so-called 'trinity', with three particular groups of actors in war – passion with the people, the play of probability and chance with the army and its commander, and reason with the government. But he also made clear, in a way which far too many modern readers neglect, that these relations were not fixed. He did not rule out a people that was both passionate and rational; indeed, much else that he wrote about early nineteenth-century warfare was conditional on the realisation that European civilisation did not preclude the need to abandon moderation in war and embrace terror. Nor was the relationship between war and policy fixed in the trinity; it too could fluctuate, with the rational element of policy submerged by passion or by the contingencies of the battlefield. The problem with recent, predominantly Anglophone readings of *On War* is their determination to nest it in a view of modern strategy that sees a linear relationship between policy and war, that believes the former invariably limits the latter, and that the making of strategy is settled by an elite relationship between politicians and generals that excludes the people. The effect is to subordinate the roles of both passion and the people.[22]

To be fair, after the defeat of Napoleon, Clausewitz colluded in this process. The blandishments of peace and of a settled domestic life moderated his Francophobic anger. The peacemakers saw the French Revolution as the fount of 20 years of war in Europe. It had transformed warfare into something protracted, destructive and, to use a neologism not then coined, total. Preventing revolution could prevent war, and separating revolution from war was high on the list of most monarchs when they met in Vienna in 1815. Friedrich Wilhelm of Prussia was among them. Unbeknownst to the king, Clausewitz's memorandum of 1812 had questioned his authority by appealing to the German nation over his head. Fortunately for Clausewitz, the memorandum was not published in either of their lifetimes. However, Friedrich Wilhelm was well aware of Clausewitz's insubordination. He had defied the king's wishes by resigning from the Prussian army to serve in that of Russia so that he could fight the French, and he continued to rile conservatives in the years immediately after the war as he and others fought to retain the military and social reforms which the need to defeat Napoleon had forced the king to adopt.

At their apex, at least for Clausewitz, stood the Landwehr, a national militia raised by conscription and hallowed in the minds of the reformers by its part in the defeat of Napoleon in 1813. For Clausewitz, the Landwehr enabled the creation of a mass army in time of war, but it also 'touche[d] the entire people', 'affect[ed] the way the people live' and was 'an expression of the absolute power of the nation'. As he summarised it:

> The ability to produce a greater – indeed a much greater – force in time of war for the same cost, with no fixed limit, to infuse the entire people with a warlike spirit, to bind the army and the people together, drawing upon the strength of the whole nation in a defensive struggle – these are the main advantages of the *Landwehr* system.

Its opponents, he argued, were snobbish noblemen who could not bear to serve in the ranks with peasants, men whom they regarded as 'not really citizens', but subjects. Nor could they abide the thought of their sons serving under officers who were the sons of grocers. He rubbished too those opponents of the Landwehr who feared that by arming the people the state would facilitate revolution. Clausewitz argued that revolution had more profound causes than this, and that 'to believe in the possibility of such a disruption of our present circumstances would be to believe in ghosts, and to ignore external danger because of this illusory evil would be to embrace death for fear of dying'.[23]

Service, citizenship and education

After 1819, Clausewitz realised that, if he wanted preferment in post-war Prussia, he had better moderate his language. He ceased writing broadsides calling for military reform that carried political and democratising implications, and in doing so he reflected a broader current in military thought. The idealistic conflation of citizenship and military service, of political awareness and the defence of the nation, was moderated after 1815, and not just in Prussia. Armies served less as instruments for national mobilisation and more as tools of counter-revolutionary domestic order. The debate about democratisation and war became bound up above all with the idea of the nation in arms, of military service and its terms. Conscription became less a manifestation of liberalism and political awareness, as in its idealised form in the 1790s, and more a mechanism for social control. The revolutions of 1830, especially in France, where locally based units joined the insurgents (as they had done in 1789–91), stoked enough fear to cause governments to double down on their efforts.[24] They succeeded. Although the action of Stendhal's great novel, *The Charterhouse of Parma*, published in 1839, is focused in Italy, it begins with its hero, Fabrice del Dongo, then a teenager, joining Napoleon in the Hundred Days; much of the plot is then played out in a world of princely courts and ecclesiastical hierarchies as Fabrice lives down the revolutionary credentials he has acquired through his youthful idealism. Broadly speaking, in 1848, as revolution whipped through Europe's major cities, armies remained loyal to their governments. In the run-up to the First World War, the mass armies of European states may have matched themselves against each other, but they had one eye fixed on the enemy within, especially as industrialisation and urbanisation fed the growth of trades unions and political socialism. In 1907, the German general staff prepared a memorandum on fighting in insurgent towns, and the army, despite its desire for more men, held back from recruiting too heavily in such areas.[25] In France, the army was the principal tool for maintaining public order until 1921. One future First World War general was asked by his mother why he wanted to follow a career which consisted of confronting and breaking strikes.[26]

Conscription became a mechanism for social control

By 1914, mass armies could be raised without so much attention being paid to the corollary that they should see themselves as politically aware partners in the making of national strategy. If the debate remained alive, it did so in Republican France, with socialists arguing that citizen soldiers would fight purely defensive wars. In *L'armée nouvelle*, published in 1910, Jean Jaurès used the example of the armies of the French Revolution to ram home this point. In 1916, by contrast, Britain adopted conscription despite the fact that the limitations on male suffrage meant that many of those called upon to defend their country were not fully fledged citizens. The association between military service and citizenship was manifested after the event, not before it, and negatively rather than positively. When the franchise was extended to all men aged over 21 in 1918, conscientious objectors were temporarily excluded.[27]

By then all the armies of the major belligerents were effectively citizen armies, subject to the currents of opinion voiced by their friends and families at home, and linked to them by leave, literacy and efficient postal services. Commanders realised that they needed to provide political education in order to sustain morale at the front. In July 1917, Germany introduced a system of patriotic instruction. Normally condemned as ineffective, such instruction is perhaps ripe for re-examination given the resilience of the German army into 1918.[28] In France, Philippe Pétain, appointed commander-in-chief in succession to Robert Georges Nivelle in May 1917, responded to the mutinies in the army with a determination to give soldiers more information on the general strategic situation.[29] British reactions to similar problems were crystallised on 1 January 1918 with an educational programme which embraced the political context of the war, British war aims and Britain's post-war vision. From summer 1918 the programme was in the hands of Major Lord Gorell, who in 1914 had been the editor of the *Times Educational Supplement*.[30] In revolutionary Russia, M.V. Frunze in particular argued that its soldiers needed to be politically aware. For the Bolsheviks, the army became a vehicle for educating peasants, not just so that they would have the skills to be better soldiers but also so that they would be committed socialists. In the civil war command was divided, with political commissars responsible for political as opposed to military direction, but from 1925 the adoption of unitary command progressively passed this responsibility on to the unit commanders. By 1932, some units devoted 200 hours a year to political education.[31] In the Second World War, most armies provided education in the war aims and value systems for which they required their soldiers to fight. Such approaches were not just the prerogatives of the Red Army or the Wehrmacht, but were adopted by the armed forces of the liberal democracies, including Britain and the United States.

The combination of compulsory military service, citizenship and political education, the aspiration of reformers and revolutionaries at the turn of the eighteenth and nineteenth centuries, peaked in the two world wars. At one level the inspiration for these schemes was positive: conscription created an educational opportunity which would in turn produce more aware and better motivated soldiers. But at another level the whole project was a manifestation of fear – fear of pacifist propaganda, fear of subversive ideology, and fear of revolution or counter-revolution. By the second half of the twentieth century, those who were motivated to fight for political reasons had become insurgents, radicals and revolutionaries. In Jean Lartéguy's novel *The Centurions*, published in 1960, Captain Jacques de Glatigny, a French aristocratic officer captured at Dien Bien Phu in the French Indo-China War, defends a brother officer who has been accused of becoming a communist while a prisoner of the Vietminh because he has learnt the principles of revolutionary war. Glatigny's senior officer asserts that the army must re-establish its traditions and to do that it must 'separate the sheep from the goats'. Glatigny replies,

> In that case, General, we're all of us goats – all who were in the maquis in France, who served in the First Army or the F.F.L., who took part in the Indo-China campaign, in the fighting units, all who believe that the army depends on the people just as a fish depends on water. That's what Mao-Tse-Tung wrote, and it's because we ignored his theories on revolutionary warfare that we deserved our crushing defeat.[32]

Lartéguy's own career in many respects mirrored that of the fictional Glatigny. By serving with the Free French in the Second World War, he fought to overthrow the Vichy government headed by Pétain himself and supported by many officers who respected the 'traditions' of the French army. Having been wounded, he covered France's wars of decolonisation as a war correspondent and journalist. However, the process by which the politically aware fighter became once again suspect, as he had been in the aftermath of the French Revolution and Napoleon, began not with the wars which Lartéguy experienced, but earlier, with the First World War itself.

War and revolution

The war of 1914–18 changed the relationship between revolution and war. Popular mobilisation and political awareness, universal suffrage and mass press made the 'people' full participants in war. However, they also made them a source of potential vulnerability. In the Napoleonic Wars, revolution had led to war; in the First World War, war led to revolution. As the crisis of July 1914 unfolded, several of its leading protagonists expressed the fear that that would be the case. The more conservative advisers to Tsar Nicholas II warned him of the danger, with good reason given that Russia's 1905 defeat in the Russo-Japanese War had been followed by revolution. The German chancellor, Theobald von Bethmann Hollweg, expressed similar views, and the belief that the lamps were going out all over Europe, attributed to the British foreign secretary, Sir Edward Grey, can also be understood in this context.[33]

They were right. From the outset of the war, Germany aimed to export revolution to the empires of its enemies, Britain, France and Russia, and it did so not just in a colonial context, but also to Dublin in 1916 and Petrograd in 1917. Britain did the same, fomenting revolution to undermine the Ottoman Empire, especially in Arabia, and by 1917–18 the allies were ready to do so in Germany and Austria-Hungary. Democracy had become a weakness as well as a strength through its capacity for mass mobilisation. After 1918, Britain's blockade of Germany became rationalised as the instrument that had persuaded the German people to turn against their Kaiser and to overthrow their government in the final stages of the war.

In 1939, Britain planned to use economic warfare against Germany once more, but by summer 1940 German forces stood on the Atlantic coast from the North Cape to western France, making a blockade on the lines of 1914–18 impossible, and a year later they commanded most of Central and Eastern Europe as well, thus rendering it largely redundant. In its stead, by winter 1941–42 the strategic bombing offensive had been fashioned into an instrument designed to target German civilian morale. The ideas of Giulio Douhet with regard to the use of airpower in modern war arose precisely from his awareness of the relationship between citizenship and modern war. The belligerent populations of 1914–18 were responsible political actors in their own right, who could therefore be attacked as active participants in war even if they were civilians and non-combatants.[34] By 1943, Italy itself provided evidence that Douhet might have been right – not least because of its experiences of attack from the air, the population in the south turned against Fascism and ejected Mussolini.[35] In 1944, Allied intelligence searched for evidence of German collapse through another 'stab in the back' on the same lines as in 1918.[36] In the First World War, Allied assessments of German opinion had divided reasonable liberals, who were open to compromise, from Prussian militarists, who were not; the Allies sought to encourage the former to prioritise their political beliefs over their national identity. Hitler and the Nazis, precisely because they believed in this explanation for Germany's defeat, sought to prevent its recurrence. In this at least they succeeded.

In the narratives of the ultimate victors in both world wars, their own populations were united, robust and loyal; it was the peoples subject to authoritarian regimes who had proved brittle and fragile. The presumption here was that the offer of democratisation would cause the people to turn against their own autocratic leaders and embrace their invaders – a presumption put to the test in the invasion of Iraq in 2003 and found wanting.

Redefining civil–military relations

Between 1945 and the end of the Cold War, the Western democracies did not have to address the role of the people in the making of strategy at any sustained or serious level. Their armed forces were actively engaged in the wars fought as part of their withdrawal from empire. The promoters of democracy were now not their own governments, but the colonial resistance movements. Students across Europe and the United States put posters of Che Guevara on their walls and read Frantz Fanon's *The Wretched of the Earth* (1961).[37] Guevara and Fanon were the icons of the enemy, not the constituent elements of a trinity in the making of national strategy.

At home, nuclear weapons made the people potential targets of attack, as they had been in the Second World War, but now they were perpetually bound as hostages to deterrence. They became passive pawns more than potentially active participants whose loyalties could be undermined by the effects of sustained conventional bombing. When they protested against their role in the nexus of deterrence, as they did through the Campaign for Nuclear Disarmament or through opposition to cruise missiles, they were identified with the subversive influences of the putative enemy, as working against the state, not strengthening it.

Nuclear weapons demobilised the democratic resilience of Western governments in two more direct ways. Firstly, they reinforced the case against the mass army. In Britain specifically, the 1957 Defence White Paper simultaneously embraced nuclear deterrence and rejected conscription. Other countries went down similar routes, but more slowly. The United States ended the draft and adopted the all-volunteer force in response to defeat in the Vietnam War. Most European states moved to professional armed forces after the end of the Cold War. In 1997–98, even France, the spiritual and intellectual home of the nation in arms, ended conscription. Democracies no longer presumed that going to war would require the active collective participation of their citizens.

That broke the physical link between citizenship and strategy; more surprisingly, the fiscal link was disrupted too. Nuclear weapons were a cheap option. They enabled states to maintain a massively destructive capability at a containable cost, while not engaging in active hostilities. In 1799, William Pitt had introduced income tax to Britain precisely to fund war; in 1842 Sir Robert Peel was the first British prime minister to apply it in peacetime, but he still saw it as an emergency and temporary measure. William Ewart Gladstone, who became president of the Board of Trade in Peel's government the following year, believed, as Peel did, that continuing to treat income tax as a war tax would suppress the British voters' appetite for war. As prime minister, he realised that was not the case, but income tax did have another effect. Given that tax rates had to be approved by Parliament, taxation provided a form of wider participation in the decision-making process which war required. By and large, late Victorians escaped direct service in the navy or the army as Britain did not adopt national service, but they did put their hands in their pockets to pay for defence, and especially for the navy.[38] The citizens of democratic states may not have had to serve their country in war, as did those of republican Rome or revolutionary France, but they funded their defence from their own hard-earned incomes, and consented in the process. That relationship was weakened in the Cold War by the savings Britain and its NATO allies made on conventional capabilities through their reliance on nuclear weapons. It was definitively broken after 2003.

One of the most remarkable aspects of the wars waged by Western democracies since the 9/11 attacks in 2001 is that they were presented as effectively cost-free. The decisions to invade Afghanistan and then Iraq were not accompanied by major statements from governments as to how they would be funded. In 2008, Joseph Stiglitz and Linda Bilmes estimated that the eventual overall expenditure, including such indirect costs as long-term medical care for the wounded, interest payments on the borrowing which war necessitated and the opportunity costs of going to war in the first place, would total $3 trillion.[39] That was for the United States alone. Similar points can be made for the United Kingdom. Neither Tony Blair nor Gordon Brown mobilised the people of Britain for the wars in Iraq and Afghanistan by asking them to fund Britain's military effort through increased taxation or austerity. Instead, the democracies hid the costs of war and struggled to answer direct questions designed to elicit them. Most modern wars have been funded largely by borrowing; the function of taxation has been to mop up excessive demand and dampen inflation. When the credit crisis of 2008–09 caused an economic crash, few turned to the wars in Iraq and Afghanistan for explanations, as governments had turned to the First World War in the Depression of the early 1920s. Democratic states, despite being conditioned to cut defence expenditure in peacetime, proved unable even to ask about the role of waging protracted war in expanding defence costs and creating national deficits.

Both directly and indirectly, the place of democracy in the making of strategy – through the active participation of the citizen soldier or through the indirect contribution of the enfranchised taxpayer – had been marginalised by the beginning of the twenty-first century. The consequence is that the making of strategy is no longer trinitarian in a Clausewitzian sense. Moreover, Western democracies have adopted a model of civil–military relations designed to reflect that – one which specifically excludes the people from the relationship, certainly insofar as it involves the formation of strategy.

In 1957, Samuel Huntington published *The Soldier and the State*, a book which remains a standard text on civil–military relations. Although it referred to the experiences of other countries, and took the examples of Germany and Japan as cautionary tales, its core problem was that confronted by the United States. At the outset, Huntington posed a specific question: 'what pattern of civil–military relations will best maintain the security of the American nation?'[40] Two of the book's three parts were devoted entirely to America. The question was fresh because, after the end of the Second World War in 1945, the United States did not simply demobilise and reduce its armed forces. In maintaining a sizeable military establishment in peacetime, it had – or so Huntington argued – introduced a significant new actor in the making of policy.

The United States of the American Revolution, like France in 1789, had had to embrace what Huntington called 'subjective military control': the idea that the citizen soldier would, by virtue of the combination of civic rights and military obligations, become the symbol of national will, and that political intent and military capability would be fused in one.[41] The militia's central position as the 'constitutional force' had British roots, but its legacy survives in the US in a way that it does not in the United Kingdom. Those who defend the Second Amendment to the Constitution, which asserts the individual's right to own arms, forget that it was originally contingent on the existence of a now defunct organisation, the militia. Its justification rested on the reciprocal civic obligation to serve.[42]

War and politics

Huntington rejected this inheritance as a model for the United States in the Cold War, reasonably enough given that the threats the country now faced were neither from loyalists to the north nor from an open frontier to the west. Instead, he stressed what he called 'objective military control', an idea which, as he acknowledged, had no foundation in the Constitution: that the armed forces are subordinated to the civilian direction of the government.[43] Governments may be elected by the people in order to serve them, but the central relationship in Huntington's objective military control is not that with the people, but that between elites, the president and his cabinet on the one hand, and the professional heads of the armed forces on the other. In 2010, this was the model of civil–military relations which required Obama to sack General Stanley McChrystal as the commander-in-chief of the International Security Assistance Force because he criticised the president's strategy in Afghanistan.

Huntington's book addressed an American problem at a particular stage of its development. It does not follow that its model still applies more than 60 years after its conception, in very different situations from the early Cold War. Today's problems are those of war, not peace, albeit not the 'major' war whose threat underpinned Huntington's thinking.

Soldiers are assumed to be apolitical

The armed forces of the United States are no longer drafted but are fully professionalised, and they now usually expect to fight with allies, many of whom – even when they are also democracies – have different political inheritances. Yet none of these considerations has prevented the export of the Huntingtonian model of objective military control. This happened quite specifically under the terms of NATO's Partnership for Peace programme as the states of Central and Eastern Europe emerged from communist rule after the end of the Cold War.[44] It has happened more subliminally in the case of established democracies such as France and Britain. Public utterances on defence matters from military professionals are condemned because they challenge a core assumption of objective military control, that the professional soldier is by definition apolitical.

In July 2017, the French chief of the defence staff, Pierre de Villiers, opposed the defence cuts proposed by the government, his off-the-record remarks being reported by *Le Monde*.[45] As a result, he drew fire from the president of the republic, Emmanuel Macron, not least in a speech the latter delivered to the armed forces on the eve of the Bastille Day parade. De Villiers resigned on 17 July, three days after the parade, saying that it had become his duty to do so, because he had a responsibility 'to tell the truth about the threats we must face and the challenges to our armed forces. In that way, the people of France will be able the better to understand.'[46] Macron called de Villiers's behaviour undignified.[47]

De Villiers was the first chief of defence to resign in the history of the Fifth Republic, but between 1946 and 1958 the Fourth Republic was, like its predecessors, dominated by tensions along the civil–military fault line, partly as a result of the legacy of the Vichy government but ignited too by the French wars in Indo-China and Algeria. Those experiences – which occurred as Huntington was writing *The Soldier and the State* – demonstrated the problems of applying objective military control in practice. As Jean Lartéguy's battle-hardened hero, Jacques de Glatigny, responds when told 'the army's one thing, politics another': 'All warfare is bound to become political, Colonel, and an officer with no political training will soon prove ineffective.'[48] De Villiers made a similar point when reflecting on the effects of contemporary conflict, which 'creates an ambiguity at all levels in identifying the enemy, in evaluating the threat, in appreciating the situation, in setting objectives, in deciding the means'. In such circumstances, 'the dealings between the political power, the sole decision-maker in the last resort, and the general staff find themselves modified. They suppose a constant relationship, a sustained dialogue, a mutual confidence.'[49]

In Britain, as in the United States and France, both sides have struggled to meet the goals set by de Villiers. In 2011, Cameron told the chief of the defence staff, David Richards, that it was Richards's job to do the fighting while Cameron himself would do the talking. The prime minister may have been irked by Richards (allegedly) reminding him that service in the Combined Cadet Force at Eton did not qualify him to judge on complex military operations.[50] There is a more serious point here. The United Kingdom's National Security Council, set up by Cameron in 2010, rests on the model of objective military control. The chief of the defence staff attends, but as an adviser, not a full member. What the council does not recognise is the principle of subjective military control. The most significant long-term strategic decision taken by the Cameron government concerned the next generation of nuclear weapons, the successor to the *Trident* missiles and the submarines on which they would be based. Their procurement renews Britain's long-term security dependence on the United States, carries significant opportunity costs for British defence in the early 2020s and implicitly puts the British population at risk should they fail as a deterrent. One might have thought that decisions of such magnitude would demand of democracy a major national debate. In reality, both government and opposition proved anxious to minimise discussion, not promote it.

Opinion polls in 2015 showed the British public to be divided on the value of a new deterrent, but with a small majority in favour.[51] That included Scotland, although it did not stop the country's former first minister, Alex Salmond, arguing on 17 September 2015 that a unilateral decision by the United Kingdom government to renew the nuclear deterrent could be one of four conditions which would justify the Scottish government in calling for a second referendum on Scottish independence.[52] Although he liked to present nuclear deterrence as a specifically Scottish issue, it is not. It divides the Labour Party, and many Conservatives think there are more important defence capabilities on which the money could be spent. Publicly, however, the political parties polarise the debate in crass oversimplifications. Those in favour of the nuclear deterrent assert that Britain does not know what threats may emerge in 50 years' time – a truism which does not address the threats of today. Those who oppose say that nuclear weapons will not deter suicide bombers – another truism but one only relevant to one sort of threat.

Strategy after the 'long war'

If electorates are not informed about and involved in the making of national strategy, they cannot be expected to identify with the objectives of that strategy. Their perceptions, that they believe soldiers are victims, not victors, and that they themselves belong to societies that are inherently casualty averse, become self-fulfilling prophecies because of the poverty of informed debate. That in turn both undermines deterrence and inhibits national leaders from timely action. If potential opponents believe that democracies are inherently risk averse and unlikely to use force, then democracies' defence policies lack deterrent strength, as both Saddam and Vladimir Putin seem to have concluded in 2002 and 2013 respectively.

After 2009 and the election of president Obama, the United States adopted a more limited means for waging what was presented as a 'long war' (the term 'global war on terror' having been formally abandoned). Instead of 'boots on the ground', Western governments preferred a mixture of air attacks, using both manned aircraft and weaponised drones, supplemented on the ground by special forces and training teams for indigenous 'proxies'. This was a solution which elevated means into ends, making viable tactical options a strategy in their own right, one most visible in northern Iraq and Syria, but developed in Pakistan and Yemen. However, it is not yet clear whether it has worked. As in Iraq and Afghanistan after 9/11, tactical and operational successes have yet to be converted into political solutions. One reason is that Obama's approach failed to address Smith's 'war among the people'. Many of those who lived in theatres of war, finding that their security concerns were marginalised, opted to migrate to Europe. Just as importantly, the strategy did not work for the people back home in Western democracies either, for four reasons.

Firstly, the articulation of the idea of limited war remained totally inadequate. The means which Western governments allocated to wars were comparatively small, but they did not adjust their ends accordingly. They used the vocabulary not of limited war, but of major war, which in turn carried the assumption that these wars would have to end in unequivocal outcomes. Limited wars do not tend to end so clearly. As a result, means and ends have remained consistently out of step and have frequently contradicted each other.

Secondly, in the Cold War, governments could engage in limited wars, often using only special forces and proxies, but did so without full disclosure to their peoples. Today, the revolution in digital communications and the mobilisation of mass media make this effectively impossible. The fear of the media's power can promote excessive caution in engaging with it, thus preventing its early and effective use. The result is a paradox: democratic governments, confronted with powerful agents for mass mobilisation and democratisation, stand transfixed in the headlights, uncertain how to use instruments largely of their own invention.

Thirdly, this approach to war relies for its execution on the efforts and readiness to die (and kill) of others – the proxies. However, these proxies – the Kurds, the Free Syrian Army, the Libyan militias, the Afghan National Security Forces and others – have their own political agendas which are not subordinated to the will of Western governments. By relying on proxies, the latter have effectively separated the waging of war from their own political objectives, and so deprived themselves of the opportunity of shaping the outcome which an army on the ground could help provide.

Fourthly, Western governments struggle to produce a narrative which reconciles overseas wars with the needs of their national security. Calling wars fought in the Middle East or Central Asia wars of choice but clothing them as wars of necessity, they fuel the scepticism of those at home to whom such narratives are addressed. After all, an effective strategic narrative cannot exist in its own right; it depends in the first place on a coherent strategy.

In one sense, the liberal democracies have recognised the challenge, but they have attributed that realisation to their opponents and so failed to recognise what it says about their own predicament. It was Russia's takeover of Crimea and intervention in Ukraine in 2014 that gave 'hybrid warfare' purchase in the public mind. The use of 'green men', whose belligerent status could not be firmly determined; the dissemination of disinformation; and the exploitation of the divisions between the United States and Europe in their policies towards the region – all were aggregated under the label 'hybrid war'. Its core themes were then linked to the doctrines of Valery Vasilyevich Gerasimov, the chief of the Russian general staff, despite the fact that his approach is probably better rendered as 'political' or 'ambiguous' warfare.

Hybrid warfare was not an idea born in Russia, but in the United States, and it is NATO which has elevated hybrid warfare to the status of Russian strategy, not least in order to unite its members in their determination to honour their commitment to allocate 2% of their GDPs to national defence. For those in Eastern Europe, from the Baltic to the Balkans, fear of an assertive Russia has good historical foundations, and was the principal reason for their joining the Alliance at the end of the Cold War. For those members further west, the talk of a resurgent Russia is a way of refocusing the Alliance after Afghanistan. The phrase 'hybrid warfare' acquired currency in Western strategic circles not in 2014, but five years earlier. It reflected the experiences of Iraq and Afghanistan, and was therefore developed specifically in the context of 'wars among the people'. Hybrid threats, in the words of its principal promoter, Frank Hoffman, 'blend the lethality of state conflict with the fanatical and protracted fervor of irregular warfare'.[53] The real point of hybrid warfare is not what it says about Russia, but what it says about the Western democracies which have given it so much attention.

Hybrid war has become a mirror for the West's own fears and for its recognition of its own vulnerabilities. The Baltic states have worried about the loyalties of their Russian populations exposed to the blandishments of Putin. Fearful of their eastern neighbour, they have had less difficulty in aligning democracy with strategy than the states to their west. Estonia embraced conscription from the moment it achieved independence from the Soviet Union. Lithuania, which abolished conscription in 2008, reintroduced it in 2015, despite its association in the minds of many with Soviet rule. In 2017, Latvia decided not to restore it on cost grounds, but did embrace 'total defence', which gives every citizen a role in the event of a national crisis. Finland, proud of the determined defence of its country against the Soviet Union in 1939–40, has taken hybrid warfare particularly seriously. It has both conscription and a scheme which, like that of Latvia, gives every institution in society, including churches and schools, a role in the event of invasion. Norway and Denmark have retained conscription, and Sweden, which abandoned it in 2010, reintroduced it in 2017.

Hybrid war is a mirror for the West's own fears

For these countries, the combination of geographical location and an imminent threat has made it easy to align national strategy with democratic debate. The people are the basis of national defence, and every citizen needs to understand his or her role in its delivery. For the democracies further west, the determination to identify hybrid warfare with Russian expansionism carries a different message: it is a reflection of how badly out of kilter their ownership of national strategy has become. In early 2018, Theresa May responded to the effects of 'fake news' and Russian misinformation by setting up the National Security Communications Unit. This could have been seen, positively and proactively, as a moment when the British government recognised the need to embrace the role of its own citizens in the debate on national strategy. It was not. Instead, the British press saw it negatively, as a device to prevent them from being suborned by Britain's adversaries. If Western governments appreciated that distinction, between active participation on the one hand and risk management on the other, they might also see that they are two sides of the same coin. The reintegration of strategy with democracy could confer the domestic resilience governments seek and so also address the external threat which hybrid warfare is meant to present. Instead of looking at a Russian adversary through a tightly focused telescope from a great distance, they might pause for a moment of self-reflection in the mirror somewhat closer to them.

Trump and the trinity

When, across the Atlantic, Donald Trump was elected president in November 2016, May quickly beat a path to his door. On her arrival in the United States, she delivered a speech on 26 January 2017 in which she said that the days of the two countries intervening in order to remake overseas governments were finished.[54] However, her own government's National Security Strategy of September 2015 had said that by 2025 it would create a joint task force, built around a carrier group, a deployable division and the appropriate air assets.[55] The British and American experiences of modern war have been – even in the two world wars – more expeditionary than existential.

The British prime minister was responding to what the new president had said on the campaign trail. Like Obama in Kabul in 2012, she was giving one message to the people of America, while formally cleaving to another policy at home. Trump's condemnation of the protracted and indecisive wars of low intensity waged by his predecessors had helped win him the votes of blue-collar workers in the Midwest, anxious that the government should attend to problems at home rather try unsuccessfully to redress the problems of others. Once in office, however, he threatened not the avoidance of war, but its escalation. North Korea, Syria and, in January 2020, Iran were confronted by a president whose tweets suggested that the United States would use its full range of assets if it came to conflict. His unpredictability lent credibility to what he said. Moreover, his approach has worked, at least thus far. His practice, to carry out an exemplary precision strike from the air, designed to cause minimal casualties, is not to escalate, but to de-escalate. When Iran responded to the killing of Qasem Soleimani on 3 January 2020 by launching strikes on US bases in Iraq, the president initially said they had had no effect. By 21 February the Pentagon acknowledged that 110 Americans had suffered traumatic brain injury,[56] and yet Trump opted not to use Iran's action as an excuse to hit the 52 targets which he said the United States had identified before 3 January.

Both as a candidate in 2016 and as president, Trump's approach appealed to his Republican base. The killing of Soleimani in 2020 shored up his core constituency as he faced impeachment in the Senate. In this respect, less separates him from Obama than he might like to claim. To an even greater extent than his immediate predecessors, he makes strategy in dialogue with public opinion. But while his approach addresses one aspect of the Clausewitzian trinity, it does terrible damage to another. His relationships at the elite level with his strategic advisers and with the professional military have become dysfunctional. While the latter urge attention to the second- and third-order consequences of America's actions, Trump sees their prudence as an excuse for not taking risks. While they stress the legitimacy given to US actions and policies by the support of America's allies, he upbraids those allies for not paying more and treats NATO in transactional terms. While they argue for the prioritisation of the principal challenge to US power, China, Trump alternately undermines and then deepens America's involvement in the Middle East.

On 20 July 2017, the US secretary of state, Rex Tillerson, and the secretary of defense, Jim Mattis, invited the president to a secure room known as 'the Tank' in the Pentagon for a briefing on American strategy, its core assumptions and its direction of travel. Trump soon 'tuned out', and then announced, 'You're a bunch of dopes and babies.' Having lauded Mattis's military reputation when he appointed him, he now said, 'I wouldn't go to war with you people.'[57]

Since Vietnam, the armed forces of the United States have rebuilt their relationship with the American people, a core element of the trinity as Colin Powell acknowledged in 1995.[58] Public support for the American military has been burnished, particularly since the 9/11 attacks in 2001. But by attacking military elites, Trump has challenged the integrity of the service and specifically the chain of command. In November 2019, he intervened in the court martial of Edward Gallagher, a SEAL in the United States Navy, who was accused of war crimes and had been demoted from chief petty officer.

Trump reversed Gallagher's demotion and ordered that his 'Trident' pin, the indicator of his special-forces status, not be removed. He exploited his position as commander-in-chief to leverage the popularity of American 'heroes' in order to undermine not only the legal process but also the authority of the navy secretary and of admirals in uniform.

Neither in the United States nor in the United Kingdom has the executive worked out how to manage civil–military relationships at the objective and subjective levels simultaneously in order to produce coherent strategy. Strategy-making suffers from a 'democratic deficit', as Trump's actions implicitly acknowledge, but his solutions are not sufficiently integrated with strategy's other elements to produce a result which is consistent and effective. A series of independent bilateral relationships creates divisions, not unity. After all, the trinity is not just a triangular construction, it also embodies three in one. The publics of Western democracies, literate and politically empowered, deserve not just strategic communication but strategy itself. Democracy should not be the problem but part of the solution.

Notes

1   The present author was in the group that visited Kabul University. What follows is derived from a valedictory lecture given at Oxford University on 22 September 2015.

2   White House, 'Fact Sheet: The U.S.–Afghanistan Strategic Partnership Agreement', 1 May 2012, https://obamawhitehouse.archives.gov/the-press-office/2012/05/01/fact-sheet-us-afghanistan-strategic-partnership-agreement.

3   White House, 'Remarks by President Obama in Address to the Nation from Afghanistan', 1 May 2012, https://obamawhitehouse.archives.gov/the-press-office/2012/05/01/remarks-president-obama-address-nation-afghanistan.

4   Rupert Smith, *The Utility of Force: The Art of War in the Modern World* (London: Allen Lane, 2005), Part Three.

5   'NATO Summit Press Conference', 20 November 2010, https://www.gov.uk/government/speeches/nato-summit-press-conference.

6   George W. Bush, speech to commemorate the 60th anniversary of Pearl Harbor, Norfolk, VA, 7 December 2001; Tom Baldwin, Philip Webster and David Charter, 'Blair Attacks Appeasement in Our Time', *The Times*, 1 March 2003, https://www.thetimes.co.uk/article/blair-attacks-appeasement-in-our-time-8jsb7wsv6zq. See also Tom Bower, *Broken Vows* (London: Faber & Faber, 2016), pp. 122–3.

7   See Patrick Wintour and Nicholas Watt, 'David Cameron's Libya War: Why the PM Felt Gaddafi Had to Be Stopped', *Guardian*, 3 October 2011, https://www.theguardian.com/politics/2011/oct/02/david-cameron-libyan-war-analysis; Tim Ross and Robert Mendick, 'David Cameron: Six Britons Feared Dead in Algeria', *Telegraph*, 20 January 2013, https://www.telegraph.co.uk/news/politics/9813914/David-Cameron-six-Britons-feared-dead-in-Algeria.html; Patrick Wintour and Emma Graham-Harrison, 'Tunisia Attack: David Cameron Pledges "Full-spectrum" Response to Massacre', *Guardian*, 29 June 2015, https://www.theguardian.com/uk-news/2015/jun/29/tunisia-attack-david-cameron-pledges-full-spectrum-response-to-massacre; and 'Tunisia Attack: Cameron Says IS Fight "Struggle of our Generation"', BBC News, 29 June 2015, https://bbc.co.uk/news/uk-33307279.

8   Aislinn Simpson and James Kirkup, 'Britain's Security Linked to Military Operations in Afghanistan, Claims Gordon Brown', *Telegraph*, 10 July 2009, https://www.telegraph.co.uk/news/newstopics/onthefrontline/5796068/Britains-security-linked-to-military-operations-in-Afghanistan-claims-Gordon-Brown.html.

9   Tony Smith's *Why Wilson Matters: The Origin of American Liberal Internationalism and Its Crisis Today* (Princeton, NJ: Princeton University Press, 2017) is good on these points.

10 Quoted by Sean M. Lynn-Jones, in Michael E. Brown, Sean M. Lynn-Jones and Steven E. Miller (eds), *Debating the Democratic Peace* (Cambridge, MA:

Harvard University Press, 1996), p. ix.

11 In his *Théorie de la guerre* (Nancy, 1777), Paul Gideon Joly de Maizeroy identified strategy as a separate level in the art of war. The first use of the word 'strategy' in English is dated to 1811 by the *Oxford English Dictionary*.

12 See T.C.W. Blanning, *The French Revolution in Germany: Occupation and Resistance in the Rhineland 1792–1802* (Oxford: Oxford University Press, 1983); and, more generally, T.C.W. Blanning, *The French Revolutionary Wars 1787–1802* (London: Hodder Education, 1996); and David A. Bell, *The First Total War: Napoleon's Europe and the Birth of Modern Warfare* (London: Bloomsbury, 2007).

13 Jacques-Antoine Hippolyte Guibert, *A General Essay on Tactics: With an Introductory Discourse upon the Present State of Politics, and the Military Science in Europe*, vol. 1 (London: J. Millan, 1781), pp. v, viii, xxi, xxiii.

14 Bell, *The First Total War*, p. 156.

15 Jean-Paul Bertaud describes this process in *The Army of the French Revolution: From Citizen-soldiers to Instruments of Power* (Princeton, NJ: Princeton University Press, 1988).

16 Bell, *The First Total War*, p. 180. See also Blanning, *French Revolutionary Wars*, p. 97; and Jean-Clément Martin, *La guerre de Vendée 1793–1800*, 2nd ed. (Paris: Points, 2014).

17 'Entwicklung der allgemeinen Ursachen des Glücks der Franzosen in dem Revolutionskriege und insbesondere in dem Feldzuge von 1794', published in *Neues militärisches Journal*, vol. 8, 1797, pp. 1–154, and reprinted in Gerhard von Scharnhorst (Hansjürgen Usczek and Christa

Gudzent, eds), *Ausgewählte militärische Schriften* (Berlin: Militärverlag Berlin, 1986), pp. 97–150. For a later iteration of similar points, see *Bemerkungen über die franzosische Armee der neuesten Zeit, oder der Epoche von 1792 bis 1807* (Königsberg: Friedrich Nicolovius, 1808; translated from the French); and, more generally, Thomas Hippler, *Soldats et citoyens: Naissance du service militaire en France et Prusse* (Paris: Points, 2006).

18   The full text of the three statements can be found in Carl von Clausewitz (Werner Hahlweg, ed.), *Schriften, Aufsätze, Studien, Briefe*, vol. 1 (Göttingen: Vandenhoeck und Ruprecht, 1966), pp. 682–750. For the quotations from Guibert, see pp. 710–11.

19   Carl von Clausewitz (Michael Howard and Peter Paret, eds and trans), *On War* (Princeton, NJ: Princeton University Press, 1976), p. 592.

20   *Ibid.*, p. 593.

21   *Ibid.*, p. 220. Here, the translators have rendered the German *Politik* as politics; they could equally have rendered it as 'policy'.

22   See Christopher Bassford, 'The Primacy of Policy and the "Trinity" in Clausewitz's Mature Thought', in Hew Strachan and Andreas Herberg-Rothe (eds), *Clausewitz in the Twenty-First Century* (Oxford: Oxford University Press, 2007).

23   Carl von Clausewitz, 'Our Military Institutions' [1819], in Peter Paret and Daniel Moran (eds and trans), *Historical and Political Writings* (Princeton, NJ: Princeton University Press, 1992), pp. 316–28, esp. pp. 323 *et seq.*

24   See Douglas Porch, *Army and Revolution: France 1815–1848* (London: Routledge and Kegan Paul, 1974).

25   Bernd Ulrich, Jakob Vogel and Benjamin Ziemann, *Untertan in Uniform: Militär und Militärismus im Kaiserreich 1871–1914. Quellen und Dokumente* (Frankfurt am Main: S. Fischer Verlag, 2001), pp. 163–5. See also Nicholas Stargardt, *The German Idea of Militarism: Radical and Socialist Critics, 1866–1914* (Cambridge: Cambridge University Press, 1994), pp. 93–6.

26   See André Corvisier (ed.), *Histoire militaire de la France*, vol. 3 (Paris: Presses Universitaires de France, 1997), pp. 13–14; André Bach, *L'armée de Dreyfus: Une histoire politique de l'armée française de Charles X à "l'affaire"* (Paris: Tallandier, 2004), pp. 209–19; and Douglas Porch, *The March to the Marne: The French Army 1871–1914* (Cambridge: Cambridge University Press, 1981), pp. 102, 106–9.

27   See Martin Pugh, *Electoral Reform in War and Peace 1906–18* (London: Routledge and Kegan Paul, 1978); and Hew Strachan, 'Liberalism and Conscription 1789–1919', in Hew Strachan (ed.), *The British Army, Manpower and Society into the Twenty-first Century* (London: Frank Cass & Co., 2000).

28   See 'Leitsätze für den vaterländischen Unterricht unter den Truppen, 29 Juli 1917', in Herbert Michaelis, Ernst Schraepler and Günter Scheel (eds), *Ursachen und Folgen: vom deutschen Zusammenbruch 1918 und 1945 bis zur staatlichen Neuordnung Deutschlands in der Gegenwart*, vol. 1 (Berlin: H. Wendler, 1958), pp. 220–3.

29   See Guy Pedroncini, *Les mutineries de*

1917 (Paris: Presses Universitaires de France, 1967), pp. 254–6.

30 See S.P. Mackenzie, *Politics and Military Morale: Current Affairs and Citizenship Education in the British Army 1914–1950* (Oxford: Oxford Historical Monographs, 1992), pp. 4–30; and Jim Beach (ed.), *Lord Gorell and the Army Educational Corps, 1918–1920* (Cheltenham: History Press, 2019).

31 Alexander Hill, *The Red Army and the Second World War* (Cambridge: Cambridge University Press, 2017), pp. 15–18.

32 Jean Lartéguy (Xan Fielding, trans.), *The Centurions* (New York: Penguin Classics, 2015 [1960]), pp. 247–8.

33 See D.C.B. Lieven, *Russia and the Origins of the First World War* (London: Palgrave Macmillan, 1983), pp. 77–80; and Hew Strachan, *The First World War: To Arms* (Oxford: Oxford University Press, 2001), p. 101.

34 See Giulio Douhet, *Command of the Air* (London: Faber & Faber, 1943 [1921]). For similar thinking, see Basil Liddell Hart, *Paris, or the Future of War* (London: E.P. Dutton, 1925). Thomas Hippler's *Bombing the People: Giulio Douhet and the Foundations of Air-power Strategy, 1884–1939* (Cambridge: Cambridge University Press, 2013) makes the democratic links clear.

35 See Gabriella Gribaudi, 'The True Cause of the "Moral Collapse": People, Fascists and Authorities under the Bombs, Naples and the Countryside, 1940–1944'; and Marco Fincardi, 'Anglo-American Air Attacks and the Rebirth of Public Opinion in Fascist Italy', in Claudia Baldoli, Andrew Knapp and Richard Overy (eds), *Bombing, States and Peoples in Western Europe 1940–1945* (London: Continuum, 2011).

36 See F.H. Hinsley et al., *British Intelligence in the Second World War: Its Influence on Strategy and Operations* (London: Stationery Office Books, 1988), vol. 3, part 2, p. 365. In 1941, Churchill hoped that by targeting morale, bombing might provoke revolution in Germany. See Richard Overy, *The Bombing War: Europe 1939–1945* (London: Penguin, 2014), p. 257.

37 Fanon, a doctor who fought with the National Liberation Front in Algeria, saw the use of violence as a necessary route to decolonisation and democratisation.

38 See Lance E. Davis and Robert A. Huttenback, *Mammon and the Pursuit of Empire: The Political Economy of British Imperialism 1860–1912* (Cambridge: Cambridge University Press, 1986), pp. 223–6; and Jon Tetsuro Sumida, *In Defense of Naval Supremacy: Finance, Technology and British Naval Policy, 1899–1914* (Boston, MA, and London: Unwin Hyman, 1989), pp. 196, 336.

39 Joseph Stiglitz and Linda Bilmes, *The Three Trillion Dollar War* (London: Allen Lane, 2008).

40 Samuel P. Huntington, *The Soldier and the State: The Theory and Politics of Civil–Military Relations* (Cambridge, MA: The Belknap Press of Harvard University Press, 1957), p. 3.

41 *Ibid.*, pp. 164–6.

42 H. Richard Uviller and William G. Merkel, *The Militia and the Right to Bear Arms, or How the Second Amendment Fell Silent* (Durham, NC: Duke University Press, 2002).

43 Huntington, *The Soldier and the State*, pp. 163–4.

44 See the essays in David Betz and John Löwenhardt (eds), *Army and State in Postcommunist Europe* (London: Frank Cass, 2001).

45 See Nathalie Guibert, 'Pierre de Villiers, un chef d'état-major dans la tourmente', *Le Monde*, 18 July 2017, https://www.lemonde.fr/politique/article/2017/07/18/pierre-de-villiers-un-chef-d-etat-major-dans-la-tourmente_5161925_823448.html.

46 Pierre de Villiers, *Servir* (Paris: Fayard, 2017), quotation from the back-cover blurb.

47 Guibert, 'Pierre de Villiers, un chef d'état-major dans la tourmente'.

48 Lartéguy, *The Centurions*, p. 247.

49 De Villiers, *Servir*, p. 225.

50 See Josie Ensor, 'Top Military Chiefs "Sidelined" after Afghanistan Row', *Telegraph*, 24 June 2011; and Dan Hodges, 'Generals Talking about Politics Should Remember Who's the Boss', *Telegraph*, 22 September 2015.

51 See, for example, Andrew Grice, 'Trident: Majority of Britons Back Keeping Nuclear Weapons Programme, Poll Shows', *Independent*, 24 January 2016.

52 Chris Green, 'Alex Salmond Interview: "If Scotland Voted on Independence Again Today, We Would Win"', *Independent*, 17 September 2015.

53 Quoted in Williamson Murray and Peter R. Mansoor (eds), *Hybrid Warfare: Fighting Complex Opponents from the Ancient World to the Present* (Cambridge: Cambridge University Press, 2012), pp. 2–3. See also Ofer Fridman, *Russian Hybrid Warfare:*

Resurgence and Politicisation (London: C. Hurst & Co., 2018); and Bettina Renz, *Russia's Military Revival* (Cambridge: Polity, 2018), pp. 160–88.

54 Theresa May, 'Prime Minister's Speech to the Republican Party Conference 2017', 26 January 2017, https://www.gov.uk/government/speeches/prime-ministers-speech-to-the-republican-party-conference-2017.

55 HM Government, 'National Security Strategy and Strategic Defence and Security Review 2015: A Secure and Prosperous United Kingdom', November 2015, p. 29, https://assets.publishing.service.gov.uk/government/uploads/system/uploads/attachment_data/file/478933/52309_Cm_9161_NSS_SD_Review_web_only.pdf.

56 '110 US Troops Suffered Concussion, Brain Injury in Iranian Strike: Pentagon', GlobalSecurity.org, 22 February 2020, https://www.globalsecurity.org/military/library/news/2020/02/mil-200222-presstv01.htm.

57 Carol D. Leeming and Philip Rucker, '"You're a Bunch of Dopes and Babies": Inside Trump's Stunning Tirade against the Generals', *Washington Post*, 17 January 2020, https://www.washingtonpost.com/politics/youre-a-bunch-of-dopes-and-babies-inside-trumps-stunning-tirade-against-generals/2020/01/16/d6dbb8a6-387e-11ea-bb7b-265f4554af6d_story.html.

58 Colin Powell with Joseph Persico, *My American Journey* (New York: Random House, 1995), pp. 207–8.

NATO 4.0: The Atlantic Alliance and the Rise of China

François Heisbourg

The transatlantic defence and security relationship has demonstrated its ability to adapt to fundamental strategic change during its 70-year existence. It has in effect lived through three phases since its creation, each filling distinct strategic purposes.

During its first 40 years, the Atlantic Alliance was the prime mover in ensuring deterrence and defence in Europe and the North Atlantic vis-à-vis the Soviet bloc. In achieving this goal of strategic containment, the Alliance helped create the conditions for Western Europe's lasting return to freedom and prosperity. It also provided the shield behind which the threat of military force was eliminated as a factor in relations among European democracies. The Cold War in Europe, from the Berlin blockade to the fall of the Berlin Wall, was perceived at the time as it is in retrospect: as a discrete era characterised by a high degree of strategic continuity.

The Atlantic Alliance was severely tested on several occasions during that period, notably by the Suez crisis between France and the United Kingdom on one hand and the United States on the other; the *Sputnik* moment and its aftermath, which threw into question the United States' ability to credibly extend deterrence; the withdrawal of France from most of NATO's military structures until 2009; and the Vietnam War, which none of America's European allies, including the UK, was willing to support. The allies weath-

François Heisbourg is IISS senior adviser for Europe and special adviser of the Paris-based Fondation pour la Recherche Stratégique (FRS). He is author of *Le Temps des Prédateurs: La Chine, les États-Unis, la Russie et Nous* [The Age of the Predators: China, the United States, Russia and Us] (Odile Jacob, 2020).

Survival | vol. 62 no. 2 | April–May 2020 | pp. 83–102   DOI 10.1080/00396338.2020.1739950

ered these storms. Over time, it was the West's strategic cohesion, political resilience and economic success that brought this first era of transatlantic purpose to a satisfying conclusion. Soviet academician Georgy Arbatov captured the zeitgeist in 1988 when he stated that the USSR's 'major secret weapon is to deprive you of an enemy'.[1]

Phase two spanned the following quarter-century, characterised by what was quickly called 'America's unipolar moment', a time during which the United States and by extension the Atlantic Alliance ceased to face a peer competitor.[2] Very much along the lines of Arbatov's forecast, the Alliance initially appeared to be bereft of purpose.

During the 1991 Gulf War, the West's first post-Cold War military confrontation, NATO was left on the sidelines.[3] As the wars of Yugoslavian succession began a few months later, US secretary of state James Baker stated that 'we do not have a dog in this fight', with NATO playing a marginal role in the Balkans for the following three years.[4] This prompted an overhasty Luxembourgeois foreign minister, Jacques Poos, speaking for the presidency of the European Community, to declare that 'this is the hour of the Europeans – not the hour of the Americans' in the Balkans.[5]

In political terms, the Alliance was similarly slow in finding a new compass, with no immediate consensus on the crucial issue of enlarging NATO. Contrary to Russia's subsequent rewriting of history, there was no agreed view in the US and NATO on this issue immediately following the disappearance of the Warsaw Pact in July 1991, or the collapse of the Soviet Union in December 1991.

By the middle of the 1990s, however, and for the following 20 years, NATO found itself fulfilling several distinct roles while not reclaiming a single purpose. NATO waged its first shooting wars – in Bosnia and then in Kosovo – largely at the expense of Serbian irredentism. The Alliance proceeded with the expansion of its membership once that political decision had been made in the early 1990s, with Washington and Bonn in the lead. Concurrently, NATO attempted to establish a direct multilateral relationship between the allies and Russia, by way of a succession of transatlantic formats: the Euro-Atlantic Partnership Council (1991), the Partnership for Peace (1994), the Permanent Joint Council (1997) and the NATO–Russia Council

(2002). In 1997, NATO stated its intention not to deploy nuclear weapons and large-scale forces (that is, brigade level or above) east of the former Iron Curtain; these commitments continue to be observed. NATO invoked Article V – collective defence – in the wake of the 9/11 attacks and subsequently conducted substantial counter-insurgency and counter-terrorism operations in Afghanistan. Furthermore, NATO decided to deploy an anti-ballistic-missile defence system located mostly on the territory of its eastern members, with the stated purpose of countering the threat of Iranian missiles.

Without a superpower threat, NATO became strategically unanchored. More ominously than a general lack of focus, the Iraq crisis of 2002–03 demonstrated that both the US, which was ready to intervene without United Nations or NATO approval, and the French–German 'axis of weasel',[6] which was not, considered that the unity of the Alliance had become eminently dispensable. Eventually, it became clear that NATO's main second-phase achievement and legacy was the establishment of a strategically homogeneous European space from Brest, France, to Brest-Litovsk, Poland.

NATO has found a clear main purpose

NATO's third and latest phase, which began in 2014, has hearkened back to the Cold War in the sense that it has found a clear and well-identified main purpose. This consists of deterring and defending against renewed aggression by a revisionist Russia, after its military seizure and subsequent annexation of Crimea, a part of Ukraine until then recognised as such by Moscow. NATO, which found itself back in its organisational and cultural comfort zone, responded swiftly to the Russian challenge. At its Wales Summit in September 2014, it decided in the short term to establish a rapid-reaction force and a rotational military presence in the Baltic republics including both European and North American soldiers. NATO contingency planning, which had essentially been suspended for more than two decades, was revived, and ambitious military exercises were held, including in areas close to Russia.[7] Perhaps most importantly in the longer run, each of NATO's members committed to spending at least 2% of their GDP on military budgets by 2025, versus a 1.5% average in 2014. Since then, European defence spending has increased across the board every year. For its part, the US has raised its troop numbers and military spending for Europe, moving forces and pre-positioned materiel eastward. Whereas the last US main battle tank had left Europe in early 2013, American armour returned after Russia attacked Ukraine.

Russia has shown no sign of abandoning its revisionist agenda, with Foreign Minister Sergey Lavrov periodically restating Russia's position as an unsatisfied power, notably at the Munich Security Conference. It is modernising its increasingly agile armed forces and aggressively using all means of attack short of large-scale war, including cyber attacks and information operations along with more traditional forms of subversion, from 'wet work' on NATO territory (including assassinations) to the funding of extremist and anti-status quo parties. Notwithstanding a GDP lower than Italy's, Russia appears to be able to afford this multifaceted effort. Furthermore, some of NATO's new members are strategically exposed and intrinsically difficult to defend. In this light, 'NATO 3.0' could have been with us for quite a number of years. However, even if the deterrence and defence goals of present-day NATO vis-à-vis the Russian threat need to be sustained, they may not constitute NATO's main purpose in the future.

There are two basic reasons for this. One, which is bounded by US constitutional limits of four to eight years for a president's time in office, is the election of Donald Trump in 2016, which represents a step change in US alliance policy. The other is the emergence and establishment of China as America's peer competitor, which will obtain over an unknowable but possibly decades-long period of time. This is leading the US to move its strategic focus from the European theatre to Asia. Over time, the traditional US–European burden-sharing disputes will give way to a debate on burden-shifting – that is, the redeployment of US military assets from Europe to East Asia.[8] Given the technological and commercial aspects of China's rise as well as its ideological, strategic and military dimensions, it will affect a broader range of issues than the Cold War rivalry with the Soviet Union did, calling for innovative approaches in terms of statecraft. The rise of China will also affect US and European interests in different, and sometimes even opposing, ways. These new realities call into question the future of NATO. Certainly they will have a mutually reinforcing disruptive effect on the Alliance. This prospect calls for a 'NATO 4.0'.[9]

America's Trumpian passage

Trump's bilateralist and transactional vision of US foreign relations, broadly defined, is long-standing and clear-cut.[10] It is also deeply held and has remained unchanged, unlike many other facets of Trump's political positioning. Similarly, there is little doubt about Trump's impulsive and vainglorious character, his disorganised and detail-free working style, his vindictive and autocratic management of human resources, his self-perception as a 'very stable genius' who also knows he's the boss, and a decision-making approach that combines streetwise cunning with recklessness and extreme short-termism, not to mention an emotional and childlike disregard for limits of any sort, including constitutional constraints or Alliance commitments.

Furthermore, his transactional approach excludes broad-based, long-term relations and endeavours, and amplifies the negative effects of his personality. For NATO, this has come to mean that the allies have to work with an ally who does not understand the meaning of the word 'ally'. They are not necessarily reassured by US reminders that America's force presence in Europe and the Gulf region has actually increased in recent years. In a Trumpian age, that presence may be transient and does not imply a lasting commitment. With the passing of time, the probability of a sudden, irreversible and catastrophic disruption has not decreased the way it normally would as a leader and his administration gathered experience and fine-tuned their policies. On the contrary, this probability has increased. Nobody can count on the so-called 'adults in the room', which Trump has largely culled from his administration, to eliminate the possibility of an early-morning Twitter message serving 'notice' that the US is pulling its troops out of Europe or leaving NATO.[11] The consequences of Trump's re-election would therefore be widely seen as spiking existing risks rather than consolidating a disagreeable but stable new normal.

Independently of broader considerations, the best that NATO can hope for after Trump is a rattled set of allies engaged in more hedging than they ever have before. If Joe Biden, who at the 2019 Munich Security Conference vowed that all would be as it was before, were elected, the Alliance might return to something close to the status quo ante relatively promptly.[12] The drafting of a NATO strategic review of the sort raised at the London Leaders' Meeting in December 2019 could be enough to breathe new life into the Alliance.[13] That, however, assumes that the 'stable genius' is not re-elected in November, that he does not do anything too rash before he leaves his desk, and that if a Democrat other than Biden is elected, he or she will somehow share the former vice president's Alliance classicism. Those are three big ifs.

China: the long pole in America's strategic tent

Washington recognised the rise of China as America's peer strategic competitor well before China's GDP had exceeded that of France in nominal terms.[14] China was the central reason for the Pentagon reforms initiated by Donald Rumsfeld, then secretary of defense, in early 2001, with the added urgency of the serious incident in April of that year in which a US spy plane was forced to land on the island of Hainan after sustaining damage in a mid-air collision with a Chinese fighter aircraft whose pilot died when his plane crashed. The Pentagon's earlier plans were shelved as 9/11 shifted US attention and effort to Afghanistan and the Middle East for the rest of the decade.

With Barack Obama's speech in Canberra in November 2011, the United States signalled that it would refocus on Asia in response to the rise of China. At the time, little changed in military terms apart from the rotational basing in 2014 of a battalion-sized US Marine Corps force in Darwin, Australia. European jitters turned out to be premature. However, Obama worked hard to remove all US troops from Iraq, a goal which was achieved in December 2011, before their return was prompted by the rise of the Islamic State (ISIS) in 2014. He practised 'leading from behind' during NATO's war in Libya in 2011, and declined to enforce his 'red line' against chemical weapons when the regime of Bashar al-Assad used them in Syria in 2013. ISIS's resurgence cut short America's apparent disengagement from the Middle East. Trump has been caught in a similar dynamic, made worse by the contradiction between his instinct to end long-running military engagements and his decision to opt out of the Joint Comprehensive Plan of Action – that is, the Iran nuclear deal – thus fuelling tension in the Gulf region.

If the US has been comparatively slow in shifting its strategic focus, Beijing has proceeded in leaps and bounds, moving briskly from regional power to superpower status. In 2009, the Chinese economy moved into second position and by 2014 its GDP expressed in purchasing power parity overtook that of the US. This parameter may be an imperfect measurement and it may take most of the new decade for China's nominal GDP to catch up. In any case, the US and China are now in a league of their own. In 2017, Chinese President Xi Jinping and the Chinese Communist Party fleshed out their understanding of the 'Chinese dream', symbolically proclaiming China's superpower standing. Its military capabilities are ramping up rapidly: both quantitatively and qualitatively, China could enjoy close to peer military status with the US by the end of the new decade, even if it will take longer for it to reach that level in net assessment terms. China's last shooting war was in February 1979 against Vietnam, and although the Chinese eventually prevailed, it was a painful victory of the sort the Soviets endured against Finland during the 1939–40 Winter War. China still lacks the organisational know-how and operational experience required to meet the Americans on equal terms.

Nevertheless, the US sees China's rise as calling for the same level of priority in its strategy that the Soviet Union required during the Cold War: it is becoming the long pole in America's strategic tent. The US consensus behind resisting China's ambitions and behaviour is also broadening, deepening and hardening in a manner that increasingly includes the business community and – exceedingly rare in the US these days – transcends partisan divides. Trump has behaved erratically towards Xi, treating him as an arch-villain one day and a deal partner the next, even publicly casting him as a potential provider of dirt on Hunter Biden's activities in China (Xi wisely refused to play the part). And Trump is focused less on what may matter most strategically, such as China's Great Digital Firewall, than on what may reward him electorally, such as soybeans. Even so, he is part of the wider hawkish consensus.

Trumpism and the US 'China consensus'

The interaction between Trumpian foreign policy and America's China consensus will likely produce outcomes of relevance to NATO both during and after Trump's presidential tenure. Firstly, there is the consolidation of the China consensus. Trump's aggressive and abrasive approach tends to harden attitudes of friend and foe alike. To the extent that Trump is part of the US mainstream with respect to China, Trumpian contingencies and Sino-American structural confrontation will be mutually reinforcing.

Furthermore, even before Trump's current term at the White House expires, America's policy as to its European and Asian allies will be increasingly shaped by US perceptions of the role allies play in helping or hindering US objectives towards China. The ongoing dispute between the US and China concerning the acquisition of 5G networks is the first major test of this proposition. America has openly threatened to curb intelligence sharing with its closest allies if they choose to entrust China's Huawei Technologies Company with setting up their 5G networks.[15] It remains to be seen what practical conclusions the US will actually draw if major allies such as France, Germany, Italy or the UK decide to 'go Chinese'.

If no key European ally chooses Huawei, following in Japan's and Australia's footsteps, that outcome will be due at least in part to the strength of America's campaign calling attention to the security and strategic implications of their 5G decisions. Given the commercial advantage enjoyed by Huawei as a result of the infrastructure it built up as part of 3G and 4G networks and what is apparently massive state aid, it could normally expect to be selected as a 5G prime contractor in many markets in the absence of broader security and strategic considerations.[16]

As China's rise consolidates and as its assertiveness increases over time, NATO will be systematically forced to choose between working with the US, without the US or against the US when it comes to relations with China. China itself well understands this. It is handling the precedent-setting 5G confrontation as a first-order political issue. Threats from Chinese ambassadors in Europe and others arose from November 2019 onwards, while the general tone of Chinese diplomacy in Europe and Canada deteriorated, with punishments imposed on a broad range of issues.[17]

Against this backdrop, the relationship between the US and its NATO allies will be increasingly prone to misunderstanding and uncontrolled disagreements. It is in the North American and European interest to work together to avoid the former and reduce the latter to manageable proportions. Because European and Canadian interests may align more closely with

China's policies than with America's on a number of key issues – such as the global financial order, the extraterritorial reach of American law and climate change – any US–Europe mechanism for coping with differences would need to have a heavily transactional cast, with or without Trump. The basic structural differences between the new international system and its bipolar and unipolar predecessors will further complicate transatlantic interactions.

NATO's 'three-body problem'

Liu Cixin, a prominent Chinese author of science fiction, has written a trilogy titled *Remembrance of Earth's Past* that includes a book called *The Three-body Problem*.[18] It provides an apt analogue to the quandary faced by NATO, and specifically by its European members. In his version of another time and cosmos, Liu describes an inhabited planet that is under the simultaneous and comparable gravitational pulls of two stars. He argues that in physics such a configuration is both unpredictable and unstable, subjecting the planet's denizens to extremes of temperature with which they have to cope with little advance warning and no sense of duration.

In its first 70 years, NATO existed as a part of stable systems. During the Cold War, the East–West bipolarity was inherently stable from the European vantage, whether as a matter of choice in NATO or as a result of coercion in the Warsaw Pact. Within each of the blocs, a single superpower exercised a quasi-monopolistic gravitational pull, before a hollowed-out Soviet Union suddenly fell into its very own black hole. The unipolar moment was also stable as a result of the absence of a peer competitor. The current system is multipolar in global terms, and multipolarity has also begun to prevail in the European context. China's pull is distorting the post-2014 force field between the US and Russia. With its combination of geo-economic, political and strategic dimensions, this system is more complex than the erstwhile East–West conflict, and it is developing rapidly as a Wilhelminian China rises against a challenged but incumbent American superpower. Most ominously for Europe, the main contest is occurring between the US and China 'stars', threatening Europe with marginalisation and even expendability.

These factors point to instability and unpredictability. John Mearsheimer's recommendation that the 'United States should go to great lengths to pull

Russia out of China's orbit and integrate it into the U.S.-led order' may be easier to state at this stage than to bring about.[19] But stranger things have happened in history – for instance, during the Seven Years War or with the Hitler–Stalin pact. From a European perspective, Mearsheimer's scenario would be unappealing were it to lead the US to dump parts of Europe into Russia's sphere of influence as part of the grand bargain to contain China. But whichever way the geopolitical bodies oscillate, present-day NATO will be of decreasing relevance in the resolution of Europe's – and America's – future security problems if it confines itself to its current Russian focus.

Wedges and hedges: Europe's options

In contrast to the US and China, the European Union as a group is not a superpower, even if its norm-setting powers are considerable and some of its competencies in trade and competition policy give it global heft. Nor are any of NATO's European members individually in a position to balance Russia, even if some of them have more than regional diplomatic and military power. Furthermore, whether in an EU or a NATO framework, the European states form a heterogeneous group, each of whose members may react differently to outside challenges: Europe is a stress-taker rather than a stress-maker, even if it has the ability to assert and enforce norms in specific areas. In Liu's universe, Europe would definitely be a planet rather than a star. For this reason, it has to contemplate the broadest possible range of options to face forces beyond its control, whereas the superpowers are in little doubt as to what their primary external focus should be – namely, managing the US–China relationship – even if that can come in many flavours.

At this stage, Europe's options are often conceived, explicitly or implicitly, as hedges in the face of the uncertainty of America's commitment under Trump and as a consequence of the rise of China. This is not only the case in continental Europe but also in post-Brexit Britain, given the statement by Ben Wallace, the UK secretary of state for defence, that the 'assumptions of 2010 that we were always going to be part of a US coalition is really just not where we are going to be'.[20] Given the nature of Trumpian decision-making, each and every hedge, and sometimes even the absence of one, carries the risk of becoming a wedge.

There are five basic options. In current practice, several are carried out concurrently as hedges of hedges – a widespread practice sometimes known as 'cakeism', an expression derived from the colloquialism 'having one's cake and eating it too' much used during Britain's Brexit debates.

The baseline option, sometimes known as Plan A in the European debate, is to try to 'hang on to nurse for fear of worse', either through constant attempts to fulfil President Trump's agenda in Europe in terms of defence spending or bilateral add-ons to NATO, such as Poland's 'Fort Trump', or through magical thinking, as in Germany's simultaneous non-fulfilment of NATO spending commitments and its refusal to think through the consequences of an American retreat when invited to do so by French President Emmanuel Macron's 'NATO is brain dead' interview.[21] This may or may not work, but what is certain is that on its own it does not provide a compass for dealing with a China-focused US either now or in a post-Trump world. Poland can build Fort Trump, but it is also a member of the China-centric 17+1 group composed of ex-communist countries plus communist China (and more recently Greece) caught up in the debate about Huawei 5G.

The most loudly expressed but also divisive hedge – Plan B – is to build up specifically European defence capabilities in case the Americans reduce their commitment, implying that the Europeans collectively, in the EU or via ad hoc ventures such the French-launched European Intervention Initiative that includes the United Kingdom (known as the E12), acquire a degree of strategic autonomy, a concept developed by France within the EU from 2015 onwards. In a non-Trumpian world, such a hedge could be acceptable to the US insofar as it would enhance NATO capabilities.

In the age of Trump this option could easily become a self-fulfilling prophecy, particularly if oil is added to his fire by way of Gallic pronouncements about a putative 'European army'. Although budget realities are often invoked to disqualify this hedge, money is not the main obstacle: a recent IISS study assesses the additional costs for Europe to offset a substantial reduction of the US commitment to NATO at no more than $470 billion, spread over a ten-year period.[22] A $47bn annual spending supplement falls within NATO's 2% of GDP target. The bigger problems are political, with a Europe deeply divided on Plan B.

Teaming up with Russia may look like an unlikely hedge, but that is what some Central European countries, such as Hungary and the Czech Republic, are tempted to do alongside their NATO and EU commitments. Macron also suggested a rapprochement with Russia in August 2019, making the strategic point that a closer Euro-Russian relationship could break up the Russia–China strategic partnership, thus diminishing China's ability to exert pressure on Europe.[23] By the same token, such an outcome could mesh with the American consensus on China. The only problem is that this modern version of an *alliance de revers* with Russia against a third power cannot be achieved. The more than two-decades-old strategic partnership between Russia and China did not develop as a result of Europe's policies vis-à-vis Russia.[24] In bilateral exchanges with France, the Russians have made it quite clear that they would be happy to pocket European concessions, and have no interest in dropping the China connection for any price that Europe is able and willing to pay.

'If you can't beat them, join them' appears to be an even more improbable option whereby the EU or selected member states, and possibly the UK, would give preference to Chinese blandishments and threats over stated American interests. As a wedge, this would presumably prompt America's retreat from Europe and with it the end of NATO, not a prospect likely to generate great enthusiasm in most European capitals. However, the idea also has uncomfortably long legs. China has much to offer along with the ability to punish. The 5G debate abundantly demonstrates that there is nothing straightforwardly and unambiguously beneficial about taking sides with the Americans, notably in otherwise strongly pro-NATO countries, including the UK. Furthermore, China has the ability to co-opt local elites as well as the broader public through money-rich, job-creating, influence-cum-investment operations on a scale that may put Russia's 'malign activities' in the shade.

In France and Germany, these are still early days, but Chinese governmental and corporate lobbying is ramping up, spurred in part by the prospect of Huawei losing key 5G battles.[25] Given the current pushback over China's recent attempts to bully the Europeans, however, this effort may not prevail. The fear of China is a broad church in Europe, combining the rejection of cyber dictatorship with that of Chinese threats to European sovereignty. But it would be wrong to write off Europe's 'join them' notion yet, if only because it plays to the greedy side of human nature and is therefore broadly feasible.

The final option, compatible with the 'cakeism' in plans A and B, is NATO 4.0.

Making NATO fit its redefined purpose

NATO should have as its main objective to make the Alliance safe from the consequences of China's rise without prejudice to NATO's ongoing policy of defending against and deterring Russia. In creating a NATO 4.0, Europe would be confirming that, come what may, its preference is to resolve its three-body problem through a renewed, lasting and broad-spectrum alliance with the United States, and the US would be committing itself to refraining from sacrificing Europe on the altar of expediency in its strategic contest with China.

From the perspective of its European members, such a repurposed NATO would ideally be compatible with the pursuit of strategic autonomy without compromising the continued presence of US forces in Europe. From the US standpoint, it should ensure maximum overlap between US and European policies towards China, and the reduction to manageable proportions of the areas of disagreement between the US and Europe, in an 'agreeing to disagree' mode.

Getting from here to there would entail overcoming substantial, and potentially show-stopping, organisational and procedural obstacles. In effect, NATO would have to combine its traditional unconditional commitments, notably Article V, with a continuously renewed give and take on policy towards China. Such a development would be out of sync with the Alliance's historical experience and organisational culture. In this light, the Chinese dimension arguably should be handled from outside NATO, in order to insulate the Alliance's incumbent Russia-specific focus. This was, after all, the Cold War dispensation. For example, the Coordinating Committee for Multilateral Export Controls (COCOM), the West's ad hoc technology-control body with no legal status, operated from 1949 to 1994 in parallel with NATO, not as part of it. Big and divisive disagreements, notably the 1982 US–European confrontation over the Siberian gas pipeline, could be dealt with at the highest political levels and handled separately from NATO.

The hardening of COCOM restrictions in the mid-1980s – one of the factors that led the Soviet Union to throw in the towel as the arms race broke its economic back – was basically a non-NATO effort and largely driven by special intelligence on Soviet technological requirements. A direct channel established between presidents François Mitterrand and Ronald Reagan from mid-1981 onwards gave the US access to the high-grade intelligence products from a Moscow-based KGB double agent code-named 'Farewell'.[26] Why not resuscitate, on a much larger scale, the Chinese version of COCOM, known as the China Committee, or CHINCOM, which was set up in 1952 during the Korean War? Such an option would admittedly be a second-best outcome. COCOM was a limited-scope operation, and high-level disagreements such as the one over the Siberian gas pipeline, or extraordinarily sensitive matters such as the Reagan–Mitterrand channel for the 'Farewell' intelligence, while appropriately handled on an ad hoc basis, were *sui generis* situations. NATO's much broader political–military remit is far more versatile.

Conversely, the Chinese challenge is big, broad and multidimensional. The failure or success of America and Europe in managing their respective approaches to China will have an increasing strategic impact for NATO's legacy role towards the Russian threat. The Huawei affair serves as a harbinger of the linkages the US will inevitably establish between Europe's choices with respect to China and US readiness to sustain its Alliance commitments. For the Alliance to survive these linkages, they must be as simple and transparent as possible, such that their strategic, political and economic transaction costs are minimised. This calls for institutional proximity.

Accordingly, it would make sense to create within the Atlantic Alliance a consultative body, supported by substantial administrative machinery, to scrutinise all aspects of China policy carrying demonstrable implications for the security and defence of NATO's members, jointly and severally. This body would not make policy but rather lay out options for the political decision-makers among its members, operating on their own account or in collective settings such as the North Atlantic Council. Because Europe's interactions with China, such as those on trade or competition policy, are handled by EU institutions as such rather than its member states, it would make sense for the European Commission and the European Council to be represented alongside NATO members. This should be politically manageable insofar as this body would have no executive power of its own. Those European countries refusing such representation in the discussions of a defence alliance would need only to declare their disinterest in the new body's proceedings and opt out. This would also make it possible to sidestep the problem posed by the non-congruent memberships of NATO and the EU. Only four EU countries (Austria, Cyprus, Ireland and Malta) are neither NATO members (which include 21 EU states) nor NATO cooperation partners (which include Sweden and Finland).

Conflict deflection is an urgent matter

Calling this body the 'North Atlantic Consultative Committee' would leave plenty of scope and flexibility for defining a broad de facto mandate. On a day-to-day basis, countries could be represented at deputy-chief-of-mission level, with the more contentious items being referred to ambassadors and the capitals.

Setting up such a conflict-deflection body is an urgent matter, and should be undertaken during the next US presidential term, whether or not Trump is re-elected. The big problem may not be that Trump would reject such an initiative; if anything, he may view it as an overly mild response to the Chinese challenge. Rather, since such a system would call for a broad array of inter-agency input, National Security Council (NSC) supervision on the US side would be required for the new mechanism to function smoothly and effectively. This implies a return to the kind and calibre of NSC structure that existed before the current dysfunction in the inter-agency process took hold under Trump. The senior-level understaffing of other US executive-branch agencies, notably the State Department, would also be significant impediments.

*   *   *

The good news is that NATO collectively has begun to take the measure of the Chinese challenge, and on both sides of the Atlantic; the trend is no longer to view China merely as a bigger Japan afflicted with a few human-rights problems. This evolution is recent, its progress is extremely uneven within given countries and from country to country, and the realisation of China's ascent to superpower status may lead some to lie down rather than stand up. But the fact remains that NATO's leaders took the portentous decision in London in December 2019 to single out China's policies in general and the 5G problem specifically as having become Alliance concerns. Despite the mushy language contained in the final declaration on this score, this constitutes an epistemological and political leap that potentially opens the way to NATO 4.0.[27]

The not so good news, in addition to Trump's vagaries, is that it will be no mean feat to keep US and European decisions relating to China in close enough coordination to prevent a collapse of the transatlantic defence relationship. The extraterritorial reach of American law – notably in the form of so-called secondary sanctions – and the exploitation of the dollar's power at the centre of a financial system that made more sense in 1944 than it does now will increasingly inspire Chinese and European countermoves. The pull of China's expanding domestic market and the push of its low-priced yet technologically advanced exports are immensely powerful. The US may wish to avoid confronting the EU and China simultaneously on trade issues, since together these two represent 30% of global trade (about 15% each) versus 15% for the US. Indeed, by 2018, China had displaced the US as the EU's main supplier.

The global effects of Trump's first-term policies also may not be easy to ameliorate. In particular, his decision to cease abiding by the terms of the Paris agreement on climate change, though it may be reversed under a new president, remains a singularly divisive issue. Beyond that, the Trump administration's wilfully ignorant and negligent environmental policies have led by negative example, encouraging disastrous climate-change policies elsewhere, notably in Australia and Brazil.

None of this is meant to minimise America's immense power to inspire and to mobilise. Nor is China without its own demographic and social fragilities, including a value system which appears increasingly repellent as it is scrutinised. It will still take political goodwill, constructive policies, heavy diplomatic lifting and some luck to prevent the rise of China from pulling apart a transatlantic compact sealed in a very different world. Today's NATO, with its quasi-exclusive focus on the Russian threat, is not equipped to deal with that task. But it could develop the necessary tools.

Notes

1   Jean Davidson, 'UCI Scientists Told Moscow's Aim Is to Deprive U.S. of Foe', *Los Angeles Times*, 12 December 1988.

2   Charles Krauthammer, 'The Unipolar Moment', *Foreign Affairs*, vol. 70, no. 1, America and the World 1990/91, pp. 23–33.

3   NATO's involvement consisted of the deployment to Turkey of elements of the Supreme Allied Commander Europe (SACEUR)'s Allied Mobile Force, including Belgian *Mirage V* combat aircraft in Diyarbakir.

4   Quoted in Elizabeth Drew, *On the Edge: The Clinton Presidency* (New York: Simon & Schuster, 1994), p. 139.

5   Quoted in Josip Glaurdic, *The Hour of Europe: Western Powers and the Breakup of Yugoslavia* (New Haven, CT: Yale University Press, 2011), p. 1.

6   This was the headline of the *New York Post* on 4 January 2003.

7   These include, on a yearly basis, the eastward-looking *Anaconda* exercises and the *Trident Juncture* exercises on the flanks.

8   I owe this expression to Thomas Kleine-Brockhoff, vice-president of the German Marshall Fund.

9   The expression 'NATO 4.0' appears to have been first used in print by Admiral (Retd) James Stavridis, a former SACEUR commander, in a March 2019 Politico colloquium on NATO: 'NATO at 70: What's Next?', Politico, 4 March 2019, https://www.politico.com/story/2019/04/03/nato-70th-anniversary-1315491. His vision of NATO 4.0 is largely focused on the Arctic.

10 For an early example, see Ilan Ben-Meir ,'That Time Trump Spent Nearly $100,000 on an Ad Criticizing U.S. Policy in 1987', Buzzfeed, 10 July 2015, https://www.buzzfeednews.com/article/ilanbenmeir/that-time-trump-spent-nearly-100000-on-an-ad-criticizing-us.

11 Trump indicated (in a tweet, naturally) that his tweets pertaining to US military action against Iran would 'serve as notification to the United States Congress' of such action. Donald J. Trump (@realDonaldTrump), tweet, 5 January 2020, https://twitter.com/realdonaldtrump/status/1213919480574812160?lang=en.

12 See 'Joe Biden Tells Europeans that America Is "An Embarrassment" (Munich Security Conference)', YouTube, 16 February 2019, https://www.youtube.com/watch?v=Ab47oh3X8I8.

13 See NATO, 'London Declaration', 4 December 2019, https://www.nato.int/cps/en/natohq/official_texts_171584.htm.

14 The IMF estimates that China reached France's GDP in purchasing-power-parity terms in 1991 and in nominal terms in 2005. International Monetary Fund, 'World Economic Outlook Database', October 2018, https://www.imf.org/en/Publications/WEO/Issues/2018/09/24/world-economic-outlook-october-2018.

15 See, for instance, Emma Vickers, 'The 70-year Spy Alliance the U.S. Says It May Cut Off', Bloomberg, 29 June 2019, https://www.bloomberg.com/news/articles/2019-06-30/the-70-year-spy-alliance-the-u-s-says-it-may-cut-off-quicktake.

16 See Cecilia Kang, 'Huawei Ban Threatens Wireless Service in Rural Areas', *New York Times*, 25 May 2019, https://www.nytimes.com/2019/05/25/technology/huawei-rural-wireless-service.html; and Kieran Corcoran, 'Huawei Attacks Wall Street Journal for Report on $75 Billion China State Aid', *Business Insider*, 26 December 2019, https://www.businessinsider.com/huawei-attacks-wall-street-journal-report-75bn-china-state-aid-2019-12?r=US&IR=T.

17 See, in chronological order, Steve Dent, 'Huawei Is Suing French Critics Who Say It's Tied to the Chinese State', Endgadget, 25 November 2019, https://www.engadget.com/2019/11/25/huawei-suing-french-critics-ties-to-chinese-state/; Jessica Murphy, 'Two Canadians Held for a Year by China Remain "Resilient"', BBC, 9 December 2019, https://www.bbc.co.uk/news/world-us-canada-50592055; Tony Czuczka and Steven Arons, 'China Threatens Retaliation Should Germany Ban Huawei 5G', Bloomberg, 14 December 2019, https://www.bloomberg.com/news/articles/2019-12-14/china-threatens-germany-with-retaliation-if-huawei-5g-is-banned; James Schotler, 'Prague Mayor Fights to Put Distance Between Prague and Beijing', *Financial Times*, 1 January 2020, https://www.ft.com/content/3f89c6ae-1ce1-11ea-9186-7348c2f183af; 'Chinese Ambassador Warns Dutch Government Against Restricting ASML Supplies', Reuters, 23 January 2019, https://www.reuters.com/article/us-netherlands-asml-china/chinese-ambassador-warns-dutch-government-against-restricting-asml-supplies-idUSKBN1ZE1Z8; and Nicolas Rolander, 'Sweden Girds for Diplomatic Crisis with China over Free Press', Bloomberg, 20 January 2020, https://www.bloomberg.com/news/articles/2020-01-20/sweden-girds-for-diplomatic-crisis-with-china-over-free-press.

18 Cixin Liu (Ken Liu, trans.), *The Three-body Problem* (London: Tor Trade, 2016).

19 John J. Mearsheimer, 'Bound to Fail: The Rise and Fall of the Liberal International Order', *International Security*, vol. 43, no. 4, Spring 2019, p. 50.

20 'Ben Wallace: UK "Must Be Prepared to Fight Wars Without US"', BBC, 12 January 2020, https://www.bbc.co.uk/news/uk-51081861.

21 'Assessing Emmanuel Macron's Apocalyptic Vision', *The Economist*,

7 November 2019, https://www.economist.com/leaders/2019/11/07/assessing-emmanuel-macrons-apocalyptic-vision.

22 Ben Barry, 'Defending Europe: Scenario-based Capability Requirements for NATO's European Members', IISS Research Paper, 10 May 2019, https://www.iiss.org/blogs/research-paper/2019/05/defending-europe.

23 'Watch Live: France's Macron Speaks to Ambassadors About Foreign Policy Strategy', France 24, 27 August 2019, https://www.france24.com/en/20190827-france-macron-conference-ambassadors-foreign-policy.

24 The Shanghai Cooperation Organisation was created in 2001, succeeding the Shanghai Five Group formed in 1995.

25 See, for instance, 'Huawei Lève une Armée de Lobbyistes et de Consultants Pour Imposer sa 5G en France', *Le Canard Enchaîné*, 24 December 2019.

26 See François Heisbourg, *Secrètes Histoires: La Naissance du Monde Moderne* (Paris: Stock, 2015).

27 NATO, 'London Declaration'. The pertinent language is: 'NATO and allies … are committed to ensuring the security of our communications including 5G … We recognise that China's growing influence and international policies present both opportunities and challenges that we need to address together as an Alliance.'

All in the Family: North Korea and the Fate of Hereditary Autocratic Regimes

Oriana Skylar Mastro

Today, hereditary autocracies – absolute monarchies, or personalistic dictatorships centred on a strongman who intends to pass power to his family or who fills government positions with blood relatives – may seem like a thing of the past, a relic of the days when the world was ruled by kingdoms and empires. The number of such regimes has fallen steadily for decades: only 12 remain, and no new ones have been established in the past 16 years.

But while few countries now have hereditary autocratic regimes, those that do happen to matter a great deal to international security. The collapse of such regimes in the Dominican Republic and Haiti led to waves of refugees fleeing political instability. If the Castro family dynasty loses power in Cuba, the United States might have to deal with another refugee surge. The fall of absolute monarchies in Iran and Iraq, and the subsequent establishment of the Hussein family dictatorship, dragged the United States into long, messy conflicts in the Middle East and threatened to disrupt energy supplies from the region's major oil-producing nations. History could repeat itself if the federation of absolute monarchies in the United Arab Emirates (UAE) loses power. Discontent with the Assad family dictatorship led to a civil war in Syria, which has torn the country apart, given birth to the Islamic State (ISIS) and sparked a refugee crisis across Europe.

In short, while hereditary autocratic regimes are rare, their impact on international affairs justifies an in-depth study into their weakest links

Oriana Skylar Mastro is an assistant professor of security studies at Georgetown University and a Resident Scholar at the American Enterprise Institute.

Survival | vol. 62 no. 2 | April–May 2020 | pp. 103–124   DOI 10.1080/00396338.2020.1739951

and patterns of collapse, and into what typically happens once they've ended. Surprisingly, despite their huge practical importance to the international system, hereditary autocracies have been the subject of little contemporary scholarship. Most research focuses on specific cases and fails to provide any broader insights into the weaknesses and evolution of hereditary autocratic regimes.[1] In comparative politics, scholars have researched hereditary regimes and autocratic regimes, but they have largely ignored the subset of *hereditary autocratic* regimes.[2] Looking at merely hereditary regimes is not enough, because the research does not distinguish between absolute and constitutional monarchies, and some researchers even include democracies that are dominated by political dynasties.[3] Lumping together all types of hereditary regimes obscures the unique features of hereditary autocracies: Syria, a family dictatorship, has far more in common with Bahrain, an absolute monarchy, than it does with the United

The transfer of power is especially challenging

Kingdom, a constitutional monarchy. Nor is it sufficient to examine autocracies more broadly,[4] as hereditary regimes face unique problems caused by their structure and sources of legitimacy, and by the limited number of possible successors to the current ruler. Finally, many researchers define a hereditary regime as one in which the ruler has successfully transferred power to an heir, a definition that excludes cases in which a leader tried but failed to pass on power.[5] If these cases are left out, it will appear that such regimes are more durable than they really are. Researchers are likely, therefore, to miss many of the conditions under which they collapse.

This article seeks to fill the gaps in the academic literature through an inductive study of the rise, fall and persistence of 31 hereditary autocracies since the end of the Second World War, based on the findings of previous research into the conditions and processes of collapse. Firstly, research has demonstrated that the transfer of power from one leader to another is especially challenging in autocratic regimes.[6] Secondly, scholarship has focused on regime durability, the onset of instability and the possibility of rapid collapse.[7] Thirdly, a strong research tradition stresses the importance of the military's role in regime durability, specifically arguing that military defection increases the chances that civil resistance will be effective.[8] Lastly, many researchers emphasise the security challenges that result from regime collapse – from civil war to the establishment of equally repressive regimes.[9]

My own research indicates that four specific patterns are applicable to, and in some cases especially severe in, hereditary autocratic regimes. Firstly, the weakest link in hereditary autocratic regimes tends to be the transfer of power, especially between generations. Hereditary autocracies lack inclusive political institutions and procedures for distributing and managing power, with the result that when the ruler dies or steps down, a crisis often results. Secondly, hereditary autocracies may last longer than other autocracies,[10] but they are prone to collapsing rapidly (within one year of signs of trouble) and often unexpectedly. Thirdly, a collapse tends to be foreshadowed by the defection of the military. Finally, democracy rarely follows the end of a hereditary autocracy, but societies that have rid themselves of such governments are moderately freer.

This article combines these patterns in hereditary autocratic regimes with existing research on the durability of autocracies more broadly to explain why the Kim regime has managed to stay in power in North Korea. Many observers in the 1990s thought the regime would not survive the collapse of the Soviet Union, its crucial supporter. Others have pointed to North Korea's horrendous economic situation and predicted that opposition would arise from within the ranks or among the population, given the direness of the situation.[11] My own research suggests that these factors – external patronage and economic circumstances – are not the primary threats to hereditary autocratic regimes, and thus it is not surprising that North Korea's regime has endured.[12] Indeed, many of the tools Pyongyang has used to stay in power – restrictive social policies to manipulate ideas and information; the use of force; co-option; the manipulation of foreign governments; and institutional coup-proofing – ensure that opposition forces do not arise during successions and that the regime is supported by the military in the unlikely event of domestic instability.[13]

Even though the Kim regime has managed to be an exception, the pattern of rapid, unexpected regime collapse among hereditary autocracies indicates a need for policymakers to be prepared. Should the North Korean regime collapse, the results could be disastrous. The country's nuclear weapons might fall into the hands of other rogue states or dangerous non-state actors. Even if the weapons themselves are secured, bad actors might get hold of nuclear material, experts or other know-how. The end of the Kim regime could also force the United States, along with South Korea, to launch contingency operations, such as seizing nuclear, biological and chemical weapons and material, or deploying troops to establish order, which could bring China and the United States to the brink of war.[14] Even if the Korean Peninsula were reunified peacefully, the process would still destabilise the Indo-Pacific. This broad region, in addition to being economically significant, is home to crucial maritime routes, shared natural resources, and burgeoning global threats such as terrorism and a rising China.

These findings suggest a number of recommendations. Firstly, for countries wishing to influence the political nature of the hereditary regime, the most effective time to do so would be during times of succession, which can be unexpected and narrow windows of opportunity. However, trade-offs should be expected. On the one hand, the military or competing elites often catalyse a regime's downfall, and therefore supporting them can be a more effective way of ending the regime than supporting civil society. However, if the military or the elites are stronger than civil society, free and democratic governments are highly unlikely to follow any change in regime.[15] Secondly, US policymakers should plan for regime collapse in all cases of hereditary autocratic regimes, even North Korea's, as history shows that such regimes can fall rapidly and with little warning. Lastly, policymakers should prioritise policies designed to create wedges between hereditary autocratic regimes and the military. As this article will show, the most important indicator of potential instability is the relationship between the military and the regime. Because North Korea is unlikely to have a succession challenge in the foreseeable future, sowing division between these two elite groups may be the most effective way of shaping Kim Jong-un's behaviour and policies.

Hereditary autocratic regimes since the Second World War

To constitute a hereditary autocracy, a regime needs to meet two conditions. Firstly, it must be autocratic. Countries in which a family member of
a previous leader gained power through legitimate means, such as Djibouti
(where Ismaïl Omar Guelleh was elected president in 1999, after his uncle,
Hassan Gouled Aptidon, stepped down), Singapore (where Lee Hsien
Loong, the son of the country's first prime minister, became prime minister himself in 2004 through a constitutional process) or the United States
(where George W. Bush was elected president eight years after his father,
George H.W. Bush, left office), are not family dictatorships. Constitutional
monarchies also do not count as autocracies, because in such countries the
political system places institutional limits on the monarch's power.

Secondly, a familial component must exist. Usually this component takes
the form of a leader who has passed, or plans to pass, power to the next
generation in his family. Sometimes the attempt to transfer power succeeds,
as it did in North Korea, Saudi Arabia and Syria. Sometimes it fails and the
ruling family loses absolute power, an outcome I refer to as regime collapse.[16]
Regime collapse has occurred in the Dominican Republic, the Democratic
Republic of the Congo (previously Zaire), Ethiopia, Haiti, Indonesia, Iran,
Iraq, Libya, Nepal, Nicaragua, the Philippines and Romania. And sometimes the handover of power succeeds, but the successor presides over a
transition into a constitutional monarchy, marking the end of the hereditary
autocratic regime, as happened in Bhutan, Bahrain and Nepal. Occasionally,
when the succession is unclear, a family dictatorship can persist if the leader
installs family members in key government positions, especially in the military and the internal security services. As long as the leader plans to pass
power to a family member and the regime is an autocracy, a country can be
characterised as a hereditary autocracy.[17]

Since the end of the Second World War, 27 countries have at some point
been ruled by hereditary autocratic regimes. Four countries – the Democratic
Republic of the Congo, Ethiopia, Iraq and Nepal – have each experienced
two separate hereditary autocratic regimes, and so count as two cases each.
Thus, these 27 countries provide 31 instances of hereditary autocratic rule.
Table 1 lists these cases, including the type of regime, its duration, the kind

Table 1: **Summary of case studies**

Country	Type	Years in power	Ended?	Regime type that followed	Freedom House rating 2018 (1=most free, 7=least free)*
Azerbaijan	Family dictatorship	2003–present	No	N/A	6.5
Bahrain	Absolute monarchy	1782–2002	Yes	Constitutional monarchy	6.5
Bhutan	Absolute monarchy	1907–2008	Yes	Constitutional monarchy	3.5
Brunei	Absolute monarchy	1400s–present	No	N/A	5.5
Cuba	Family dictatorship**	1959–present	No	N/A	6.5
Dominican Republic	Family dictatorship	1930–1961	Yes	Presidential republic	3.0
Democratic Republic of the Congo/Zaire	Family dictatorship	1965–1997	Yes	Family dictatorship	6.5
	Family dictatorship	1997–2006	Yes	Semi-presidential republic	
Equatorial New Guinea	Family dictatorship	1979–present	No	N/A	7.0
Ethiopia	Absolute monarchy	1268–1936	Yes	Italian occupation	6.5
	Absolute monarchy	1941–1974	Yes	Military junta	
Gabon	Family dictatorship	1967–present	No	N/A	6.0
Haiti	Family dictatorship	1957–1986	Yes	Semi-presidential republic	5.0
Indonesia	Family dictatorship	1967–1998	Yes	Presidential republic	3.0
Iran	Absolute monarchy	1921–1979	Yes	Islamic republic	6.0
Iraq	Absolute monarchy	1921–1958	Yes	Family dictatorship	5.5
	Family dictatorship	1979–2003	Yes	Federal parliamentary republic	
Libya	Family dictatorship	1969–2011	Yes	Provisional government/civil war	6.5
Nepal	Absolute monarchy	1846–1951	Yes	Constitutional monarchy	3.5
		1955–2015	Yes	Federal parliamentary republic	
Nicaragua	Family dictatorship	1936–1979	Yes	Presidential republic	4.5
North Korea	Family dictatorship	1948–present	No	N/A	7.0
Oman	Absolute monarchy	1951–present	No	N/A	5.5
Philippines	Family dictatorship	1965–1986	Yes	Presidential republic	3.0
Qatar	Absolute monarchy	1916–present	No	N/A	5.5
Romania	Family dictatorship	1965–1989	Yes	Semi-presidential republic	2.0
Saudi Arabia	Absolute monarchy	1932–present	No	N/A	7.0
Swaziland (eSwatini)	Absolute monarchy	1968–present	No	N/A	6.5
Syria	Family dictatorship	1970–present	No	N/A	7.0
Togo	Family dictatorship	1967–2015	Yes	Presidential republic	4.0
UAE	Federation of monarchies	1971–present	No	N/A	6.5

*Freedom House, 'Freedom in the World 2018', https://freedomhouse.org/report/freedom-world/freedom-world-2018.
**While Raúl Castro is no longer the president of Cuba, he remains head of the Communist Party of Cuba and unofficial head of the military. His son and daughter also hold prominent party memberships.

of government that followed and the Freedom House rating of the country in 2018. Of the 31 cases, about 60% were family dictatorships and 40% were absolute monarchies. Today, six family dictatorships and six absolute monarchies remain in power.

Although family dictatorships and absolute monarchies are both hereditary regimes, they tend to follow different trajectories and have different vulnerabilities. At first glance, family dictatorships seem to be more prone to collapse. Twelve of the 18 family dictatorships since the Second World War have collapsed (about 67%), compared with seven of the 13 absolute monarchies (about 54%). Perhaps even more significant, family dictatorships do not last as long as absolute monarchies: family dictatorships that ended in collapse endured for an average of 32 years, less than one-fifth the average duration of absolute monarchies that experienced collapse (184 years).

Why have absolute monarchies tended to last longer than family dictatorships? One reason might be the number of small states ruled by such monarchies. While the vast majority of absolute monarchies collapsed before the Second World War, those in very small states or emirates, such as Brunei, Oman, Qatar, Swaziland and the UAE, have tended to survive. Absolute monarchies might also gain an advantage if they are founded at the same time as the country they rule. Five of the seven surviving absolute monarchies – Brunei, Oman, Qatar, Saudi Arabia and the UAE – were formed upon the founding of the nations in the twentieth century, which may have conferred bonus legitimacy on the ruling family.[18] The difference in durability may also be a product of historical trends – most states founded before the end of the First World War, such as Bahrain, Bhutan, Brunei, Ethiopia, Nepal and Qatar, have lasted hundreds of years (more than 700 for Ethiopia), while 38% of those founded after the First World War have since collapsed, lasting on average 52 years.

Modern scholarship has also concluded that determining whether a regime is led by civilians or the military is the key to understanding its behaviour and stability.[19] Hereditary autocratic regimes are almost equally split between those that were established by military leaders and those run by civilians, but the regimes with military leaderships have a higher rate of collapse: 76%, compared with 35% for civilian regimes. Recent scholarship on autocratic regimes in general has shown that the cause of regime death has shifted away from military coups and toward popular revolt.[20] But in case studies of hereditary autocratic regimes, the two factors interact with each other – popular protests tend to lead to the end of the regime, but only if the military also retracts its support for the leader. Such a move is most likely when military commanders perceive the current leader as weak and when the leader gives them responsibility for regime stability.[21]

Although family dictatorships and absolute monarchies have different average durations, when they do collapse, they often do so for similar reasons, in similar ways and with similar results. Most collapses come during transitions of power, and most happen quickly. In both regime types, the loss of the military's support is frequently enough to bring down the regime, in contrast to popular protests, which are not sufficient by themselves. Once the old regime has fallen, the results tend to be messy.

Difficulties of succession

As noted, hereditary autocratic regimes are uniquely vulnerable during succession periods. Successful hereditary transitions rely on the support of the state's elites.[22] There may be resistance to hereditary succession, particularly if an autocrat who rose to power through an existing party structure subsequently tries to transfer power to an heir.[23] Moreover, the need to pick a blood relation to succeed a ruler creates two challenges. Firstly, the likelihood of finding an individual who both enjoys the support of the elite and is seen as the most competent candidate is relatively low, due to the small pool of candidates. Secondly, the difficulty of organising collective action under autocratic regimes is a key reason why such regimes endure, but opposition groups form more readily when there are visible alternative candidates for power.[24]

Collapse usually happens when power is passing from a dead, incapacitated or retired dictator to a family member, or when the dictator is ageing and a handover of power is expected to take place in the near future. These are times of instability. In some cases, the leader designates a successor and grooms the next generation during his lifetime, a practice more common in absolute monarchies such as Saudi Arabia than in family dictatorships. In other cases, a family member tries unsuccessfully to consolidate power after the unexpected death of the original leader – as did Ghazi bin Faisal in Iraq, Ramfis Trujillo Martínez in the Dominican Republic, Joseph Kabila in the Democratic Republic of the Congo and Jean-Claude Duvalier in Haiti after the deaths of their fathers. The successor often enjoys little credibility among the ruling elites, as his main source of legitimacy is his bloodline.

While all transitions of power are dangerous, some are more dangerous than others. The riskiest moments are when the second ruling generation attempts to hand power to the third in a family dictatorship. Since the end of the Second World War, only two family dictatorships, the Somozas of Nicaragua and the Kims of North Korea, have managed to do so. Nicaragua's case is unique because the Somozas installed puppet governments, allowing the family to maintain its grip, albeit indirectly, during times of regime weakness.

The difficulty in handing power to the third generation is partly to do with leadership. The generation that founds a dictatorship is typically headed by a strong and charismatic leader who, by sheer force of personality, can groom a successor from within the family and remove any obstacles to his or her rise to power. The founding dictator may also enjoy strong loyalty from his supporters, who may well transfer that loyalty to his successor. But a second-generation dictator rarely enjoys the same legitimacy or loyalty as the founder, a weakness that can leave him unable to pass power to another family member. Family dictatorships also face an acute adverse-selection problem. They are among the most corrupt autocracies in the world,[25] so they tend to attract opportunists who are principally motivated by greed rather than loyalty, a problem that only worsens over time, either because the leader amasses unparalleled power or because the original revolutionary ideology fades but the elites still need to be co-opted. Corrupt bureaucrats both delegitimise the regime and weaken the authority of the second-generation dictator because the ruler cannot count on their support if the money runs out. These problems – weak second-generation rulers and adverse selection – mean that family dictatorships rarely survive long enough for the second generation to pass power to the third.

Leaders of hereditary autocracies realise that transitions are dangerous, so they are usually reluctant to hand over power during their lifetimes.

Instead, most leaders plan to wait until their health has deteriorated to deal with succession, or they refuse to do so at all while they are alive. (In absolute monarchies, of course, the standard procedure is to wait for the death of the king for the Crown prince to rise to the throne, but there are clear succession rules in place to prevent power grabs.) Waiting is a risky strategy, however. The regime weakens as its leader ages. In the cases studied here, the average founder of a family dictatorship lost or ceded power when he or she was 68.5 years old. This may not sound ancient, but because younger leaders tend to be forced out rather than step down voluntarily, the average figure understates the tendency of leaders to cling to power even after they have become physically and mentally unable to rule. First-generation leaders who die natural deaths expire at an average age of 71; those who are over-thrown or assassinated go out at just 59. In only three cases – Azerbaijan, Cuba and Togo – did the leader pass power to his successor before dying. As the leader ages, his ability to maintain control over government factions, the military and the people declines, hurting the legitimacy of the family regime and making it even harder for the second generation to take the reins of government.

For now, North Korea has managed to beat the odds by being the only clear case of a family dictatorship in its third generation. When Kim Jong-il first disappeared from the public eye in 2008 after a severe stroke, it was not immediately clear who would succeed him, as his sons were largely seen as unqualified to rule. Eventually the youngest, Kim Jong-un, became the chosen one, despite the Korean tradition of naming the eldest as the successor.[26] To ensure a smooth transition, Kim senior toured with Kim junior around North Korea to vest authority in his son.[27] But unlike Kim Jong-il, who spent 20 years ruling the country with his father before taking over the leadership role, Kim Jong-un had less than three years to consolidate power in key institutions such as the Workers' Party of Korea, the military, and the security and intelligence agencies. Kim Jong-un now leads North Korea with an iron fist and is not afraid to punish traitors at all levels of society, as evidenced by the execution of his uncle in late 2013 and the assassination of his half-brother in Malaysia in 2017. Currently, the 36-year-old leader has no clear successor.

Patterns of rapid collapse

Kim is known to be in bad health: US and South Korean intelligence teams have speculated that due to his weight gain and behaviour, 'he may suffer from a range of conditions including gout, diabetes, high blood pressure, a sexually transmitted disease and psychological issues'.[28] Nevertheless, because he is only 36, there is little prospect of a succession crisis in North Korea in the near future. But this does not mean the regime is stable. The second common characteristic of hereditary autocratic regimes is rapid and often unexpected collapse. Most regimes that fall disintegrate completely within about a year of the first signs of a crisis. The Marcos regime in the Philippines, for example, collapsed less than a year after fraudulent election results sparked the People Power Revolution. More and more military groups defected until Ferdinand Marcos fled to Hawaii and Maria Corazon Cojuangco Aquino took over the presidency. The overthrow of Romania's Nicolae Ceauşescu during the Romanian Revolution of 1989 was accomplished within weeks after he was criticised for abuses of power and economic policies.

Suharto's Indonesia offers another example of rapid collapse. Suharto's regime can be characterised as a family dictatorship because in its later years, the president appointed family members to his cabinet who prospered financially by monopolising key sectors of the economy.[29] For example, he appointed his daughter the social-affairs minister and his son-in-law the commander of the elite Kostrad force.[30] In February 1998, sustained student protests began at the University of Indonesia in Jakarta, and quickly spread to all the country's major universities. The students called on the government to cut the prices of basic commodities and reject corruption, collusion, nepotism and Suharto's 'New Order' reform programme.[31] By May, the protests had spread to other sectors of society and turned into riots, causing about half a billion dollars' worth of damage. Suharto's support among elites began to crumble, and he was forced to resign on 28 May, less than four months after the protests had begun.

Before the Indonesian students took to the streets, there were few signs of mass discontent. Indeed, one of the policy challenges when dealing with hereditary autocratic regimes is that there are rarely clear indicators that they might be in danger. Such indicators are not always entirely absent, however. In some cases, there are political protests, as in the Philippines in 1974 and 1978. Pressure from protesters is often one factor that leads to political reforms, new elections and the eventual toppling of the regime. In Bahrain, for example, largely Shi'ite protesters took to the streets to challenge the undemocratic nature of the regime; security forces arrested more than 2,500 protesters in 1995.

Additionally, a country's economic and social state can also serve as a catalyst for regime collapse. In countries where there is a clear divide between the rich and the poor, and where the people are discontented with the resources provided by the state, collapse is more likely. Ethiopia and Haiti were consumed by natural disasters, famine, drought and poverty; Romania had no heat or food; and Iraq faced economic hardship and a visible gap between the rich and the poor. These circumstances facilitated the fall of their regimes. International pressure can also drive a regime toward collapse. The Democratic Republic of the Congo came under international pressure to liberalise its government, and the Philippines faced both domestic and foreign calls for new elections. If the leader is weak, such pressure and discontent can be enough to end the regime.

However, while bad domestic situations, international opprobrium and public discontent often foreshadow the collapse of a regime, in most cases the regime endures even when these conditions are present. The key factor is whether the autocratic regime maintains sufficient control of its repressive apparatus to control the country. Military support tends to be a critical element of such control. The family dictatorships that endure can all, to varying degrees, be characterised as police states that suppress internal discontent and elite scheming. For example, in Bahrain in 2011, a popular pro-democracy movement was crushed by the monarchy through force, and since then the monarchy has cracked down on political and civil liberties to avoid future mobilisation.[32] By contrast, in cases where the military turns on the political leadership, as it did in Haiti, Faisal's Iraq, Romania and the Philippines, protests tend to signal the end of the regime. Thus, the support of the military is critical for the durability of family dictatorships and absolute monarchies – and its withdrawal often marks the end of the regime.

Whenever a weak successor rises to the top of a hereditary regime, an opportunity opens up for the military (or a strongman unrelated to the family) to seize power. The military might depose the regime and install military rule, as it did in Ethiopia in 1974, Haiti in 1986, the Dominican Republic in 1961 and Hashemite Iraq in 1958. Alternatively, the military might throw its support behind another elite group (or the political opposition) to topple the hereditary regime, as in Romania in 1989, the Philippines in 1986 and Iran in 1979.

One of the reasons the Kim regime has managed to stay in power through three different leaders is that it has made a number of policy decisions to ensure that the military will not challenge it. For example, the North Korean military is confined to intervening in decisions related to national security.[33] Moreover, North Korea has chosen a decentralised security structure with multiple coercive institutions that are constrained by a system of checks and balances. Thus, the Kims seem to have guarded against threats such as military coups or assassination by the security services even more effectively than it has guarded against threats from the masses.[34] Lastly, Kim Jong-il's focus on building nuclear weapons, as part of his revival of the 'military first' (*songun*) strategy, likely made him popular among military elites.

The low likelihood of democracy post-collapse

Policymakers in liberal democracies may be heartened by the fact that only 12 hereditary autocracies remain, and that no new ones have been established in the past 16 years. However, even when hereditary autocracies come to an end, the regimes that follow are often little better. Since the Second World War, family dictatorships have rarely transitioned into thriving democracies. Instead, the collapse of a dictatorship tends to produce a period of acute instability or even civil war, followed by the establishment of yet another autocratic regime. In many cases, after the leader is overthrown, close associates gain control of the government and its institutions remain relatively unchanged, as happened in the Dominican Republic, Indonesia, Nepal and Romania.[35] In countries where the opposition overthrew the government through violence, such as Zaire, Ethiopia and Iran, family regimes were replaced with equally repressive governments. In Zaire, another family dictatorship took over (and renamed the country the Democratic Republic of the Congo); in Ethiopia, a brutal military regime seized power; and in Iran, an equally repressive regime emerged. Currently, the average Freedom House rating for an autocratic hereditary regime is 6.375 out of 7 ('not free'), while the average rating for countries that have transitioned from such regimes is 4.6 ('partly free').[36] Since the 1940s, about 46% of the autocratic regimes that have collapsed have been replaced by democracies;[37] but for hereditary autocratic regimes, only 32% have been followed by democracies, of which half are considered only 'partly free'. What happens after a collapse depends on many variables, the most important of which are usually the power and cohesiveness of the opposition. In most cases, however, long periods of ruthless repression mean that when the regime collapses, it leaves behind a political vacuum that democracy struggles to fill.

Collapse leaves a political vacuum

In some cases, such as Iraq in 1958 and Libya and Syria in 2011, the end of the hereditary regime (or its attempted overthrow) coincides with the outbreak of a civil war. In Iraq, the country's monarchy was followed by two brutal dictatorships, a civil war and then, after Saddam Hussein was overthrown by US forces in 2003, a federal parliamentary republic, albeit a frequently dysfunctional one. Eight years after Muammar Gadhafi was killed, Libya remains under the rule of a provisional government. The second Libyan civil war began in 2014 and continues to this day; a unified, central government has yet to emerge from the chaos. Bashar al-Assad continues to serve as the president of a disintegrating Syria; an estimated 13.1 million Syrians are in need of humanitarian assistance, with 6.1m people displaced internally and a further 5.4m registered as Syrian refugees abroad.[38] Yet Syria has multiple opposition groups, such as the National Coordination Committee for Democratic Change, that are at least partially prepared to take power if the Syrian civil war ends with the ouster of the Assad family. Where a civil war has followed a regime collapse, third parties have had to step in, as the United Nations did in the Democratic Republic of the Congo in 1999, brokering a peace agreement after rebels led by Laurent Kabila overthrew the country's long-time dictator, Mobutu Sese Seko. In that case, the result was another family dictatorship, this time led by Kabila for nine more years. Although this family dictatorship ended in 2006, the country's current Freedom House rating is 6.5/7, or 'not free'.[39]

In the few countries that have attempted to transition to democracy after a hereditary dictatorship, even if only for show – the Dominican Republic, Haiti, Indonesia, Iraq, Nicaragua, the Philippines and Romania[40] – the fall of the family regime was followed by years of instability, transitional governments or rigged elections. In all these countries, the governments that followed were still corrupt; power remained concentrated in a few hands; and the people's quality of life improved little. Indeed, no country that had experienced the collapse of a family dictatorship since the Second World War was considered a democracy in 2006.[41] According to the Economist Intelligence Unit, only the Dominican Republic, Indonesia, the Philippines and Romania merited the designation of 'flawed democracy' by 2017.[42]

The experience of hereditary autocracies since the Second World War suggests that the way a regime falls affects the nature of the regime that follows. Violent overthrow usually leads to military rule; spontaneous popular uprisings in countries without an organised opposition leave a vacuum that members of the former regime or other autocrats scramble to fill; and when an organised political opposition helps bring down the regime, that group either becomes the sole authority (Congo, Iran, Nicaragua) or replaces one autocrat with another, failing to transform the political system (the Philippines). In short, although not all regime collapses look alike, none of them have good short-term outcomes.

Should the North Korean regime collapse, significant resources and involvement will be required from the United States and South Korea, and potentially even China, Japan and Russia, to make sure the country does not fall into this vicious cycle. But there are reasons to believe that a North Korean collapse scenario may deviate from the norm. While hereditary autocratic regimes are rarely followed by democracy, South Korea, a mature democracy, would probably absorb North Korea after a collapse, which means that democracy is a plausible post-collapse scenario for the people of North Korea.[43]

Reunification would bring challenges, however. Firstly, it promises to be expensive for the people of South Korea, which may be one reason public support for reunification is waning.[44] The process will also be arduous, as South Korea's market-based economy will need to incorporate North Korea's unskilled labour force and reform the North's virtually non-existent economy (North Korea's GDP is reported to be less than 1% of the South's).[45] Social and humanitarian issues will also abound: 18–25m North Koreans currently face chronic food insecurity, 10.5m are malnourished and more than 100,000 are imprisoned in labour camps that are known to be hotbeds for epidemic diseases.[46] Lastly, to ensure the stability of a reunified Korea, it will be essential to prevent the proliferation of North Korea's weapons of mass destruction while they are being eliminated. The Korean People's Army will need to be demobilised and its members redirected to other sectors.[47]

* * *

While it is 'impossible for analysts to know how or when the Kim family will cease to rule North Korea', as Michael O'Hanlon put it more than ten years ago, the experiences of countries with similar political systems can shed light on the range of policy options available to the United States and other liberal democracies in the event of its collapse.[48]

The first lesson is that US and international pressure would probably play only a minor role in instigating North Korea's collapse. The history of hereditary autocracies suggests that when a regime is strong, external pressure has a negligible effect, and similarly, when the regime is weak, external support can do little to help it maintain power. Moreover, the United States should not encourage insurgencies or military coups, since regimes that are brought down in those ways tend to be replaced by equally repressive governments. This principle applies even to cases, such as North Korea, in which the regime is so repressive that encouraging political opposition or grassroots movements is not a viable option. The United States would have to weaken Kim's control over the repressive apparatus, including the military, to increase the likelihood of his regime's demise.

There is, however, one point at which outsiders could have a significant influence: during a succession. At that point, the structural weaknesses of hereditary regimes come to the fore, and foreign governments can do much to encourage political opposition, grassroots movements and even insurgencies or military coups. Western policymakers should also bear in mind that when collapse happens, it happens fast, opening a small window in which the outcome might be influenced. At the end of Marcos's reign in the Philippines, for example, the White House quickly moved to support those who opposed him, despite Marcos's close friendship with the US president at the time, Ronald Reagan.

It is difficult to determine the stability of the North Korean regime. It is possible that it will endure for a long time. Despite international sanctions and restrictions on foreign trade, North Korea's economy seems to be holding; the won has remained stable against the US dollar and the Chinese renminbi.[49] Foreign products that were visible prior to sanctions have been replaced with locally made options, and citizens have even seen improvements in their daily lives, including a more reliable supply of electricity and cheaper coal to heat homes, as coal can no longer be exported.[50] But the speed with which similar regimes have – with few early indicators – collapsed in the past suggests that scholars and strategists should continue to plan for the demise of the Kim regime, however stable it may seem. History also suggests that US planning for a post-Kim North Korea should go beyond the military, which has been preparing for this contingency since the end of the Korean War, because a peaceful, stable Korean Peninsula will require the building of a new civil society. Such planning, therefore, should involve greater coordination across government agencies, for example between the South Korean Ministry of Unification and the US State Department. Even though the likelihood of imminent collapse is low, these preparations may be the only way to prevent instability, civil war and the installation of a new but equally repressive regime.

Notes

[1] See Patrick McEachern, 'Comparative Authoritarian Institutionalism, Regime Evolution, and Stability in North Korea', *Asian Journal of Comparative Politics*, vol. 3, no. 4, 2018, pp. 367–85; Daniel Byman and Jennifer Lind, 'Pyongyang's Survival Strategy: Tools of Authoritarian Control in North Korea', *International Security*, vol. 35, no. 1, 2010, pp. 44–74; Charles Armstrong, 'One-family Rule: North Korea's Hereditary Authoritarianism', *World Politics Review*, 18 February 2014; Joshua Stacher, 'Reinterpreting Authoritarian Power: Syria's Hereditary Succession', *Middle East Journal*, vol. 65, no. 2, 2011, pp. 197–212; and Carlos M. Vilas, 'Family Affairs: Class, Lineage and Politics in Contemporary Nicaragua', *Journal of Latin America Studies*, vol. 24, no. 2, May 1992, pp. 309–41.

[2] See Milan W. Svolik, *The Politics of Authoritarian Rule* (Cambridge: Cambridge University Press, 2012); Axel Hadenius and Jan Teorell, 'Authoritarian Regimes: Stability, Change, and Pathways to Democracy, 1972–2003', Kellogg Institute, 2006; Barbara Geddes, Joseph Wright and Erica Frantz, 'Autocratic Breakdown and Regime Transitions: A New Data Set', *Perspectives on Politics*, vol. 12, no. 2, 2014, pp. 313–31; and Jose Antonio Cheibub, Jennifer Gandhi and James Raymond Vreeland, 'Democracy and Dictatorship Revisited', *Public Choice*, vol. 143, no. 1–2, 2010, pp. 67–101.

[3] See Ernesto Dal Bo, Pedro Dal Bo and Jason Snyder, 'Political Dynasties', *Review of Economic Studies*, vol. 76, no. 1, 2009, pp. 115–42.

[4] For broad studies, see Gordon Tullock, *Autocracy* (Boston, MA: Springer, 1987); and Jason Brownlee, 'Hereditary Succession in Modern Autocracies', *World Politics*, vol. 59, no. 4, 2007, pp. 595–628.

[5] See Timothy Besley and Marta Reynal-Querol, 'The Logic of Hereditary Rule: Theory and Evidence', *Journal of Economic Growth*, vol. 22, no. 2, 2017, pp. 123–44.

[6] See John Herz, 'The Problem of Successorship in Dictatorial Regimes: A Study in Comparative Law and Institutions', *Journal of Politics*, vol. 14, no. 1, 1952, pp. 19–40; and Geddes, Wright and Frantz, 'Autocratic Breakdown and Regime Transitions'.

[7] See Ricardo Sanhueza, 'The Hazard Rate of Political Regimes', *Public Choice*, vol. 98, no. 3–4, 1999, pp. 337–67; and Laurence Whitehead, 'The "Puzzle" of Autocratic Resilience/Regime Collapse: The Case of Cuba', *Third World Quarterly*, vol. 37, no. 9, September 2016, pp. 1,666–82.

[8] See Kara Kingma Neu, 'Do Military Defections Help or Hinder Pro-democracy Civil Resistance?', International Center on Nonviolent Conflict, 31 July 2018, https://www.nonviolent-conflict.org/blog_post/military-defections-help-hinder-pro-democracy-civil-resistance/; Satoshi Ikeuchi, 'Explaining Authoritarian Collapse and Persistence: Regime–Military–Society Relations in the Face of the Arab Spring', paper presented at the 2013 Annual Meeting of the Western Political Science Association,

Hollywood, CA, March 2013, http://www.wpsanet.org/papers/docs/Explaining%20Authoritarian%20Collapse%20and%20Persistence%20WPSA%202013.pdf; Jean-Baptiste Gallopin, 'Protest Is Not Enough to Topple a Dictator: The Army Must also Turn', *Aeon*, 31 July 2019, https://aeon.co/ideas/protest-is-not-enough-to-topple-a-dictator-the-army-must-also-turn; Eva Bellin, 'Reconsidering the Robustness of Authoritarianism in the Middle East: Lessons from the Arab Spring', *Comparative Politics*, vol. 44, no. 2, 2012, pp. 127–49; and Milan W. Svolik, 'Power Sharing and Leadership Dynamics in Authoritarian Regimes', *American Journal of Political Science*, vol. 53, no. 2, 2009, pp. 477–94.

9   See Geddes, Wright and Frantz, 'Autocratic Breakdown and Regime Transitions'; Bellin, 'Reconsidering the Robustness of Authoritarianism in the Middle East'; and Joseph Wright and Abel Escriba-Folch, 'Authoritarian Institutions and Regime Survival: Transitions to Democracy and Subsequent Autocracy', *British Journal of Political Science*, vol. 42, no. 2, 2012, pp. 293–309. Additionally, Edward Mansfield and Jack Snyder show that new democracies that emerge from collapsed authoritarian regimes often become more aggressive and war-prone due to power struggles between elites from the old authoritarian order and new democratic elites. Edward Mansfield and Jack Snyder, 'Democratization and the Danger of War', *International Security*, vol. 20, no. 1, Summer 1995, pp. 5–38.

10   See Sanhueza, 'The Hazard Rate of Political Regimes'.

11   See CIA Director of Central Intelligence, 'Implications of Alternative Soviet Futures', CIA National Intelligence Estimate, 1991.

12   Existing literature has characterised North Korea as a single-party personalist regime, or argued that the Kim regime is best understood as originally military (1948–1993) and then civilian. See, for example, Geddes, Wright and Frantz, 'Autocratic Breakdown and Regime Transitions'; Beatriz Magaloni and Ruth Kricheli, 'Political Order and One-party Rule', *Annual Review of Political Science*, no. 13, 2010, pp. 123–43; and Cheibub, Gandhi and Vreeland, 'Democracy and Dictatorship Revisited'.

13   Byman and Lind, 'Pyongyang's Survival Strategy', p. 45.

14   See Oriana Skylar Mastro, 'Conflict and Chaos on the Korean Peninsula: Can China's Military Help Secure North Korea's Nuclear Weapons?', *International Security*, vol. 43, no. 2, Fall 2018, pp. 84–116.

15   Hereditary autocratic regimes tend to be slightly less free than autocratic regimes in general (6.60 vs 6.11 on a scale in which 7 is the least free), which may create additional challenges for democratisation post-collapse. See Drew Desilver, 'Despite Global Concerns About Democracy, More than Half of Countries Are Democratic', Pew Research Center, 14 May 2019, https://www.pewresearch.org/fact-tank/2019/05/14/more-than-half-of-countries-are-democratic/; and Freedom House, 'Freedom in the World 2018', https://freedomhouse.org/report/freedom-world/freedom-world-2018.

[16] It is tricky to categorise regime transitions in absolute monarchies that are voluntary. A transition to a constitutional monarchy might not be considered a collapse because the family voluntarily relinquishes absolute power while retaining symbolic legitimacy and lucrative perks. In this study, however, I characterise this type of transition as a collapse.

[17] Researchers use several terms – 'hereditary authoritarianism', 'hereditary rule', 'dynastic dictatorship' and 'oligarchic familial control' – to refer to such political systems. See Armstrong, 'One-family Rule'; Besley and Reynal-Querol, 'The Logic of Hereditary Rule'; and Kathy Fogel, 'Oligarchic Family Control, Social Economic Outcomes, and the Quality of Government', *Journal of International Business Studies*, vol. 37, no. 5, 2006, pp. 603–22.

[18] In most cases, the same family had been ruling the region for many years before it officially became a country. Examples include Qatar, the UAE, Saudi Arabia, Swaziland and Oman.

[19] See Barbara Geddes, *Paradigms and Sand Castles: Theory Building and Research Design in Comparative Politics* (Ann Arbor, MI: University of Michigan Press, 2003).

[20] See Andrea Kendall-Taylor and Erica Frantz, 'How Autocracies Fall', *Washington Quarterly*, vol. 37, no. 1, 2014, pp. 35–47.

[21] See Holger Albrecht and Dorothy Ohl, 'Exit, Resistance, Loyalty: Military Behavior During Unrest in Authoritarian Regimes', *Perspectives on Politics*, vol. 14, no. 1, 2016, pp. 38–52.

[22] See Jack Goldstone, 'Understanding the Revolutions of 2011: Weakness and Resilience in Middle Eastern Autocracies', *Foreign Affairs*, vol. 90, no. 3, May 2011, pp. 8–16.

[23] See Brownlee, 'Hereditary Succession in Modern Autocracies'.

[24] See Tullock, *Autocracy*.

[25] See Transparency International, 'Corruption Perceptions Index 2018', https://www.transparency.org/cpi2018.

[26] See Armstrong, 'One-family Rule'.

[27] See Jonathan D. Pollack, 'Kim Jong-il to Kim Jong-un: North Korea in Transition', Brookings Institution, 19 December 2011, https://www.brookings.edu/opinions/kim-jong-il-to-kim-jong-un-north-korea-in-transition/.

[28] Hollie McKay, 'US, South Korean Intelligence Probe Reports of Kim Jong Un Health Woes', Fox News, 8 March 2018, https://www.foxnews.com/world/us-south-korean-intelligence-probe-reports-of-kim-jong-un-health-woes.

[29] See Michael R.J. Vatikiotis, *Indonesian Politics Under Suharto: The Rise and Fall of the New Order*, 3rd ed. (New York: Routledge, 1998), pp. xviii–xix.

[30] *Ibid.*, p. 219.

[31] The 'New Order' programme focused on economic development and rapid industrialisation, which alleviated the worst of Indonesia's poverty, but was oppressive and allowed little room for dissent.

[32] See Freedom House, 'Freedom in the World 2017: Bahrain', https://freedomhouse.org/report/freedom-world/2017/bahrain.

[33] See Svolik, 'Power Sharing and Leadership Dynamics in

Authoritarian Regimes'.

34 See Sheena C. Greitens, *Dictators and Their Secret Police: Coercive Institutions and State Violence* (Cambridge: Cambridge University Press, 2016).

35 In the case of Nepal, the same king remained in power, but the political system transitioned from an absolute to a constitutional monarchy. The next king attempted to revert to absolutism, only to be forced by public discontent to embrace constitutionalism once more. In 2015, however, the king gave up power and a federal, secular, parliamentary republic was established.

36 Freedom House, 'Freedom in the World 2018'.

37 Geddes, Wright and Frantz, 'Autocratic Breakdown and Regime Transitions', p. 316.

38 UNICEF Syria, 'Syria Crisis: 2017 Humanitarian Results', pp. 1, 2, https://www.unicef.org/mena/media/1421/file/SYR-SitRep-End17.pdf.pdf.

39 Freedom House, 'Congo, Democratic Republic of (Kinshasa)', https://freedomhouse.org/report/freedom-world/2019/congo-democratic-republic-kinshasa.

40 External pressure by the United States may have encouraged these countries to take the democratic route.

41 Freedom House, 'Freedom in the World 2006', https://freedomhouse.org/report/freedom-world/freedom-world-2006.

42 Economist Intelligence Unit, 'Democracy Index 2017', 2018, https://infographics.economist.com/2018/DemocracyIndex/. The index gives the Democratic Republic of the Congo

a score of 1.61 (with 10 being a full democracy); the Dominican Republic, 6.66; Ethiopia, 3.42; Indonesia, 6.39; Iraq, 4.07; Nepal, 5.18; Nicaragua, 4.66; the Philippines, 6.71; Romania, 6.44; and Togo, 3.05.

43 See Bruce Bennett, 'Alternative Paths to Korean Unification', RAND Corporation, 2018.

44 One group of economists estimated expenditures of at least $3 trillion. See 'Korean Reunification to Cost over $3 Trillion', *Korea Times*, 14 September 2010, http://www.koreatimes.co.kr/www/news/nation/2010/09/113_73029.html.

45 See 'North Korea vs. South Korea', IndexMundi, https://www.indexmundi.com/factbook/compare/north-korea.south-korea; and Benjamin K. Silberstein, 'The North Korean Economy, August 2019: Why China Will Continue to Dominate', 38 North, 10 September 2019, https://www.38north.org/2019/09/bkatzeffsilberstein091019/.

46 Frank Aum, 'North Korea and the Need for a US–ROK–PRC Dialogue', United States Institute of Peace, Special Report 412, August 2017, p. 5; Roberta Cohen, 'Time to Address North Korea's Prison Labor Camps', Brookings Institution, 5 July 2013, https://www.brookings.edu/research/time-to-address-north-koreas-prison-labor-camps/; and Victor Cha and Lindsay Lloyd, 'The Gulags of North Korea', *Foreign Policy*, 10 June 2014, https://foreignpolicy.com/2014/06/10/the-gulags-of-north-korea/.

47 See *Ibid.*; and Chung Min Lee and Kathryn Botto, 'Reconceptualizing US–ROK Cooperation in Korean

Unification: A Stabilization Framework', Carnegie Endowment for International Peace, 30 April 2019, https://carnegieendowment.org/2019/04/30/reconceptualizing-u.s.-rok-cooperation-in-korean-unification-stabilization-framework-pub-78737.

[48] Michael E. O'Hanlon, 'North Korea Collapse Scenarios', Brookings Institution, 9 June 2009, https://www.brookings.edu/opinions/north-korea-collapse-scenarios/.

[49] Peter Ward, 'The North Korean Economy in October 2018: An Overview', NK Pro, 11 November 2018, https://www.nknews.org/pro/the-north-korean-economy-in-october-2018-an-overview/.

[50] Eun-Young Jeong and Dasl Yoon, 'The New Look of North Korea's Economy: "It's All Capitalism There Now"', *Wall Street Journal*, 25 February 2019, https://www.wsj.com/articles/sanctions-were-supposed-to-cripple-north-koreas-economy-theyre-not-working-11551116032.

Forging Stability in Cyberspace

Lu Chuanying

Great-power relations and strategic stability are two critical factors for order and peace in cyberspace. Yet views are divided. Some scholars do not recognise states as the main actors in cyberspace, but argue for an open, transparent, bottom-up and multi-stakeholder model of governance.[1] Others seek to apply Cold War lessons about nuclear stability to cyberspace. The stark differences between these two approaches make harmonising policy a tall order.[2] Meanwhile, cyber conflicts between great powers are rising and cyberspace militarisation is accelerating, posing grave threats to global strategic stability and potentially affecting security and political trust among states, the global trading system, technology development and the integrity of global supply chains.[3]

The balance of power in cyberspace

Three phases can be observed in the development of the virtual domain. The first one was a kind of anarchy, in which first-generation internet organisations largely controlled critical internet resources while nation-states stayed on the sidelines. The internet experienced rapid and sustained growth. An open, transparent, bottom-up and multi-stakeholder model played a vital role, bolstering the argument for self-regulation.[4] Conventional balance-of-power dynamics, dominated by state actors, had yet to gain purchase in the virtual world.[5]

Lu Chuanying is director and senior research fellow of the Cyberspace International Governance Research Center at the Shanghai Institutes for International Studies and a visiting fellow at the Center for Strategic and International Studies.

Survival | vol. 62 no. 2 | April–May 2020 | pp. 125–136   DOI 10.1080/00396338.2020.1739959

In the second phase, human activities in the security, political and economic realms increasingly migrated online. The United States asserted its technological advantage.[6] Its TCP/IP protocol was superior to the X.25 protocol supported by some European states and became the foundation of the global internet.[7] With the growth of Silicon Valley entrepreneurship, American internet companies came to dominate the internet ecosystem, from hardware to operating systems, software and applications. The United States was the single hegemonic power in cyberspace and dictated its commercial, political and security order.[8]

The third and current phase is cyber balkanisation, in which a US-dominated, universalised cyberspace has begun to splinter as national governments move to protect their cyber sovereignty.[9]

There are several reasons for this shift. Firstly, with cyberspace taking on greater strategic significance, states have become more active in exercising sovereignty online, making it increasingly difficult to balance interests and build a global cyberspace order.[10] Starting in 2018, both the European Union and China imposed broad data-protection and -transfer regulations. Secondly, the United States' perceived exploitation of its technological advantages to serve its own strategic interests diminished its legitimacy as a standard-setter in cyberspace. For example, during the Arab Spring, the US insisted that social-media platforms, such as Facebook and Twitter, support the mobilisation of opposition groups as well as ramping up signals-intelligence surveillance operations as expected. Thirdly, asymmetric cyber capabilities aggravated cyber-security challenges for the US, impelling it to devote more resources to protecting domestic security, step up cyber militarisation and urge like-minded states to foster a common cyber order.[11]

Behaviour patterns

Cyberspace has changed the standard national-security calculus. States have become more aggressive in pursuing security in cyberspace, more distrustful in their political relations, and more hands-on in commercial and technical matters, manifesting a tendency towards technological nationalism that crowds out international cooperation.[12] Furthermore, cyber attacks are not restricted to military targets, but threaten the entire critical infrastructure of a state, much of it operated by private businesses. Shielding all of them from attacks would be unrealistic and extremely costly. Passive defence is generally considered insufficient to cope with cyber attacks. Accordingly, state strategies are generally weighted towards offence.

Russian hackers' interference in elections and Cambridge Analytica's activities are prime examples of the new challenges.[13] Deepening mistrust among great powers makes political security tenuous and political commitments hard to implement. Great powers also find it more difficult to reach a consensus on cyberspace issues. More often than not, they are divided internally and cannot find a unified voice to engage externally. For instance, the US government, which considers internet surveillance legitimate, tends to downplay business and public concerns about intellectual property and privacy, rendering international consensus on cyber espionage hard to establish.[14] The plausible deniability of many cyber attacks is another obstacle to enforcing political commitments.

In the commercial realm, technological nationalism has displaced economic efficiency and the global distribution of labour as the determinants of global supply chains. This phenomenon was already fairly common in the military area. Yet cyber and information technologies are used more for civil than for military purposes. Thus, technological nationalism in the cyber domain will have a more profound and far-reaching impact on the global economy. Edward Snowden warned that American multinational companies such as Google, Microsoft and Amazon, which have greater technological resources than most governments, could become strategic tools of the US government.[15] Reliance on these companies puts other governments in a highly risky position. They are therefore inclined to favour local internet products and services.

Elusive strategic stability

The concept of strategic stability has been associated primarily with nuclear weapons.[16] But it also applies to cyberspace, and strategic stability there, where great-power rivalry has created security dilemmas and political suspicion, is fragile indeed.[17] Especially since the Snowden leak in 2013, great powers have been reluctant to share knowledge and information that is critical to cyber security. Breaches such as the Sony Pictures hack and Russia's meddling in the 2016 US election have only increased that reluctance. Worries that Beijing will use the Chinese technology company Huawei's capabilities to spy on Western nations have further impeded cooperative efforts to establish collective security and given rise to unilateralism, pre-emptive approaches and strategic self-reliance among great powers. The US Department of Defense, in particular, has developed the operational concepts of 'defense forward' and 'persistent engagement', effectively extending its security antennae into the sovereign jurisdictions of other states.[18] Following this doctrine, the US has conducted cyber operations against the critical infrastructure of Iran, North Korea and Russia in retaliation for their alleged incursions on US cyber security.[19] While the United States considers these operations defensive, Iran, North Korea, Russia and the international community at large do not.[20]

Dialogue on confidence-building measures between China and the US, and Russia and the US, have hit a wall. Several years ago, the US and Russia did establish a joint cyber-security task force and produce a tentative agreement on confidence-building measures, but these were discarded when Russia granted Snowden political asylum.[21] Russia's hacking of the 2016 US election and offensive US cyber operations against Russia have only made matters worse. In 2013, China and the US also set up a cyber-security working group and sought to put in place confidence-building measures. But the endeavour was suspended indefinitely when the US indicted five Chinese military officers for engaging in cyber espionage. High-level bilateral dialogues on countering cyber crimes and on law enforcement and cyber security have yielded little substantive progress because the two militaries were not directly involved, and in any case ground to a halt with the outbreak of the US–China trade war.

Potential shocks

Cyber security now is a serious source of risk to nuclear stability. The command-and-control systems of nuclear weapons and satellite communications are vulnerable to cyber attacks, leaving states anxious about the reliability of their respective nuclear deterrents.[22] This could lead to dangerous escalation in a crisis, insusceptible to established tools of crisis management. Artificial intelligence has also raised new risks, as have precision-strike weapons. Non-kinetic cyber arsenals constitute an increasingly important operational component of great-power militaries, and their targets are different from those of traditional forces. While they can make wars less violent, they also threaten to make a wider impact by targeting critical civilian infrastructure.[23] Opinions are divided on how international law, including the Charter of the United Nations and international humanitarian standards, apply in this new area.[24] The existing international security architecture, including that for arms control and disarmament, cannot accommodate the new technologies.[25]

The current international political system is unprepared for these challenges. Some Western governments doubt the UN's ability to drive the development of a cyberspace order, and non-state actors challenge its legitimacy owing to their exclusion from its decision-making processes and to its bureaucratic unwieldiness.[26] The UN has yet to prove its effectiveness even in bringing about and implementing international consensus on the basic questions in cyberspace governance. In the past five sessions, the UN Group of Governmental Experts has only been able to reach agreement three times and on a limited scale.[27]

An increasing number of states demand data localisation for security reasons, restricting the global flow of data and inhibiting globalisation. Without rules for the digital economy, this trend threatens to tear apart the global economic system. Digital geo-economic blocs may emerge in cyberspace. The global economic-governance system is also struggling to handle the challenges arising from technological innovations. For example, virtual currencies enabled by blockchain are now popular tools for money laundering, blackmail and fraud.

Establishing strategic stability in cyberspace

In physics, stability is defined as the ability of an object to regain its previous state after enduring a disruption. States need to develop an appreciation for cyberspace stability and refrain from disruptive activities, and a cyberspace-security architecture must be put in place to restore stability after a disruption.

Four qualities of cyberspace should be framed and recognised: strategic, interconnected, cross-sectoral and disruptive. Cyberspace is a strategic frontier in which all states are making their own plans to gain the upper hand and refusing to compromise their strategic interests. It is interconnected in the sense that all devices, from nuclear weapons to wearable gadgets, share protocols, media and codes in cyberspace, and a problem for one could mean a problem for all. Cyberspace is cross-sectoral because relevant topics are interrelated and cut across areas of security, technology and commerce. And cyber activity can obviously have uniquely disruptive effects, a general point being that real-time data transmission defies geographical and time limitations that normally apply in the physical world.

Stability is feasible only if several conditions are met. Firstly, the global internet must remain resilient in cyber conflicts. Secondly, state cyber strategies and policies cannot result in cyber balkanisation. Thirdly, limits must be set such that military cyber operations cannot target critical infrastructure in peacetime. Fourthly, command-and-control systems of nuclear weapons must be off-limits for cyber operations. These stipulations should determine the framework for national cyber strategies.

Great powers should also recognise certain general constraints to make strategic rivalries manageable.[28] In particular, the integrity and interconnectivity of cyberspace should always be protected. The Global Commission on the Stability of Cyberspace's call for protecting the public core of the internet is an attempt to address this concern. Policymakers must also bear in mind the cross-sectoral impact of a single decision or action with respect to cyber security, the digital economy, and information and communication technology. States must understand the harmful effect of excessive security measures and the militarisation of cyberspace as a whole. For instance, an extreme degree of data localisation for personal privacy and national-security purposes could suffocate the free flow of data.

An international security architecture for cyberspace

State competition and conflict in cyberspace make institutional guarantees even more crucial. As noted, however, previous efforts based on conventional security practices to increase cyberspace transparency, develop confidence-building measures and manage crises have failed.[29] It is clear from this failure that, for a new architecture to make a real difference, it must be able to address the need to protect global critical infrastructure, establish specific responsibility for cyber attacks and other transgressions, share information on vulnerabilities and ensure global supply-chain security.

A lack of mutual trust has been the principal stumbling block. American officials indicated that the US would never disclose to anyone the scale and distribution of its critical infrastructure. Yet withholding all information will stifle possibilities for cooperation. Establishing norms and protective measures for energy, transportation and finance might be useful and achievable first steps.

The difficulty of attributing cyber activities to identifiable actors – and thus assigning responsibility and culpability for such activities – is a major impediment to progress on security. At present, there is no objective and neutral international organisation to investigate cyber-security incidents. As a result, most attacks on states have gone unpunished, which encourages others to follow suit and threatens security and stability in cyberspace. Some scholars argue for UN-based arrangements for investigating and deterring attacks.[30] But only a handful of states possess the technologies required to establish attribution, and they have not been willing to share them or to help the UN build its own capacity. International organisations and other stakeholders must show a clear determination to overcome such obstacles and support a central role for the UN.

Also required is an international vulnerabilities-equities process. Vulnerabilities are program bugs in computers that can be exploited to develop cyber weapons and launch attacks. At the national level, a vulnerabilities-equities process determines whether zero-day exploits should be brought to the attention of software suppliers or withheld temporarily for national-security purposes. At the international level, though, vulnerabilities are seen as the means to gain a strategic advantage and remain undisclosed. Increasing international cooperation in this area would provide an important technical foundation for establishing trust among great powers, and building an international security architecture.

Finally, global supply-chain security would preclude cyber balkanisation. The products and services that nourish the internet flow from highly intricate global supply chains that constitute a singularly complex and efficient technical and commercial network. Without a global-governance system, great powers resort to technology nationalism, trusting only products that are locally produced and excluding those from other sources on national-security grounds. This practice obstructs foreign investment and sustains monopolies over technologies and products. Instead, security standards for cyberspace devices and products should be enhanced to allow the global supply chain to remain intact.[31] States should focus more on shoring up cyber security and cyber services, and refrain from rejecting foreign products and investments in ways that undermine global trade. In particular, they should work towards an intergovernmental ban on embedding back doors and vulnerabilities in cyber-security products used for civilian purposes.

*   *   *

Strategic stability is a new and important item on the agenda of global cyberspace governance. Only with sustained effort along the lines suggested here, however, can it become a cornerstone of the future cyberspace order.

Acknowledgements

This paper is a product of the 'Big-power Relations in Cyberspace and Strategic Stability' programme (No. 19BGJ083), supported by the Chinese government's National Social Science Fund.

Notes

[1] See Laura DeNardis and Mark Raymond, 'Thinking Clearly about Multistakeholder Internet Governance', GigaNet: Global Internet Governance Academic Network, 14 November 2013, pp. 1–2, https://papers.ssrn.com/sol3/papers.

cfm?abstract_id=2354377.

[2] See Joseph S. Nye, Jr, 'Nuclear Lessons for Cyber Security', *Strategic Studies Quarterly*, vol. 5, no. 4, Winter 2011, pp. 18–36.

[3] See Zhou Hongren, 'Strategic Stability in Cyberspace: A Chinese View', *China*

Quarterly of International Strategic Studies, vol. 5, no. 1, 2019, pp. 81–95.

4   David Johnson and David Post, 'Law and Borders: The Rise of Law in Cyberspace', *Stanford Law Review*, vol. 48, no. 5, May 1996, pp. 1,368–78.

5   See Milton L. Mueller, *Networks and States: The Global Politics of Internet Governance* (Cambridge, MA: MIT Press, 2010); and Miles Kahler (ed.), *Networked Politics: Agency, Structure and Power* (Ithaca, NY: Cornell University Press, 2009), p. 34.

6   See John B. Sheldon, 'Geopolitics and Cyber Power: Why Geography Still Matters', *American Foreign Policy Interests*, vol. 36, no. 5, September 2014, pp. 286–93.

7   Jeremy Malcolm, *Multi-stakeholder Governance and the Internet Governance Forum* (Wembley: Terminus Press, 2008), pp. 44–69.

8   See Madeline Carr, 'Power Plays in Global Internet Governance', *Millennium: Journal of International Studies*, vol. 43, no. 2, January 2015, pp. 640–59.

9   See Camino Kavanagh, *The United Nations, Cyberspace and International Peace and Security: Responding to Complexity in the 21st Century* (Geneva: United Nations Institute for Disarmament Research, 2017).

10   The United States failed to gain universal support for the principles of countermeasures and state responsibility it proposed, which impeded the UN Group of Governmental Experts' effort to build cyberspace norms. See Michele G. Markoff, 'Explanation of Position at the Conclusion of the 2016–2017 UN Group of Governmental Experts (GGE) on Developments in the Field of Information and Telecommunications in the Context of International Security', US Department of State, 23 June 2017, https://s3.amazonaws.com/ceipfiles/pdf/CyberNorms/Multilateral/GGE_2017+US+State+Department+Position.pdf.

11   Michael P. Fischerkeller and Richard J. Harknett, 'Persistent Engagement, Agreed Competition, Cyberspace Interaction Dynamics, and Escalation', Institute for Defense Analyses, May 2018, https://www.ida.org/-/media/feature/publications/p/pe/persistent-engagement-agreed-competition-cyberspace-interaction-dynamics-and-escalation/d-9076.ashx.

12   Lu Chuanying, 'Cyberspace Security Dilemma and Governance Structure', *Contemporary International Relations*, vol. 11, 2011, pp. 55–9.

13   See Clint Watts and Andrew Weisburd, 'How Russia Wins an Election', Politico, 13 December 2016, https://www.politico.com/magazine/story/2016/12/how-russia-wins-an-election-214524.

14   Jack Moore, 'Intelligence Chief: OPM Hack Was Not a "Cyberattack"', Nextgov, 10 September 2015, https://www.nextgov.com/cybersecurity/2015/09/intelligence-chief-clapper-opm-hack-was-not-cyberattack/120722/.

15   See Dennis Broeders, Sergei Boeke and Ilina Georgieva, 'Foreign Intelligence in the Digital Age: Navigating a State of "Unpeace"', The Hague Program for Cyber Norms, 2019 Policy Brief, September 2019.

16   See Robert Jervis, 'Some Thoughts on Deterrence in the Cyber Era', *Journal of Information Warfare*, vol. 15, no. 2, June

2016, pp. 66–73.

17 See James N. Miller, Jr, and Richard
    Fontaine, 'A New Era in U.S.–
    Russian Strategic Stability: How
    Changing Geopolitics and Emerging
    Technologies are Reshaping Pathways
    to Crisis and Conflict', Center
    for a New American Security, 19
    September 2017, https://www.cnas.
    org/publications/reports/a-new-era-
    in-u-s-russian-strategic-stability;
    and International Security Advisory
    Board, 'Report on a Framework
    for International Cyber Stability',
    US Department of State, 2 July
    2014, https://2009-2017.state.gov/
    documents/organization/229235.pdf.

18 US Department of Defense, 'Summary
    – Department of Defense Cyber
    Strategy 2018', https://media.defense.
    gov/2018/Sep/18/2002041658/-1/-1/1/
    CYBER_STRATEGY_SUMMARY_
    FINAL.PDF.

19 See, for example, David E. Sanger and
    Nicole Perlroth, 'U.S. Escalates Online
    Attacks on Russia's Power Grid', *New
    York Times*, 15 June 2019, https://www.
    nytimes.com/2019/06/15/us/politics/
    trump-cyber-russia-grid.html.

20 See Alexander Klimburg, 'Mixed
    Signals: A Flawed Approach to Cyber
    Deterrence', *Survival*, vol. 62, no. 1,
    February–March 2020, pp. 107–30.

21 Ellen Nakashima, 'U.S. and Russia
    Sign Pact to Create Communication
    Link on Cyber Security', *Washington
    Post*, 17 June 2013, https://www.
    washingtonpost.com/world/
    national-security/us-and-russia-
    sign-pact-to-create-communication-
    link-on-cyber-security/2013/06/17/
    ca57ea04-d788-11e2-9df4-
    895344c13c30_story.html.

22 See Beyza Unal and Patricia
    Lewis, 'Cyber Threats and Nuclear
    Weapons Systems: Threats,
    Vulnerabilities and Consequences',
    Research Paper, Chatham House,
    https://www.chathamhouse.org/
    sites/default/files/publications/
    research/2018-01-11-cybersecurity-
    nuclear-weapons-unal-lewis-final.pdf.

23 See UNIDIR, 'The Weaponization
    of Increasingly Autonomous
    Technologies: Concerns,
    Characteristics and Definitional
    Approaches', UNIDIR Resources, No.
    6, 2017, https://www.unidir.org/files/
    publications/pdfs/the-weaponization-
    of-increasingly-autonomous-
    technologies-concerns-characteristics-
    and-definitional-approaches-en-689.
    pdf.

24 See Michael N. Schmitt (ed.), *Tallinn
    Manual 2.0 on the International
    Law Applicable to Cyber Operations*
    (Cambridge: Cambridge University
    Press, 2017).

25 See Jeremy Rabkin and John Yoo,
    *Striking Power: How Cyber, Robots, and
    Space Weapons Change the Rules for War*
    (New York: Encounter Books, 2017).

26 See Mueller, *Networks and States*.

27 'Group of Governmental Experts
    on Developments in the Field of
    Information and Telecommunications
    in the Context of International
    Security', UN General Assembly
    Document A/70/174, 22 July 2015.

28 See Joseph S. Nye, Jr, 'Deterrence
    and Dissuasion in Cyberspace',
    International Security, vol. 41, no. 3,
    Winter 2016/17, pp. 44–71.

29 See Daniel Stauffacher (ed.)
    and Camino Kavanagh (rap-
    porteur), 'Confidence Building

Measures and International Cyber Security', ICT4Peace Foundation, 2013, https://ict4peace.org/wp-content/uploads/2019/08/ICT4Peace-2013-Confidence-Building-Measure-And_Intern-Cybersecurity.pdf .

30 See Martin C. Libicki, *Cyber Deterrence and Cyberwar* (Santa Monica, CA: RAND Corporation, 2009), https://www.rand.org/content/dam/rand/pubs/monographs/2009/RAND_MG877.pdf.

31 National Institute of Standards and Technology, 'Best Practices in Cyber Supply Chain Risk Management', US Resilience Project, US Department of Commerce, https://csrc.nist.gov/CSRC/media/Projects/Supply-Chain-Risk-Management/documents/case_studies/USRP_NIST_Intel_100715.pdf.

Right-wing Extremism: The Russian Connection

Shelby Butt and Daniel Byman

Russian interference in US and European politics is well documented, with Moscow seeking to influence the West's elections and undermine its social cohesion. Yet Russia's efforts go beyond trying to shape mass opinion and twist democracy. One of Moscow's most pernicious efforts is its support for white-supremacist and other far-right groups, encouraging them with propaganda, providing them with a haven, and otherwise making them stronger and more dangerous. Such support makes the challenge white supremacists pose to the United States and Western democracies all the more potent by threatening to deepen social and political divisions, and increase violence in democratic countries. In the short term, this allows Moscow to contrast the resulting chaos with the stability it seeks to foster at home, undermining the appeal of Western democracy. As its support for the extreme right continues, however, the danger to international security overall will increase and the risk of violence will grow.

As with so many things Russian, the specifics are often maddeningly opaque. Numerous actors are involved, including the Kremlin, covert branches of the state, regime-linked oligarchs and state-tolerated right-wing groups in Russia itself that sometimes work with the government but at times oppose it. These diverse actors all have their own goals. Some are true believers in a white-supremacist and right-wing agenda, others seek to

---

Shelby Butt is an undergraduate research scholar in Georgetown University's Center for Security Studies. **Daniel Byman** (@dbyman) is a professor in the School of Foreign Service at Georgetown University and a senior fellow at the Brookings Institution.

Survival | vol. 62 no. 2 | April–May 2020 | pp. 137–152   DOI 10.1080/00396338.2020.1739960

weaken perceived enemies in the West, and still others are cynically advancing their political agendas at home. Despite such divergent motives, it is hard to avoid the conclusion that Russia is cultivating extreme right-wing support to undermine the West, using a variety of actors to woo different partners.

Russia's vast right-wing conspiracy

It is easy to jump to conspiracy scenarios in the absence of specific information, but the overall picture does suggest that Russia is running an active-measures campaign to cultivate right-wing support to undermine the West. Russian President Vladimir Putin himself is an ex-intelligence officer, and Russia ran such a campaign to influence the 2016 US presidential election, which turned out as the Kremlin hoped it would.[1]

Russia has cultivated a range of political parties in Europe in an attempt to strengthen extremes of the political spectrum and weaken the middle. These include the far-right Alternative for Germany (as well as the neo-Nazi National Democratic Party and anti-immigrant PEGIDA party there), the National Rally in France, and like-minded parties in Austria, Greece, Hungary, Italy and other countries. Many of these right-wing parties oppose NATO, are hostile to European Union integration and otherwise seek to weaken European institutions, a central Russian goal.[2] In the Balkans, Russia has sought to dilute support for NATO and EU membership, portraying Europe and the United States as seeking to break up the Balkan states along ethnic lines, defending Muslims rather than Orthodox Christians, and pushing for lesbian, gay, bisexual, transgender and queer (LGBTQ) rights. Far-right parties have also backed Russia's invasion and annexation of Crimea in the European Parliament and offered support for Moscow's narrative in Ukraine.[3]

Many Russian efforts are implemented peacefully and involve the far left as well as the far right. Russia's social-media campaign to influence the 2016 US election supported not only Donald Trump, but also Green Party candidate Jill Stein.[4] Russia's aim was broadly to divide. It thus blithely supported both ends of the political spectrum to turn them against each other. At best, from Moscow's point of view, supporting left-wing candidates would fatally undermine Hillary Clinton's presidential run and help pro-Russia candidate Trump. At the very least, it would delegitimise Clinton among some voters and help foment unrest. In Houston, for example, Russian-linked Facebook pages backed duelling pro- and anti-Muslim protests outside an Islamic centre in May 2016.[5] Moscow also has ties to the left-wing Syriza party in Greece and Podemos party in Spain.[6]

In addition to dividing the West, Putin seeks to placate, shape and co-opt potential opposition at home. Although Putin has won over or silenced potential opposition in Russia, he seeks to consolidate the country's political right and nationalistic forces in general. Giving such groups a degree of freedom to help their European and American counterparts, and in effect turning them into instruments of the state, keeps them loyal and useful.

Russia also directly supports numerous far-right groups in Europe and the United States. In some cases the support takes the form of money and loans, and in others propaganda elevating radical voices and even, usually through non-state actors aligned with the Russian state, paramilitary training to commit acts of violence. In addition, the Kremlin exports its own networks of paramilitary forces, far-right ideologues and financial backers to cultivate allies in European states.[7] A 2016 Center for Strategic and International Studies report highlighted an 'unvirtuous cycle' in countries such as Hungary, Bulgaria and Serbia, where loans from Russian banks, investment by Russian companies and other financial ties are used to bolster pro-Moscow politicians, who in turn use their political power to back Russia's agenda.[8] Moscow's support for extreme political causes is well known from investigations into Russian election tampering in the United States and Europe, and investigative reporting on Russian attempts to divide its democratic enemies by exacerbating internal tensions through propaganda, often via social media. Such campaigns have had grim consequences for mainstream politics, but their impact on the extreme fringe of society is potentially even graver. The 2019 Department of Homeland Security strategic framework warned that 'foreign states' are exploiting social media not only to polarise American society and foment strife, but also to 'spur vulnerable individuals or groups to commit acts of violence'.[9] As seen from mass shootings and acts of violence inspired by radical online content, words can kill.

Russian media performs an open and leading role, playing up migrant crime in Europe and other white-nationalist hot-button issues. The ubiquitous 24-hour, government-funded news station RT regularly hosts far-right commentators, helping to infiltrate their ideas into the mainstream. These commentators have included Holocaust deniers, members of the US-based Christian Patriot movement who reject federal authority, American far-right leader Richard Spencer and other voices once confined to the information wilderness.[10]

Russia also exploits social media, a critical outlet for white supremacists and other extremists, and knowingly hosts white supremacists on Russian-based platforms. In recent years, Facebook and other social-media companies have become more aggressive about purging white nationalists on their sites. Even less well-known sites traditionally more tolerant of white-supremacist views such as Gab have expelled some extremists.[11] After Facebook removed many accounts following the August 2017 'Unite the Right' rally and bloodshed in Charlottesville, Virginia, a new group called 'FB Alt-Right Expats' appeared on the Russian Facebook equivalent, VKontakte (VK), which allows, and seems to even welcome, racist posts. One white-supremacist and anti-LGBTQ VK community called 'Sober and Angry Youth' assaulted a Roma camp in Ukraine.[12] Around 100 right-wing American groups are on VK, comprising perhaps 10,000 members in all, and they have successfully recruited new members via this site.[13] Other white-nationalist groups have established domain names in Russia or otherwise tried to circumvent US companies, which impose greater content restrictions.[14] The Russian state does not operate these platforms, but while it suppresses content it regards as potentially hostile to Putin's government, it does little to discourage discourse among foreign white supremacists.

Putin and Russia, of course, have their American and Western admirers, affording Russia a form of soft power. White-supremacist demonstrators appeared in Charlottesville only weeks after the August 2017 incident chanting 'Russia is our friend'.[15] Ex-Ku Klux Klan head David Duke lived in

> *Russian platforms knowingly host white supremacists*

Russia for several years.[16] In Europe, the admiration for Russia among far-right groups is deeper and the ties more extensive, with Russia portrayed as a model of masculine, Christian traditional values, in contrast to 'globalists' and 'elites' (often code for Jews) who advocate multiculturalism.[17] Russia, the narrative goes, is unlike European states in that it values its sovereignty and traditional culture and morals, with a particular hostility toward the LGBTQ community. In Europe, opposition to NATO is also a far-right theme.[18] Marine Le Pen, the head of France's National Rally, praised Putin for doing 'what is good for Russia and the Russians', and her party is the only major European far-right party to accept Russian financial aid openly.[19] The head of Britain's UK Independence Party described Putin as 'brilliant' and the world leader he admired most.[20]

Many key actors have indirect links to the Russian state and ties to Russian intelligence. Although not directly linked to violence, the Russian Orthodox Church augments fringe right-wing voices and has worked closely with Putin's regime.[21] Church representatives have their own ties to European right-wing parties, doing the Kremlin's bidding by playing up purported cultural threats posed by the LGBTQ community and at times providing a platform for radical right-wingers at church-sponsored conferences.[22] Wealthy oligarchs close to Putin also apparently carry out significant Russian influence operations. For example, Ukraine has accused the conservative oligarch Konstantin Malofeev of financing Russian rebels in Ukraine. Malofeev is also known for his harsh anti-LGBTQ agenda and promotion of what he sees as Orthodox Christian values.[23] The far-right Rodina party in Russia is a rival of Putin's yet often backs him, and some claim it was set up to help him siphon votes away from the Communist Party.[24] It has hosted fringe groups at conferences where largely unknown organisations, such as those calling for Texas to leave the United States ('Texit'), present themselves as legitimate.[25]

Often the support is more clandestine and diffuse. Russian intelligence has set up fight clubs promoting *systema* (a Russian martial-arts style) in a number of European countries to attract violent young men and spread Russian influence.[26] Russian soccer hooligans also are an entry point, with the Kremlin using sports solidarity as a pretext for sending in undercover intelligence officers to build ties to violent young men.[27] According to the BBC, Russian intelligence had a liaison with Moscow's soccer clubs, in part to prevent violence during the World Cup matches in Russia but also to stir up far-right fervour; one hooligan leader declared his fellow thugs to be 'foot soldiers of Putin'.[28] The pro-Putin, Russian Orthodox motorcycle gang Night Wolves, which has thousands of members, coordinates with Russian military intelligence and also has active chapters in Germany, Latvia and other countries. The Night Wolves have also toured countries in Eastern Europe to show solidarity with pro-Russian causes.[29]

At times, Russian-backed far-right groups serve as outright Russian government proxies, especially as the theatre shifts closer to Russia and away from more consolidated Western democracies. The Montenegrin government claims that Russian military intelligence sought unsuccessfully to stage a coup there during the 2016 elections, which ushered in a government that finished bringing the country into NATO in 2017.

Russia covertly provides military training

Russia reportedly helped organise the plot and provided money and weapons, working with far-right groups in part so Moscow could maintain deniability.[30]

Russia covertly provides military training to young men within its borders and abroad, concentrating on far-right groups. Russian special-operations forces trained one such group, the Slovak Conscripts, whose members later battled alongside Russian proxies in Ukraine. In Hungary, Russian military-intelligence officials attended combat-training sessions held by the Hungarian National Front, a neo-Nazi group.[31] One Hungarian neo-Nazi who shot a policeman is suspected of being supported by Russian intelligence.[32] Russian intelligence has also tried to recruit veterans sympathetic to right-wing causes. German servicemen who are members of far-right groups have met with Russian intelligence officials and elite military-unit members.[33]

Russia has also provided support to The Base, an American neo-Nazi group, by hosting its American-born leader in St Petersburg. The Base has planned to murder anti-fascist activists, kill police officers and vandalise synagogues, among other crimes. In January 2020, investigations by the BBC and the *Guardian* revealed that Rinaldo Nazarro, the group's leader, had moved from New York to Russia in 2018, around the same time as the founding of The Base. Though Nazarro has gone by several aliases over the past few years, he was listed under his birth name as a guest at a Russian government security exhibit in Moscow last year and is married to a Russian citizen. The presence of The Base and the Atomwaffen Division, another violent far-right extremist group, in Russia indicates that the country has become a safe haven for American paramilitary fascist groups and global fascist networks. Given the high level of domestic surveillance in Russia, it is improbable that Nazarro could be living in St Petersburg and operating The Base from there without the knowledge of Russia's security services, especially given the group's close ties to other far-right groups and ideologues in Russia.[34]

While the Russian state is often a direct participant in right-wing activities, Russia is also home to a number of white-supremacist and other far-right groups that act in concert with, or with the mere toleration of, the Russian state in supporting like-minded extremists abroad. Since the fall of the Soviet Union, Russia has experienced five times more right-wing violence than the United States and 750% more than Western Europe, according to scholar Johannes Due Enstad. Many of the far-right groups involved target migrants from Central Asia, most of whom are Muslim.[35] They tend to see Putin as too soft, and his government in turn seeks to both co-opt and control them, fearing they might work with opposition groups or take to the streets on their own if not accommodated and directed. The Putin regime saw them as a potential defence against a colour revolution in the early 2000s, and then accorded them a certain amount of freedom that has endured. They are permitted to organise, march and otherwise assert themselves. The only red line is that they cannot act against the Russian state.

Although such groups are strongly and often violently opposed to Muslim minorities, in recent years their violence has focused more on the LGBTQ community.[36] The Russian Imperial Movement (RIM) is a monarchist and zealously Orthodox organisation that does not have overt Kremlin backing but is tolerated by the authorities and works with extremists in the

United States, such as the Rise Above Movement, and in Europe against a 'globalised elite' who reject traditional values.[37] In Scandinavia, the Nordic Resistance Movement has close ties to the RIM.[38]

An operational example of this dangerous nexus is the RIM's one-week Partizan paramilitary course in St Petersburg, presumably offered and run with the covert approval and perhaps support of Russian security agencies. The group trains civilians to prepare for 'global chaos' and has attracted many European white supremacists. Partizan trained the Swedish neo-Nazis who bombed a refugee centre in Gothenberg.[39] Individuals trained by Partizan and associated with the RIM and its paramilitary unit, the Imperial Legion, also fought in Ukraine.[40] Some from other European countries have received weapons training through the RIM. The RIM's activities broadly serve the state's interest, but it is not explicitly connected to Moscow, which therefore enjoys plausible deniability should the group be exposed as a perpetrator of violence or other illicit activities.

Growing impact

Russia's current involvement with the most extreme right-wing supporters is marginal, but it is still dangerous and has the potential to grow. Russia's discrete efforts among multiple actors, ranging from a few neo-Nazis to more mainstream groups such as France's National Rally, appear to be elements of a broader active-measures campaign to intensify political polarisation in both the United States and Europe, undermining social cohesion.[41] Russia's contribution to actual violence perpetrated by far-right groups is more diffuse, and even more difficult to measure and assess. Its information operations are part, but only part, of a toxic mixture of misinformation and incitement that has led white supremacists to attack religious and racial minorities, leftist politicians and other enemies. More directly, Russia has enabled some radicals to become more lethal and almost certainly has a few under its direct operational control.

The long-term risks are substantial. Russian support is making these groups and individuals more violent and capable, increasing the chances that successful attacks will occur and exact higher death tolls. Even a few additional attacks can generate a cycle, inspiring other white supremacists or creating a backlash from Muslim communities, lending weight to jihadists' argument that Islam is under attack. Foreign leaders who ignore Russian behaviour increase risks to international security. Furthermore, Trump's apparent indifference to Russian covert operations empowers Russia and its minions, and encourages other authoritarians to support extreme voices and violent groups, jeopardising the security of America's traditional allies.

Countering Russian support

At this point, Russia is not seeking to inspire white supremacists to commit mass murder in the West, but its efforts to stir the pot and support or tolerate extremists are likely to lead to an increase in violence and create significant long-term risks. The West's vulnerabilities with respect to racial divisions, anti-immigrant sentiment and issues such as LGBTQ rights make it relatively easy prey for Russia. But the danger can be reduced. The United States and its allies can and should take stronger measures to counter Russian support for violent right-wing extremists.

Shaming and exposing Russia itself is worth doing, but the world should not expect significant change in Moscow's conduct. In both the United States and Europe, official bodies and press accounts have exposed Moscow's backing of white supremacists, to little effect. Likewise, Russia has not stopped election interference or disinformation campaigns, notwithstanding the unambiguous and celebrated revelation of its nefarious role in the 2016 US presidential election. The exposure of Russia's activities might constitute a more effective deterrent if paired with increased public appreciation of the dangers posed by those activities. The Department of Homeland Security, for example, has proposed a 'Media/Information Literacy Toolkit' to help citizens identify information operations that are fostering extremism and work with trusted community voices to counter the attempted manipulation.[42] However, there are limits to self-education, especially in the toxic US political environment, in which it is acceptable for people to dismiss facts that do not cater to their political viewpoints.

Given the limited scope for modifying Russia's behaviour, it would make sense for Western partners to mount concerted efforts to directly target seditious organisations that have accepted Russian training. US partners in Europe and other parts of the world that are also victims of Russian meddling will need assistance. Traditional intelligence-sharing and security cooperation are essential. As in the past, intelligence collection should target Russia and inform efforts to disrupt any extremist activities it is supporting. In addition, however, domestic-intelligence and law-enforcement agencies should focus sharply on right-wing groups and individuals themselves, investigating and prosecuting them for seditious and violent activities.

Beyond targeting Russia and the outfits it supports, US and allied counter-terrorism organisations must recognise the wide variety of other actors involved and tailor their responses to their actions. Russian oligarchs, street gangs and other non-traditional actors are all players in Moscow's schemes. Sanctions and other penalties should extend beyond the Russian state, and enforcement and deterrence efforts beyond extremist groups and their members. In particular, the United States and its allies should establish counter-influence task forces to examine links between Moscow and Western businesses and politicians.[43]

Social-media companies can also play an important role. They can help identify and block Russian disinformation and hinder efforts by extremists to forge international connections. Such companies, however, are often loath to interfere with extreme right-wing accounts owing to their connections to mainstream Western politicians who will decry supposed censorship.[44] The US and the EU should increase legal penalties on technology and social-media companies that do not remove or block violent right-wing content and strengthen efforts to share information on Russian manipulation of these platforms. Covertly, the United States should also consider cyber operations to counter Russian intelligence platforms that are fomenting unrest as well as spreading disinformation in the US and among its allies.

Treating violent right-wing groups with international links like genuine terrorists is another important policy measure. The United States rarely designates such organisations as terrorist groups, even if they have international connections.[45] So designating them would make it illegal for individuals or organisations to finance, join or otherwise support these groups, depriving them of resources and affording investigators and prosecutors significantly greater leverage. Finally, the right-wing threat warrants increases in the resources flowing to the FBI and other law-enforcement and intelligence agencies for counter-radicalisation programmes. Russia's hostile manipulation of American and European politics is migrating from the information sphere to the street itself, and requires a concerted strategic response.

Notes

1   See Special Counsel Robert S. Mueller, III, 'Report on the Investigation into Russian Interference in the 2016 Presidential Election' (Washington DC: US Department of Justice, 2019), https://www.justice.gov/storage/report.pdf.

2   See Rossella Cerulli, 'Russia's Involvement in Far-right European Politics', American Security Project, 12 July 2019, https://www.americansecurityproject.org/russias-involvement-in-far-right-european-politics; Tony Patterson, 'Putin's Far-right Ambition: Think-tank Reveals How Russian President Is Wooing – and Funding – Populist Parties Across Europe to Gain Influence in the EU', Independent, 25 November 2014, https://www.independent.co.uk/news/world/europe/putin-s-far-right-ambition-think-tank-reveals-how-russian-president-is-wooing-and-funding-populist-9883052.html; Alina Polyakova, 'Strange Bedfellows: Putin and Europe's Far Right', World Affairs, vol. 177, no. 3, September/October 2014, pp. 36–40; and Alina Polyakova, 'Putinism and the European Far Right', Institute of Modern Russia, 19 January 2016, https://imrussia.org/en/analysis/world/2500-putinism-and-the-european-far-right.

3   See Paul Stronski and Annie Himes, 'Russia's Game in the Balkans', Carnegie Endowment for International Peace, 6 February 2019, https://carnegieendowment.org/2019/02/06/russia-s-game-in-balkans-pub-78235; and Alina Polyakova et al., 'The Kremlin's Trojan Horses', Atlantic Council, 15 November 2016, https://www.atlanticcouncil.org/in-depth-research-reports/report/kremlin-trojan-horses/.

4   See Robert Windrem, 'Russians Launched Pro-Jill Stein Social Media Blitz to Help Trump Win Election, Reports Say', NBC News, 22 December 2018, https://www.nbcnews.com/politics/national-security/russians-launched-pro-jill-stein-social-media-blitz-help-trump-n951166.

5   See Claire Albright, 'A Russian Facebook Page Organized a Protest in Texas. A Different Russian Page Launched the Counter Protest', Texas Tribune, 1 November 2017, https://www.texastribune.org/2017/11/01/russian-facebook-page-organized-protest-texas-different-russian-page-l/.

6   See Rick Noack, 'The European Parties Accused of Being Influenced by Russia', Washington Post, 17 November 2017, https://www.washingtonpost.com/news/worldviews/wp/2017/11/17/the-european-parties-accused-of-being-influenced-by-russia/?arc404=true.

7   See Polyakova et al., 'The Kremlin's Trojan Horses'.

8   Heather A. Conley et al., 'The Kremlin Playbook: Understanding Russian Influence in Central and Eastern Europe', Center for Strategic and International Studies, October 2016, pp. 17–22, https://csis-prod.s3.amazonaws.com/s3fs-public/publication/1601017_Conley_KremlinPlaybook_Web.pdf.

9   US Department of Homeland Security, 'Strategic Framework for Countering Terrorism and Targeted Violence', September 2019, p. 8, https://www.dhs.gov/sites/default/files/publications/19_0920_plcy_strategic-framework-countering-terrorism-targeted-violence.pdf.

10 See Anton Shekhovtsov, *Russia and the Western Far Right: Tango Noir* (New York: Routledge, 2018).

11 See Neil MacFarquhar and Adam Goldman, 'A New Face of White Supremacy: Plots Expose the Danger of "The Base"', *New York Times*, 22 January 2020, https://www.nytimes.com/2020/01/22/us/white-supremacy-the-base.html?smid=nytcore-ios-share.

12 See Oleksiy Kuzmenko, 'The Straight-edge Neo-Nazi Group that Attacked a Ukrainian Roma Camp', Bellingcat, 26 June 2018, https://www.bellingcat.com/news/uk-and-europe/2018/06/26/straight-edge-neo-nazi-group-attacked-ukrainian-roma-camp/.

13 See Masood Farivar, 'US White Nationalists Barred by Facebook Find Haven on Russia Site', VOA News, 10 April 2019, https://www.voanews.com/usa/us-white-nationalists-barred-facebook-find-haven-russia-site.

14 Pavel Merzlikin (Kevin Rothrock, trans.), 'The American and European Far Right Are Migrating En Masse to Russian Social Media. "There's Less Censorship There"', *Meduza*, 17 August 2017, https://meduza.io/en/feature/2017/08/18/the-american-and-european-far-right-are-migrating-en-masse-to-the-russian-internet-there-s-less-censorship-there.

15 See Jackson Landers, 'White Supremacists Return to Charlottesville Chanting, "Russia Is Our Friend"', Daily Beast, 8 October 2017, https://www.thedailybeast.com/richard-spencer-and-white-supremacists-return-to-charlottesville-chanting-you-will-not-replace-us.

16 See Alexander Reid Ross, 'America's Neo-Nazi Terrorists Have a Powerful New Patron: Vladimir Putin', *Haaretz*, 2 February 2020, https://www.haaretz.com/us-news/.premium-america-s-neo-nazi-terrorists-have-a-powerful-new-patron-vladimir-putin-1.8471461.

17 See Alan Feuer and Andrew Higgins, 'Extremists Turn to a Leader to Protect Western Values: Vladimir Putin', *New York Times*, 10 April 2019, https://www.nytimes.com/2016/12/03/world/americas/alt-right-vladimir-putin.html; Landers, 'White Supremacists Return to Charlottesville Chanting, "Russia Is Our Friend"'; and Marlene Laruelle, 'Russian and American Far Right Connections', PONARS Eurasia Policy Memo No. 516, March 2018, http://www.ponarseurasia.org/sites/default/files/policy-memos-pdf/Pepm516_Laruelle_March2018.pdf.

18 See Polyakova et al., 'The Kremlin's Trojan Horses'.

19 *Ibid.*

20 Polyakova, 'Strange Bedfellows';

and Polyakova, 'Putinism and the European Far Right'.

21 See Andrew Higgins, 'In Expanding Russian Influence, Faith Combines with Firepower', *New York Times*, 13 September 2016, https://www.nytimes.com/2016/09/14/world/europe/russia-orthodox-church.html.

22 See Hélène Barthélemy, 'The Strange Alliance Between Russian Orthodox Monarchists, American Christian Evangelicals and European Fascists', Southern Poverty Law Center, 18 September 2018, https://www.splcenter.org/hatewatch/2018/09/18/strange-alliance-between-russian-orthodox-monarchists-american-christian-evangelicals-and.

23 See Joshua Keating, 'God's Oligarch', *Slate*, 20 October 2014, https://slate.com/news-and-politics/2014/10/konstantin-malofeev-one-of-vladimir-putins-favorite-businessmen-wants-to-start-an-orthodox-christian-fox-news-and-return-russia-to-its-glorious-czarist-past.html.

24 See Tom Parfitt, '"Racist" Russian TV Advert Investigated', *Guardian*, 10 November 2005, https://www.theguardian.com/world/2005/nov/10/russia.tomparfitt.

25 See Neil MacFarquhar, 'Right-wing Groups Find a Haven, for a Day, in Russia', *New York Times*, 23 March 2015, https://www.nytimes.com/2015/03/23/world/europe/right-wing-groups-find-a-haven-for-a-day-in-russia.html.

26 See Michael Carpenter, 'Russia Is Co-opting Angry Young Men', *Atlantic*, August 2018, https://www.theatlantic.com/ideas/archive/2018/08/russia-is-co-opting-angry-young-men/568741/.

27 See John R. Schindler, 'The Hidden Russian Hand Behind Germany's Violent Right-wing Riots', *Observer*, 30 August 2018, https://observer.com/2018/08/is-vladimir-putin-behind-right-wing-riots-in-chemnitz-germany/.

28 Simon Parkin, 'The Rise of Russia's Neo-Nazi Football Hooligans', *Guardian*, 24 April 2018, https://www.theguardian.com/news/2018/apr/24/russia-neo-nazi-football-hooligans-world-cup.

29 See Andrew Higgins, 'Russia's Feared "Night Wolves" Bike Gang Came to Bosnia. Bosnia Giggled', *New York Times*, 31 March 2018, https://www.nytimes.com/2018/03/31/world/europe/balkans-russia-night-wolves-republika-srpska-bosnia.html; and Laurence Peter, 'Slovakia Alarmed by Pro-Putin Night Wolves Bikers' Base', BBC News, 31 July 2018, https://www.bbc.com/news/world-europe-45019133.

30 See RFE/RL's Balkan Service, 'Key Witness Identifies Russian Suspect in Funding of Alleged Montenegro Coup Plot', Radio Free Europe/Radio Liberty, 27 October 2017, https://www.rferl.org/a/montenegro-russia-serbia-coup-plot-witness-identifies-suspect-funding/28819658.html; and Andrew Higgins, 'Finger Pointed at Russians in Alleged Coup Plot in Montenegro', *New York Times*, 26 November 2016, https://www.nytimes.com/2016/11/26/world/europe/finger-pointed-at-russians-in-alleged-coup-plot-in-montenegro.html.

31 See Carpenter, 'Russia Is Co-opting Angry Young Men'; and Andrew

Higgins, 'Intent on Unsettling E.U., Russia Taps Foot Soldiers from the Fringe', *New York Times*, 12 December 2016, https://www.nytimes. com/2016/12/24/world/europe/ intent-on-unsettling-eu-russia-taps-foot-soldiers-from-the-fringe.html.

32 See Andrew Byrne, 'Shootout Raises Fears over Russian Ties to Hungary's Far Right', *Financial Times*, 27 November 2016, https://www.ft.com/ content/66d3993a-b0b8-11e6-9c37-5787335499a0.

33 See Bojan Pancevski, 'On Edge from Attacks, Germany Finds Far-right Radicals Within Security Services', *Wall Street Journal*, 11 October 2019, https://www.wsj.com/articles/ on-edge-from-attacks-germany-finds-far-right-radicals-within-security-services-11570786206.

34 See Ross, 'America's Neo-Nazi Terrorists Have a Powerful New Patron: Vladimir Putin'; Andrei Soshnikov, Ali Winston and Daniel De Simone, 'Neo-Nazi Rinaldo Nazzaro Running US Militant Group The Base from Russia', BBC News, 24 January 2020, https://www.bbc.com/news/ world-51236915; and Jason Wilson, 'Revealed: The True Identity of the Leader of an American Neo-Nazi Terror Group', *Guardian*, 23 January 2020, https://www.theguardian.com/ world/2020/jan/23/revealed-the-true-identity-of-the-leader-of-americas-neo-nazi-terror-group.

35 See Johannes Due Enstad, 'Right-wing Terrorism and Violence in Putin's Russia', *Perspectives on Terrorism,* vol. 12, no. 6, December 2018, pp. 89–103.

36 See Mariya Petkova, 'The Death of the Russian Far Right',

Al-Jazeera, 16 December 2017, https://www.aljazeera.com/ indepth/features/2017/11/death-russian-171123102640298.html.

37 See Jeff Seldin, 'White Supremacists Lead Wave of Foreign Fighters', VOA News, 30 September 2019, https://www.voanews.com/usa/ white-supremacists-lead-new-wave-foreign-fighters.

38 See Elizabeth Grimm Arsenault and Joseph Stabile, 'Confronting Russia's Role in Transnational White Supremacist Extremism', Just Security, 6 February 2020, https://www. justsecurity.org/68420/confronting-russias-role-in-transnational-white-supremacist-extremism/.

39 See Josephine Huetlin, 'Russian Extremists Are Training Right-wing Terrorists from Western Europe', Daily Beast, 2 August 2017, https://www.thedailybeast.com/ russian-extremists-are-training-right-wing-terrorists-from-western-europe; and 'Two Men Charged over Refugee Home Blast "Received Military Training in Russia"', The Local, 9 June 2017, https://www.thelocal. se/20170609/gothenburg-sweden-two-men-charged-over-refugee-home-bomb-attack-received-military-training-in-russia.

40 See Andrew Roth, 'A Right-wing Militia Trains Russians to Fight the Next War – With or Without Putin', *Washington Post*, 2 January 2017, https://www.washingtonpost.com/ world/europe/a-right-wing-militia-trains-russians-to-fight-the-next-war--with-or-without-putin/2017/01/02/ f06b5ce8-b71e-11e6-939c-91749443c5e5_story.html; and The

Soufan Center, 'White Supremacy Extremism: The Transnational Rise of the Violent White Supremacist Movement', 27 September 2019, https://thesoufancenter.org/research/white-supremacy-extremism-the-transnational-rise-of-the-violent-white-supremacist-movement/.

[41] See Philip Bump, 'Actually, the Mueller Report Showed that Russia Did Affect the Vote', *Washington Post*, 19 April 2019, https://www.washingtonpost.com/politics/2019/04/19/actually-mueller-report-showed-that-russia-did-affect-vote/.

[42] Department of Homeland Security, 'Strategic Framework for Countering Terrorism and Targeted Violence', p. 27.

[43] See Polyakova et al., 'The Kremlin's Trojan Horses'.

[44] See Joseph Cox and Jason Koebler, 'Why Won't Twitter Treat White Supremacy Like ISIS? Because It Would Mean Banning Some Republican Politicians Too', Vice, 25 April 2019, https://www.vice.com/en_us/article/a3xgq5/why-wont-twitter-treat-white-supremacy-like-isis-because-it-would-mean-banning-some-republican-politicians-too.

[45] See Mary B. McCord and Jason M. Blazakis, 'A Road Map for Congress to Address Domestic Terrorism', Lawfare, 27 February 2019, https://www.lawfareblog.com/road-map-congress-address-domestic-terrorism; and Daniel L. Byman, 'Is Right-wing Terrorism Rising?', *National Interest*, 13 August 2019, https://nationalinterest.org/feature/right-wing-terrorism-rising-73241.

Castro's Revolutionary Coming of Age

Russell Crandall and Jack Richardson

Cuba Libre! Che, Fidel, and the Improbable Revolution that Changed World History
Tony Perrottet. New York: Blue Rider Press, 2019. £20.00/$28.00. 367 pp.

Young Castro: The Making of a Revolutionary
Jonathan M. Hansen. New York: Simon & Schuster, 2019. £25.00/$35.00. 484 pp.

Fidel Castro's legendary amphibious landing at Playa Las Coloradas in 1956 was a textbook example of Murphy's Law. When he and 81 fellow revolutionaries set sail from Tuxpan, Mexico, on 25 November, the expedition was supposed to take five days and, on paper, their arrival was to coincide with coordinated attacks across Cuba on 30 November. These attacks were intended to ignite revolutionary fervour among the populace and signal the end of US-backed dictator Fulgencio Batista's rule. However, Fidel's 'invasion craft', a dilapidated pleasure yacht named *Granma*, did not reach Cuba until 2 December. Since there had been no way to inform the co-conspirators on land of the *Granma*'s delay, their attacks had been unsuccessfully carried out two days prior, doing little except to heighten government awareness of rebel activity in El Oriente (the eastern tip of Cuba). On the morning of

Russell Crandall is a professor of American foreign policy and international politics at Davidson College in North Carolina, and a contributing editor to *Survival*. His most recent book is *The Salvador Option: The United States in El Salvador, 1977–1992* (Cambridge University Press, 2016). **Jack Richardson** graduated from Bowdoin College in 2019.

Survival | vol. 62 no. 2 | April–May 2020 | pp. 153–164   DOI 10.1080/00396338.2020.1739961

2 December, the *Granma* nearly ran out of fuel, forcing the vessel to make ground at the edge of a mangrove swamp. Some members of the expedition questioned whether the landing site was Cuba at all, and Fidel had to be reassured that they were not in Jamaica. With the planned landing site nowhere to be found, the hapless revolutionaries were forced to disembark in waist-deep water and stagger through a hellish thicket of mangroves. In the words of Che Guevara, 'it was less an invasion than a shipwreck' (*Cuba Libre!*, p. 13). After trudging for hours through the swamp, the revolutionaries were greeted by dry land and a not inconsiderable number of Servicio de Inteligencia Militar agents. These members of Batista's infamous intelli-

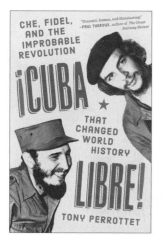

gence service were soon joined by army regulars, who had orders to destroy Fidel and the rebels. The fortunes of the fledgling insurgency further deteriorated as 17 of their number were captured, and more than a dozen were executed while attempting to surrender. It is hard to imagine a less auspicious start to the revolution that would soon conquer Cuba.

The *Granma* landing serves as an inflection point for two recent books: Tony Perrottet's *Cuba Libre!* and Jonathan Hansen's *Young Castro*. In *Cuba Libre!*, the landing arises a quarter of the way through the text, as Perrottet recounts the guerrillas' struggle in some detail. Hansen's book, on the other hand, is primarily concerned with recreating Fidel's childhood and tracing the events that led him to that fateful December day. Thus, Fidel's landing in Cuba is not chronicled until well into the second half of the book. Although each has a distinct focus, *Cuba Libre!* and *Young Castro* share a similar purpose. Hansen aims to recreate Castro's life 'as he actually lived it, moving forward, without the benefit of hindsight' (p. xv). *Cuba Libre!*'s stated goal is to 'turn back the clock to recapture the atmosphere of Cuba in the 1950s, when the actors were unknowns, history was unformed, and the fate of the revolution hung in the balance' (p. 7). Both narratives ask that their readers suspend any preconceived notions of the polarising revolution in order to peer into the zeitgeist of this pivotal, fascinating chapter of Cuban history.

The two authors approach their task from very different backgrounds. Hansen, a professor of Latin American Studies at Harvard University, has produced several scholarly works, including *Guantánamo: An American History*. He adopts a focused and meticulous approach as he strives to build a definitive history of Fidel's formative years. Perrottet, on the other hand, comes across as an unlikely authority on the subject, even though he cut his journalistic teeth in the 1980s covering Peru's Maoist Shining Path insurgency and Colombia's struggles with paramilitary warfare and the drug trade. His previous books include *Napoleon's Privates: 2,500 Years of History Unzipped* and *The Sinner's Grand Tour: A Journey Through the Historical Underbelly of Europe*. Nevertheless, Perrottet is adept at uncovering obscurities, and he has an eye for entertaining anecdotes – qualities that allow him to present an undeniably fascinating account of the revolution. While Hansen's *Young Castro* seeks to add to the academic literature, Perrottet aims to provide something 'entertaining and readable, unsaturated by ideology' (p. 360).

Birth of a revolutionary

Young Castro begins with an account of Fidel's father, Angel Castro, who grew up in Galicia, Spain, and was sent to Cuba in 1895 after being drafted into the Spanish army. At that time, Cuba was in full-blown insurrection against Spanish rule. As the Spanish rank and file sent to the island to suppress the insurrection succumbed to the twin calamities of Cuban guerrillas and tropical diseases, the locals began to gain the upper hand. Yet Washington's victory over Spain in 1898 would wrong-foot the Cuban independence movement, as control over the island passed from one imperial power to another. This was not the liberation that Cuban nationalists such as the matchless José Martí had imagined. Following the United States' intervention, the Cuban economy became 'dominated by foreign corporations', and Angel took advantage of the situation to make a small fortune in agriculture (p. 30). His mastery of the volatile sugarcane market earned him the respect of American overseers and Cuban labourers alike, as well as significant wealth. Unlike most speculators, Angel diversified his crop portfolio, which allowed him to withstand the economic gyrations that ruined many of his fellow growers. Thus, the patriarch of the Castro clan provided his children with a stable upbringing that largely insulated them from the poverty of their peers. To be sure, Fidel was to grow up observing how Cuba's political and economic maladies contributed to 'social fatalism', as evidenced by the children around him whose subpar primary education ensured that they remained impoverished. But he would later admit that his home life made him one of the world's least likely revolutionaries (*Cuba Libre!*, p. 33). As a young man, his main focus was 'playing sports, exploring the countryside, climbing mountains, chasing girls, [and] riding horses high into the hills to go hunting' (*Young Castro*, p. 50).

Fidel had a stubborn, irascible nature

Cuba Libre! emphasises Fidel's later exploits as a revolutionary leader, according only perfunctory treatment to his family and childhood. Indeed, Cuban history leading up to the revolution is dispatched in only 19 pages. That said, the book's brief introduction to Cuba's pre-revolutionary history indicates the author's willingness to explore tangents and oddities. For instance, Perrottet describes how Martí, the Cuban revolutionary who would serve as a model for Fidel, enjoyed a stint as a Manhattan poet who inspired the works of pop-culture icons such as Celia Cruz and Pete Seeger. And rather than considering, as Hansen does, the economic and political effects of the American presence in Cuba after 1898, Perrottet frames American hegemony in cultural terms. Baseball supplanted bullfighting, and the intermingling of American consumer goods with Cuban commodities produced a new repertoire of cocktails, including the legendary Cuba Libre (rum and Coke) and the daiquiri.

As a youngster, Fidel had a stubborn, irascible nature that drew him into conflict with his stoic, hardworking father, and he was sent off to boarding school for remediation. After stints living with and being tutored by the Feliú family in Santiago de Cuba (a time of 'hunger and ennui', according to Hansen – p. 56) and attending the boarding school Colegio de La Salle (where his time was cut short on account of his bad behaviour), Castro finally landed at the Colegio de Dolores – then one of the most prestigious secondary institutions in Cuba. It became evident that Fidel was an exceptionally gifted child: one who excelled in the classroom, competed fiercely on the basketball court and baseball diamond, and won over his peers with his easy-going, charismatic demeanour. Despite his petulance as a youth, upon graduation from Dolores, there was no doubt that Fidel had a bright future ahead of him.

In 1945, Fidel began his studies at the University of Havana, where he quickly acquired a new-found political awareness. The university played host to an 'alphabet soup of gangs' that sought money and influence (*Young Castro*, p. 89). Emphasising action over ideology, these groups were armed to the teeth and unafraid to inflict violence on their peers. With weapons stashed all over campus, the university was as much a battleground as a place of learning. In this turbulent setting, Castro emerged as a political leader. A skilled orator with unwavering confidence, Castro appeared primed for a rapid ascension in Cuban politics after graduation. But Batista put an end to Fidel's political aspirations (and everyone else's) by staging a coup in March 1952. Ever the man of action, Fidel did not sit idly in the wake of Batista's takeover – he enlisted 160 members of the leftist Orthodox Party (of which he had been a high-profile member during his university days) to assault the Moncada barracks in the Oriente. In a foretaste of things to come, the fighters were poorly equipped, and the plan of attack promptly fell apart when the assault began. Some Orthodox Party members were killed in the heat of battle; scores were captured and later executed by the Moncada soldiers.

Fidel himself caught a break. Instead of being summarily dispatched, he was captured and thrown into Presidio Modelo, a notorious prison in Nueva Gerona. It was here that Fidel and 25 of his fellow soldiers would serve out their sentences – in Fidel's case, 15 years. Determined to make the best of the situation, Fidel and his cohort used the long hours of prison life to further their education, with Fidel instructing the group on philosophy and history, among other subjects. Determined to expand his own horizons, Fidel 'read voraciously, giving himself virtual PhDs in Western literature and political science' (*Cuba Libre!*, p. 60).

According to Perrottet, all this reading caused Fidel to become 'more radical in his opinions' (p. 60). This observation might have benefited from a little more ideological examination. What was he reading that 'radicalised' him? How did these new ideas mesh with his previous ideological outlook? Earlier in the book, Perrottet asserts that, although Fidel carried the writings of Vladimir Lenin on his person during the Moncada attack, the former's 'political language was purely nationalist … He wanted power above all else; ideology came a distant second' (pp. 48–9). Might it be possible that some form of ideology was bubbling beneath the surface of Fidel's national-ist exterior? While Perrottet's decision not to weigh down the action with ideological discussion makes for exceptional readability, the unexplained changes in Fidel's outlook can be jarring. How did he go, for instance, from being a 'political illiterate' in his youth (p. 37) to a man who, in a courtroom speech titled 'La historia me absolverá' ('History Will Absolve Me'), quoted Thomas Paine, Jean-Jacques Rousseau and Honoré de Balzac? The reader is left to guess where he acquired this familiarity with the Western canon.

Given Perrottet's reluctance to indulge in ideological discussions, *Young Castro*, which meticulously fleshes out Fidel's political views, is a valu-able companion volume. Letters written between Fidel and his lover, Naty Revuelta, elucidate the imprisoned man's political development. Fidel read Immanuel Kant's *Critique of Pure Reason*, which made him think hard about questions of individual experience and the relativity of knowledge. Lenin and Karl Marx also figured prominently in his readings, with Marx's *The Eighteenth Brumaire of Louis Napoleon* and *The Civil War in France*, and Lenin's *State and Revolution*, being among the volumes Castro pored over during his imprisonment. Rousseau's *Discourse on Inequality* was also an inspiration. These works helped Fidel to grapple with issues of revolu-tion, wealth distribution and nationalism. For instance, as Hansen puts it, 'Kant's insistence that some concepts endure (the categories of space and time, for instance), jibed with Castro's appeal to timeless virtues like nationalism, patriotism, and self-sacrifice' (p. 227). For a revolutionary who would eventually have to determine whether to appropriate Batista's state apparatus, the questions Marx raised in *The Communist Manifesto* were especially pertinent.

Mounting public pressure induced Batista to release the Moncada prisoners on 6 May 1955. However, granting Fidel amnesty did little to placate him, and within six weeks of his release he was in Mexico planning another attempt to overthrow the Cuban strongman. Fidel's group, now calling itself Movimiento 26 de Julio (M-26-7) to commemorate the supposedly storied attack at Moncada, was able to establish itself in Mexico City, which was generally hospitable to leftist groups. (Batista nevertheless pressured Mexican police to harass the group.) It began to amass weapons, cash and more members who, although lacking military experience, made for an interesting cast of characters. These included Argentinian doctor Ernesto 'Che' Guevara and Fidel's brother, Raúl. With an infusion of cash from sympathisers in the United States, the addition of new recruits and an ascetic training regimen, the group started to look more like a fighting force – albeit one that still seemed to stand no chance against a battalion of Batista's seasoned troops

Ultimately, a raid by Mexican authorities precipitated the Cubans' operation. Although they were released from custody, staying in Mexico would have risked their being arrested again, and possibly extradited. They had no choice but to leave Mexico, and so, in the early morning of 25 November, 82 men boarded the creaky *Granma* and settled in for the 2,000-kilometre journey.

Beating the odds

Cuba Libre! underscores the unbelievable odds that the guerrillas had to overcome to overthrow Batista. It was already miraculous that they had survived Moncada, been released from prison and survived the turbulent journey on the barely seaworthy *Granma*. The landing party had devolved into smaller groups by the time it arrived in Cuba, but this proved to be a saving grace, as it allowed group members to more easily avoid detection. For five days, Fidel and two other M-26-7 comrades, cut off from the contingent Fidel was supposed to be commanding, hid in a cane field, where they sweltered in the sun and froze at night. They eventually escaped into the Sierra Maestra mountain range, where they were reunited with 12 of their *compañeros*, including Che and Raúl. Still, it was an inauspicious start: only two weeks after the landing, less than one-sixth of the original force remained.

The odds faced by the remaining fighters were so poor that they might as well have been stepping up to a roulette table at one of Havana's famed casinos. Anteing up with their lives, the inexperienced if fearless guerrillas needed several decisive moments to turn out in their favour, whereas Batista needed only one – such as the chaotic landing in Cuba or the saturation bombing of the Sierra Maestra – to swing his way to wipe out the insurgency. As the revolution continued, however, Fidel and company learned from their early disasters and adapted accordingly. As a result, skill gradually supplanted luck as the decisive factor for M-26-7.

The Oriente of Fidel's childhood, vividly described in the opening pages of *Young Castro*, had changed little when the insurgents took up refuge in its hills. It was still isolated from the rest of Cuba, meaning that Batista had committed few resources to its defence. Besides Moncada, there were no major military bases in the region, and isolated outposts made for easy attacks, even for inexperienced and ill-equipped M-26-7 forces. Still, the movement was running low on men, supplies and funds. The efforts of Celia Sánchez, an early organiser for M-26-7, helped to alleviate shortages in the short term, but it became clear that she alone would not be able to summon the materiel needed to defeat Batista. Fortunately for M-26-7, Fidel, who was a promising politician before he turned revolutionary, understood that perception was everything, and that if he could convince the public to believe in him, he would be able to recruit fighters and raise funds on a large scale. Thus, in mid-February 1956, less than three months after his landing in Cuba, he invited veteran *New York Times* journalist Herbert Matthews to interview him during the first meeting of M-26-7's national leadership. At this point in the war, Fidel's fighting force was green and hardly impressive, numbering in the low double digits. Perrottet describes how Fidel ordered these men to dress up in different uniforms and parade through the camp to give the impression that their numbers were in the hundreds. Some have questioned whether this 'outrageous deception' actually took place, as the topography of the camp was not well suited to such a scheme (*Cuba*

Libre!, p. 125). In any event, the reporter left Cuba with a lofty impression of the rebels, informing his readers that 'General Batista cannot possibly hope to suppress the Castro revolt' (*Cuba Libre!*, p. 131). Fidel followed up on this success by bringing CBS correspondent Robert Taber to film the rebels a couple of months later. The resulting 30-minute documentary, *Rebels of the Sierra Maestra*, reached tens of millions of American television sets and drummed up broad support for the rebels in the United States as well as Cuba.

Perrottet keeps his finger on the pulse of American and Cuban newspaper and film coverage of the revolution throughout the second half of his book, thereby giving readers an idea of how outsiders saw the rebels. The author is sometimes willing to take apocryphal information at face value. For instance, *Cuba Libre!* describes how Che, while in Mexico City preparing for the invasion of a country he had never visited, 'pushed himself to climb the 17,930-foot volcano Popocatépetl, battling asthma to the ice-covered summit' (p. 73). Hansen, in *Young Castro*, gives a more nuanced view of the event, writing: 'Accounts differ about whether Guevara ever summited Popocatépetl (Castro, ever competitive, says he did not), but Castro admired the determination that drove Guevara to return to the mountain multiple times' (p. 283). This is illustrative of the authors' differing approaches. Hansen prefers to avoid embellishment in favour of bare facts, while Perrottet embraces a sort of folk-history style.

Because many of the accounts of the revolution that appeared in newspapers and on television had Fidel as their source and were filtered by journalists such as Taber and Matthews, the public received a distorted picture of events. Perrottet, by embracing these possible distortions instead of discarding them, successfully recreates the revolution as people saw it at the time. Given that his ultimate goal is to entertain, this approach makes sense – a raconteur's version of events will usually be more enthralling than a clinical recitation of facts. This is not to say that *Cuba Libre!* is grossly inaccurate, but the information it presents sometimes differs from that in *Young Castro*. Hansen wants to recreate events as precisely as possible, which is why he expends the effort to untangle apocryphal tales and to assess their veracity. Early in the book, for instance, Hansen discusses an incident in which Fidel allegedly beat a worker while Angel watched. Noting that the source of the story was one of Fidel's former schoolmates, 'an exile and sworn enemy of the Castro regime' (p. 43), Hansen takes the time to evaluate the accuracy of the account, systematically splitting fact from fiction. *Young Castro* has many myths to unpack – some spun by Fidel, others by his detractors.

Given that Hansen's focus is primarily on Fidel's earlier years, *Cuba Libre!*'s account of the insurgents' time in the Sierra Maestra is inevitably more robust. Perrottet offers an excellent 'on the ground' perspective on the day-to-day survival of the guerrillas as they were hunted by Batista's forces. Some of the problems the guerrillas experienced were typical for any fighting force: materiel shortages, dysentery, eroding morale and so on. Others were peculiar to M-26-7. The fact that the movement was co-ed led to romances and trysts that could make for an awkward camp. Additionally, Fidel could be a tempestuous leader: in a letter to Sánchez, for example, he complained that 'I'm eating hideously. No care is paid to preparing my food … I won't write any more because I'm in a terrible mood' (p. 214). His mood must have reached new depths when, as part of *Operation FF* (*Fin de Fidel*), Batista sent 10,000 soldiers into the Sierra Maestra, covered by air support and naval long guns, to search for and destroy the rebel army's 280 members. At one point, the rebels found themselves confined to an area measuring only ten square kilometres. Still, the Sierra Maestra's harsh terrain and vegetation shielded them while slowing the advance of Batista's forces. Harassing sniper fire and psychological warfare eroded the morale of the conventional forces. Castro's kidnapping of Americans (including 28 marines and sailors returning to the US naval station at Guantanamo Bay) negated the conventional forces' air superiority: Batista could not risk killing citizens of the country that was supplying his aircraft and bombs.

Hansen supplements *Cuba Libre!*'s detailed account of the war in the Sierra Maestra with an examination of the forces that were working against Fidel and M-26-7. Furious debate was raging within the US State Department and the CIA as to whether Castro was a communist, and whether supporting Batista was defensible. While the United States had supplied Batista with his planes and bombs, the Eisenhower administration distanced itself from the increasingly despised, foundering Batista, and eventually suspended arms shipments as the American public became acquainted with the rebels' struggle through the enchanted media. US officials, however, were less than enthusiastic about the prospect of Fidel taking power. Would he be the Caribbean's answer to Franklin Roosevelt, as many hoped? Or would he turn Cuba into a tropical version of Prague? Both outcomes were very much in play. Additionally, public sentiment in Havana and Santiago de Cuba was originally lukewarm towards the rebellion, and the lack of popular support doused Fidel's hopes of urban uprisings taking pressure off of his guerrilla forces.

Public opinion did start to shift as Fidel's resilient band of guerrillas succeeded in holding off the dictator's advances. Emboldened by Batista's failed siege on their mountainous refuge, the revolutionaries started conducting operations in the plains of the Oriente, and later tested the waters farther west. Fidel's forces, while still badly outnumbered by Batista's, achieved unexpected victories that sapped the opposition's will to fight. Eventually realising that his regime was doomed, Batista fled the country on 1 January 1959. The rebels whose mission had seemed so impossible two years earlier claimed their improbable victory.

*   *   *

Because they cover different territory, *Cuba Libre!* and *Young Castro* add to our understanding of Fidel and his revolution in ways that avoid repetition and contribute unique insights. The two volumes complement each other: *Young Castro* covers Fidel's first two decades in much greater detail, while *Cuba Libre!* concentrates on his military campaign. Hansen's tone is scholarly and direct, while Perrottet's is playful and buoyant. Hansen addresses a more academic audience, while Perrottet targets the casual reader.

The personality traits revealed in *Young Castro* are clearly recognisable in the revolutionary figure presented in *Cuba Libre!* Fidel's stubborn nature and inability to submit to authority during his youth surfaced later in life during his repeated attempts to dislodge Batista. Even after the failed but fateful Moncada attack led to his capture and incarceration, Fidel refused to admit defeat, returning to the drawing board within six weeks. The unwavering self-confidence and charm that won over his classmates at Colegio de Dolores would hold M-26-7 together even when the outlook was bleak. The photographic memory that won him the honour of class valedictorian at Dolores would also come in handy in the Sierra Maestra, as his detailed knowledge of the terrain helped him to outmanoeuvre and entrap Batista's forces. Thus, while his upbringing in the relative comfort of Birán might have made him less likely than others to become a revolutionary, his temperament in many ways made him the perfect man to lead a guerrilla campaign. Reading *Young Castro* shows how the successful revolutionary depicted in *Cuba Libre!* came into being. Both books are well worth a look.

Book Reviews

Politics and International Relations
Steven Simon

The Allure of Battle: A History of How Wars Have Been Won and Lost
Cathal J. Nolan. Oxford and New York: Oxford University Press, 2017. £20.00/$34.95. 709 pp.

Cathal Nolan's timely book does not so much break new ground as assemble in a systematic, chronological fashion evidence for the proposition that generals and the battles they fight do not matter very much. The author, a historian at Boston University, makes a persuasive case because he has marshalled ample evidence drawn from several disciplines, presents a narrative of sweeping scope that somehow never becomes unwieldy, and writes so damn well. In its broadest terms, the argument is that in most instances, from medieval Europe through the Second World War, wars have been won not by bold manoeuvre or aggressive attack, but by the cumulative impact of attrition. (Nolan's argument reprises Stephen Van Evera's brilliant 1984 essay, 'The Cult of the Offensive and the Origins of the First World War', which he cites, but situates it in a larger diachronic context.) By and large, the winners simply had the greater stamina for a long-term, grinding fight. The prospective victor generally grasped the fact that wars of movement and daring offensives, fuelled in the best case by brilliant leadership and *élan vital*, were more costly than shooting from behind the parapet. Battles won, in other words, were not necessarily going to win wars and, as the March 1918 German offensive showed, might even lose them.

In the modern era – say, from the Napoleonic Wars to the end of the twentieth century's 30-year war – either the wrong lessons were learned from the Crimean War, the American Civil War, and the Franco-Prussian and Russo-Japanese

Survival | vol. 62 no. 2 | April–May 2020 | pp. 165–170   DOI 10.1080/ 00396338.2020.1739962

wars, or no lessons at all. Trench warfare and artillery were key to combat in Crimea and the eastern theatre of operations in the Civil War, and machine guns took a heavy toll in Russian lives in 1905. The German successes against Austria and France in 1866 and 1870 were exceptions that proved the rule, a point that the elder Helmut von Moltke, who devised the campaign plan that swept the French from Sedan, subsequently tried to press, but without much success. Indeed, it was the brilliance of his achievement in 1870 that seduced his successors into the fantasy of beating a stronger coalition of adversaries via the clever coup.

Although this book would have been useful to politicians and soldiers dreaming of a decisive war that would conclude more quickly than the subsequent victory parade in any era, it might have been especially useful to American officials in the post-Cold War world. In that era, the promise of the 'revolution in military affairs' – precision weapons, cutting-edge explosives, and advances in reconnaissance and surveillance that would enable commanders to 'get inside the enemy's decision cycle' – seemed to be fulfilled in the 100-hour Gulf War of 1991 and on the Thunder Run to Baghdad in 2003. But what eventuated was a Thirty Years War that even the United States lacked the stamina to win.

Trading in War: London's Maritime World in the Age of Cook and Nelson
Margarette Lincoln. New Haven, CT: Yale University Press, 2018. £25.00/$35.00. 304 pp.

Alfred Thayer Mahan's *The Influence of Sea Power Upon History, 1660–1783* was largely focused on the vital importance of controlling sea lines of communication and the need for a navy that was capable of fending off threats to these routes. It is still worth reading. But Mahan went farther in his analysis to stress the crucial role of secure seaports, or what we would now label infrastructure. 'The ships', he wrote, 'that thus sail to and fro must have secure ports to which to return.' Indeed, he advised that a maritime nation have no fewer than two such ports, in part to create uncertainty among pursuers of the destination of ships headed for home. Margarette Lincoln's book is a marvellous account of the development of the London dockyards along the River Thames in the latter part of the eighteenth century. While the study could be read as a contribution to Atlantic history and thalassology, or riverine and maritime studies, it is usefully read as an analysis of the role of ports in a state's security strategy in a particular place and time.

The moment chosen by the author was encumbered by severe pressure on Britain's ability to secure its vital interests. On the one hand, it was fighting a long war in North America against rebellious colonists supported by France at the end of a 6,400-kilometre logistics tail. On the other, Britain was embroiled, by 1780, in a war against three rivals, the French, Spanish and Dutch, the latter a supplier to the French war effort. These back-to-back challenges necessitated a pace of operations in the dockyards that simply astonishes. Ship construction was just one element, but it alone was a marvel of organisation, with upwards of 500 shipwrights allocated to the construction of a single vessel when hundreds of warships were commissioned and put to sea every year. The dockyards also had to source vast quantities not just of lumber for hulls, masts and planking, but also of consumables (beeswax, pitch, fodder, beef and biscuits), spares and equipment ranging from anchors to hourglasses. The archival record Lincoln refers to is extraordinarily rich and reveals the methodical, centralised, highly detailed and thoroughly bureaucratic process that regulated this enormous enterprise.

As an account of mobilisation for war this book is enlightening. It is equally instructive on the social aspects of war preparation along the Thames. The author is clearly concerned to intertwine 'little history' with large events. Thus, she has assembled an array of anecdotes and data regarding daily life in the dockyard environment, which seethed with intense industrial activity next door to dairy farms, asparagus production and rural pasture. As such, it is a tale of social exploitation and opportunity. Large-scale employment created by the building and victualling of an enormous fleet was undoubtedly a good thing. But wages went unchanged for a century during a period of steadily rising food prices; and the impressment of sailors, or the wilful abandonment of families by men seeking escape through naval service, forced women and their families into internal displacement or life in poorhouses. This spurred subversive manoeuvring, which was put down without mercy. The book closes with the creation of the West India dock complex in the early nineteenth century, the corresponding decline of private dockyards, the forced relocation of the indigent residents and the increasing regimentation of the workforce. Not an especially happy ending.

Antisemitism: Here and Now
Deborah Lipstadt. London: Scribe Publications, 2019. £14.99.
304 pp.

Anti-Semitism is a hot topic now, perhaps unsurprisingly, since there is a lot of it around. In the recent UK elections, one of the myriad factors in the Tory demolition of Labour was the widespread perception that the Labour Party was a hotbed of anti-Semitic beliefs and rhetoric, and that Jeremy Corbyn, the party leader, refused to acknowledge the problem, let alone act to counter it. Jewish Labour activists and members of Parliament defected, while the Conservative incumbent was served by a chorus of surrogates who showcased Corbyn's seeming indifference to anti-Semitism within his ranks.

The United States is far from immune. The president can scarcely be considered an anti-Semite – his son-in-law is an observant Jew and his daughter is a convert to Judaism – and he has won the loyalty and services of prominent Jewish advisers and Cabinet members. Yet he has trafficked in anti-Semitic themes and symbols that do not require an Umberto Eco to decode; and he has walked a fine if ugly line to maintain the support of his base, which encompasses conspiracy theorists, motorcycle gangs and a nativist middle class in Midwestern and Southern suburbs. His assertions that there were 'fine people on both sides' in 2017 when a Nazi torchlight rally in Charlottesville, Virginia, turned violent, culminating in the murder of a counter-demonstrator, elevated him to redeemer status among American fascists. Since then, Jews have been attacked violently on several occasions, the worst of course being the 2018 massacre of 11 Jews at the Tree of Life Synagogue in suburban Pittsburgh by a heavily armed gunman in tactical kit. On college campuses in the US, Jewish supporters of Israel and opponents of the pro-Palestinian boycott, divestment and sanctions (BDS) movement have been subjected to abuse.

Amid these dismaying developments, Deborah Lipstadt, a renowned historian who was sued in London by the British Holocaust denier David Irving (who lost the ensuing court battle), has written a book on this issue in the 'here and now'. This is not, therefore, a book about the Holocaust or a history of anti-Semitism. It is a scholarly, but approachable and sensitive, assessment of the sources and manifestations of contemporary anti-Semitism and, importantly, responses to them. The format of the book is a bit unconventional: it is epistolary and narrates a dialogue between a highly accomplished Jewish woman at a university and a non-Jewish law professor who perceives himself as tolerant and progressive. My first thought was that this structure was somewhat jejune, but if an imagined didactic dialogue on complex questions was good enough for Plato, it ought to be good enough for Lipstadt. The letters revolve around topics such as 'Antisemitism and Racism: The Same Yet Different'; 'Inverting Victims and Perpetrators'; 'De-Judaizing the Holocaust'; 'BDS: Antisemitism or Politics?'; and 'Speaking Truth to Friends: Beyond Victimhood'.

The author raises two important trends in the context of her broader analysis. The first is that social-media platforms play an important role not just because they are difficult to police and disseminate toxic content over an infinite range at the speed of light, but because they facilitate the normalisation of anti-Semitic discourse. The second is that the Jews and the political left appear to be going their separate ways, ending their historical pattern of mutual reliance. This is an adverse development for Jews because it leaves them sandwiched between detractors on the right and left; and for the left because it will reinforce radical impulses that, in the American system, are not politically viable at the national level. Although beyond her remit, it would have been salutary to hear the author's take on Muslim anti-Semitism in a European setting, and her thoughts on whether and how some sort of intercommunal armistice might be fostered.

The Light that Failed: A Reckoning
Ivan Krastev and Stephen Holmes. London: Allen Lane, 2019.
£20.00. 247 pp.

The literature on the rise of populism and authoritarianism is virtually oceanic. This is understandable. The timing, simultaneity, similarities, intensity and seeming ubiquity of these transitions were, like the Arab Spring or the revolutions of 1848, so unexpected and of such apparent import as to demand a coherent explanation. Many scholars, journalists and social commentators have risen to the occasion, converging on a set of conditions that preceded or were coextant with the rise of populism and evident decline of the old liberal verities, forms and institutions. In their assessment, key factors included stagnant wages; the near-disaster of the 2008 financial crisis; rising wealth inequality, particularly in the United States; immigration and cultural anxieties; and middle-class bitterness rooted in the rise of a wealthy, self-congratulatory, patronising urban economic and cultural elite flying high over increasingly meaningless territorial borders. There are undoubtedly other variables, but we haven't got all day.

Ivan Krastev, a Bulgarian social scientist whose previous book, *After Europe*, is much admired, and Stephen Holmes, a law professor who ranges widely and authoritatively in multiple disciplines, have joined forces to offer their interesting explanation for this post-Cold War reversal of fortune. Although they have a distinctive view, they are very much alive to the welter of explanations, descriptions and imputed causes that crowd the airwaves, nor do they seem to take issue with much of the emerging conventional wisdom. Rather, in pursuit of parsimony and elegance, they posit a more specific, unitary cause, which they call 'imitation'. According to the authors, the collapse of the Soviet Union was accompanied ineluctably by American encroachment linked to the explicit or tacit – depending on the situation – imitation of a corpus of policies and their underlying 'Western' political postures. Each of the object countries responded to the imitation imperative in different ways. Some, like Russia, feigned imitation from the outset; others, like Poland, imitated but ultimately declined to convert. The imitation crisis never penetrated China, according to Holmes and Krastev, because the Chinese rejected the comprehensive concept, opting instead to imitate the technologies of the West and not bother even to pretend to imitate Western politics or social arrangements.

The reason, argue the authors, that this became a serious problem was the flip side to the demand for imitation, namely resentment. This was probably inevitable, given the superior stance struck by Western states, the impediments to the material paradise promised by the West and the very inauthenticity implied by imitation. Even worse, from an Eastern perspective, was the Fukuyama doctrine internalised by Western powers, which held that there was no alternative to Western-style liberal democracy. No one wants to be told that there are no alternatives, especially when there are nationalists on the right insisting that there are other modes, and that these are more faithful to the values of the imagined community of which they are an integral part. The fact that the West itself was undergoing a grave economic crisis and experiencing, with Donald Trump's election in 2016, political tremors that could be measured on the Richter scale only made imitation more repugnant, and opened the door to right-wing politicians across Europe, but especially in the east. With Trump's accession to power, the American political, strategic and cultural insistence on imitation by others has been repudiated at the source.

Looking ahead, the book concludes that, more than 50 years after Daniel Bell's *The End of Ideology*, international competition, particularly between the United States and China, will no longer be infused by ideological rivalry. The authors' forecast curiously resists pessimism, but for reasons that are opaque to the reader.

Middle East

Ray Takeyh

The Last Card: Inside George W. Bush's Decision to Surge in Iraq
Timothy Andrews et al., eds. Ithaca, NY: Cornell University
Press, 2019. $34.95. 416 pp.

Iraq is a war without patrons. Nearly all of its original supporters have repented, while its opponents feel vindicated. As the war fades from memory, it may be possible for historians to dispassionately examine its origins and various trajectories. *The Last Card*'s mission is a limited one: to assess the surge of troops in 2007. The book encompasses a unique collection of oral histories supplemented by a series of articles by prominent scholars. While those who contributed oral histories naturally seek to justify their actions, the academic observers take a dimmer view of the entire episode.

In one sense, the notion that the United States needed more troops to manage Iraq is not all that remarkable. In February 2003, General Eric Shinseki, the army's chief of staff, ruffled feathers by stressing that the stabilisation of Iraq would require 'something in the order of several hundred thousand soldiers'. None of the contributors to *The Last Card* explore why this call was ignored, but the reason has to do with the justifications that were offered for what was a contentious war of choice. Proponents of the intervention had promised that the war would be quick and that the US would be welcomed as a liberator. The occupation was treated as an afterthought. That being the case, it was difficult to suddenly acknowledge that the war would be a hard slog, the occupation prolonged and the costs more significant than initially promised. It was hoped, despite a slew of academic writing to the contrary, that an inclusive political process would calm the sectarian conflict tearing Iraq apart.

Despite all this, the surge's importance should not be dismissed. Administrations rarely change strategies even when they sense the shortcomings of their existing approach. Lyndon Johnson and his advisers continually agonised about the Vietnam War, but in the end held tight to their strategy of attrition and massive bombing even when intelligence reports indicated that Hanoi would not budge. George W. Bush and his aides should be commended for their willingness to revisit their assumptions, change tactics and embrace an unpopular option at a time when the nation had become weary of war.

The Last Card strives to create the impression that a flawless bureaucratic process generated comprehensive policy options, but different government agencies concealing information from each other does not strike this reviewer

 DOI 10.1080/ 00396338.2020.1739965

as such a 'textbook' process. Still, the surge's success is beyond dispute. Less certain is whether that success was bound to be ephemeral. For the architects of the surge, Barack Obama's withdrawal of American forces in 2011 squandered important gains. For the war's opponents, the entire enterprise was doomed from the beginning, irrespective of fluctuations in the levels of violence.

Today, the surge seems like a minor episode in a war that the US is desperate to forget. Iraq is still divided along sectarian lines. Predatory outside powers, particularly Iran, dominate its politics, while American politicians of both parties complain about forever wars. Nevertheless, it is essential to learn the right lessons from the Iraq War, and *The Last Card* is an important first step in what one hopes will be a much longer journey of discovery.

Beirut 1958: How America's Wars in the Middle East Began
Bruce Riedel. Washington DC: Brookings Institution Press, 2020. $24.99. 136 pp.

The year 1958 has been called a year of revolutions. Led by Egyptian leader Gamal Abdul Nasser, Arab radicals sought to displace the conservative monarchies and assert their own brand of post-colonial nationalism. The British, having been defeated in the Suez war of 1956, were evicted from the Arab east and confined to the Persian Gulf. In the US, Dwight Eisenhower acknowledged the importance of the Middle East, but hoped that its allies would patrol the region on the United States' behalf. A parsimonious Cold Warrior, Eisenhower cared as much about balancing the budget as containing the Soviet Union.

In this compact and compulsively readable book, Bruce Riedel details a dramatic year that culminated in Eisenhower's decision to dispatch 14,000 troops to stabilise the tottering Lebanese government in America's first military intervention in the Middle East. (Few are more qualified to tell this story than Riedel, a scholar at the Brookings Institution who has served both Republican and Democratic presidents as a senior government official and has written a number of well-received history books.) In 1958, it was easy to believe that the conservative monarchies were a relic of a discredited past and that pan-Arabism was the wave of the future. Nasser had unified Egypt and Syria on his terms, creating the United Arab Republic. He was pressuring King Hussein of Jordan to sever his ties to the British Empire, and he had cornered the Saudi monarch, King Saud, whose ham-fisted attempt to assassinate the Egyptian president led to his own effective removal from power by a princely class concerned about his recklessness. The CIA uncovered a coup plot against King Hussein just in time, but in July 1958 a coup attempt against the Hashemite dynasty in Iraq succeeded. The mutilated bodies of the monarch and his prime minister were dragged through the streets.

This was when everyone panicked. The Saudis did what they do best, insisting that the United States take charge or they would come to terms with Nasser. British paratroopers were dispatched to rescue the 'Plucky Little King' in Jordan – an ironic turn of events considering that King Hussein had dismissed the commander of the famed Arab Legion as a means of placating Nasser. Washington needed to take a stand, and it chose Lebanon as the scene of its power play. The Lebanese president, Camille Chamoun, was doing his best to extend his term in office by playing the communist card. It is hard to believe that Eisenhower was convinced by his machinations, but he had to display American power to calm the nerves of his jittery allies.

Thus, in 1958, the US chose sides in the Arab Cold War and conferred its approval on conservative leaders who often led stagnant governments. The Arab radicals that it feared so much soon began to squabble among themselves. The Syrians fled the union with Nasser, and the Iraqi revolutionaries made clear that Baghdad, not Cairo, should lead the region. In 1967, Israel put an end to it all when it destroyed Nasser's army. The crestfallen Lion of Arabism had to make peace with the same Saudi monarchy that he had so relentlessly attacked. Petrodollars, in the end, spoke louder than ideological mandates.

Iran Reframed: Anxieties of Power in the Islamic Republic
Narges Bajoghli. Stanford, CA: Stanford University Press, 2019.
$22.00. 176 pp.

The Islamic Republic of Iran devotes considerable time and money to cultural and political propaganda. Documentaries, magazines and books extolling the virtues of the regime are in constant production. A topic of particular concern for the guardians of the state is Iran's war with Iraq. The Sacred Defence, in their telling, was a time of heroic sacrifice and national solidarity. In *Iran Reframed*, Narges Bajoghli attempts to untangle such regime-manufactured narratives.

The book's principal message is that while the Iranian regime makes many documentaries, these films have a limited and dwindling audience. The producers understand that their products have little popular appeal, and wrestle endlessly with the question of how to refashion their art for a new and indifferent generation. How can the regime concoct a persuasive narrative when its claims are routinely ignored by a sceptical public tired of being lied to by official organs?

There is a considerable gap between how the regime talks about the war and the realities of a conflict that still haunts many Iranians. For the clerical oligarchs, the war was a triumph for Iran against all odds. Yet their ritualistic celebration of the conflict's martyrs seems hollow to the many Iranians who have questioned why the war persisted after 1982, when Iraq was evicted from Iranian territory and Baghdad seemed poised to end the war. Tehran may even have been able to obtain reparations from Arab sheikhdoms eager for the war to end. In any case, can an armistice that led to no real exchange of territory properly be called a victory? Questions have also been raised about the reconstruction aid that was misappropriated by the same Revolutionary Guard that today extols its own heroism.

The author's discussion of Iran's war documentaries would have benefited from more detail about the controversies that continue to surround the conflict. The Islamic Republic still has not come to terms with the longest war in Iran's modern history, and continues to avoid painful questions regarding its leaders' miscalculations and misjudgements. Iranian officials may bicker and at times blame each other, but no real accounting of the war features in the regime's official presentations. So long as this remains the case, the films the regime produces will struggle to find an audience, no matter how sophisticated their production values.

The Shah of Iran, the Iraqi Kurds, and the Lebanese Shia
Arash Reisinezhad. London: Palgrave Macmillan, 2019. £79.99.
357 pp.

Many Middle Eastern countries host a multitude of ethnic and religious groups within their borders while having little in the way of representative governments that address all of their concerns. This has encouraged despotic regimes and external powers alike to fear fifth columns. The Sunni dictatorships are suspicious of their Shia populations, for example, while all the major players in the Middle East have had doubts about the Kurds. In a region where the concept of sovereignty has carried little weight, these concerns are not entirely misplaced. After all, many Middle Eastern regimes *have* sought to extend their influence beyond their own borders.

Iran is no exception. In *The Shah of Iran, the Iraqi Kurds, and the Lebanese Shia*, Arash Reisinezhad focuses on the activities of the Pahlavi dynasty in Iraq and Lebanon. Iran's Iraqi neighbour has always posed a strategic challenge, and the Persian monarchs, no less than the Islamists who replaced them, saw in Iraq's internal religious and ethnic composition a means of pressuring Baghdad. The shah's cynicism was on full display, for instance, when he instigated various Kurdish uprisings against the Ba'athist regime as a means of readjusting the boundary between the two states. Once he obtained his desired demarcation, he simply cut off the Kurds and left them at the mercy of Saddam Hussein's war machine.

The shah also tried to influence the politics of Lebanon, but somehow the complexities of that nation always eluded him, and he had little desire to spend much money in the Levant. His objectives there were limited to the critical Persian Gulf waterways. Lebanon was not central to his ambition in the same way that Iraq was.

The shah was a Persian nationalist, and unlike his Islamist successors, he was less concerned about spreading an ideology than securing core security objectives. He could be cruel and cynical, but he was never an ideologue with impractical aspirations. If he were somehow resurrected today, he would be amazed by what his successors have achieved in Iraq and Lebanon. He would be impressed by the Islamic Republic's colonisation of Iraq, but he would be flabbergasted by the billions of dollars that the mullahs have spent to nurture Hizbullah in Lebanon, and by their reckless involvement in the Syrian civil war. More than four decades after his overthrow, it is good to see that his reign is starting to be subjected to reasoned historical assessment that rises above polemical screeds.

China and the Islamic World: How the New Silk Road is Transforming Global Politics
Robert Bianchi. Oxford: Oxford University Press, 2019.
£19.99/$29.95. 376 pp.

Among the leadership of the exhausted American imperium, China is widely perceived to be the new superpower. American defence planners have described it as the United States' foremost strategic competitor, and its attempt to knit Asia and the developing world together through its Belt and Road Initiative has provoked fears not just in Washington but in other Western capitals too. Certainly, China brings considerable assets to the emerging geopolitical competition. It has economic clout, and unlike many Western governments, it avoids moral judgements about the despots and crackpots that it encounters in pursuit of its aims.

It may come as a surprise, therefore, to discover that Beijing has yet to crack the code of the Islamic world. The Chinese cannot disentangle the politics of Pakistan any more than the Americans can. China is baffled by Nigeria and remains sceptical of Egypt. Its complex relations with Indonesia and the country's many ethnic groups militate against easy ties with this important nation. China can be arrogant in its search for resources and has irked local stakeholders as its workers have rushed to claim mines and oilfields. All this is lucidly and judiciously detailed in Robert Bianchi's *China and the Islamic World*.

Perhaps the most telling example of China's difficult balancing act is its attempt to forge ties with Iran. On the surface, as revolutionaries who emancipated their country from the clutches of Western imperialism, the Chinese would make good role models for Iran's mullahs. But this has not been the case. Contemporary Chinese premiers are perplexed by the tendency among Iran's clerical oligarchs to take their revolution seriously, having themselves long since abandoned Mao Zedong's destructive postulations. Beijing may want Iran's oil, but it is wary of finding itself in the cross hairs of the US–Iran conflict, and has voted for sanctions against Iran for its nuclear infractions even as it has sustained commercial ties to Tehran. It sees Iran as an important linchpin in the Middle East, but worries about getting too close to a government that may not last. In this sense, the Chinese are more fearful of regime change in Iran than the Western liberals who insist on the Islamic Republic's durability.

China may present the West with its share of challenges, but it is also important to appreciate its limitations. It is still a nation struggling with vast pockets of poverty, environmental problems and a restive middle class. China may have more than 5,000 years of experience as a nation-state, but that does not mean it has figured out all the secrets of statecraft. *China and the Islamic World* is an important contribution to an ongoing attempt to achieve a more nuanced understanding of China and its foreign relations.

Environment and Resources
Jeffrey Mazo

Chernobyl: The History of a Nuclear Catastrophe
Serhii Plokhy. New York: Basic Books, 2018. $32.00. 420 pp.

It has been a generation since Reactor No. 4 at the Vladimir Ilyich Lenin Nuclear Power Plant near the Ukrainian town of Chernobyl suffered an uncontrolled nuclear reaction on 26 April 1986, resulting in a major steam explosion, fire and radioactive release. It was and remains the world's worst nuclear accident, and rivals the Bhopal chemical-plant tragedy in India two years earlier for the worst man-made disaster ever to occur.

Historian Serhii Plokhy, director of the Ukrainian Research Institute at Harvard University, experienced the event and its aftermath at relatively close hand as a young university lecturer in southern Ukraine. In *Chernobyl*, he draws on newly released Communist Party and government documents, including many only available since the Ukrainian revolution of 2014, to produce 'the first comprehensive history of the Chernobyl disaster from the explosion of the nuclear reactor to the closing of the plant in December 2000' (p. xiv).

The narrative of the accident from the initial explosion on 26 April to the drop-off in radioactive emissions on 4–5 May (pp. 59–169) reads like a thriller, but is less important than both his background section on the pre-Chernobyl history of the Soviet nuclear industry (pp. 7–56), and his discussion of the social and political consequences of the disaster (pp. 233–352). In particular, he explores the ways in which the disaster shook confidence in the system; emboldened dissidents; widened rifts between Moscow and the various republican governments, especially Ukraine and Belarus; stimulated glasnost; and ultimately contributed significantly to the fall of the Soviet Union. The importance of Chernobyl in this respect is widely recognised, but Plokhy documents it in detail.

He identifies the roots of the accident in the 'interaction between major flaws in the Soviet political system and major flaws in the nuclear industry' (p. 347). The immediate cause of the accident was human error – a series of missteps during a planned safety test that required disabling the emergency cooling system. But a significant factor behind the disaster was a design flaw in this type of reactor, known to its designers and others in the Soviet nuclear industry since an accident similar to Chernobyl was narrowly averted in Leningrad in 1975 (pp. 66–8). Modifications to the fuel rods were quietly suggested as a result of the Leningrad incident, but no reason was given, and those responsible for other reactors of this type were never told of the urgency of the changes.

Survival | vol. 62 no. 2 | April–May 2020 | pp. 177–182   DOI 10.1080/00396338.2020.1739967

Pressure from higher-ups to delay the test and, in the longer term, to neglect needed maintenance in order to meet targets were also important.

But these flaws, including stovepiping, short-termism, secrecy and wilful denial of risks, while stereotypical traits of the Soviet bureaucracy, are by no means absent from modern Western societies or the industrialising nations that are increasingly looking to nuclear power to help leapfrog their development. Modern nuclear reactors may not have the design flaws peculiar to reactors such as those at Chernobyl. But there are still ten such reactors (albeit modified) in operation in Russia, with planned lifetimes of two to 30 years, and the 2011 Fukushima accident shows that there is more than one path to nuclear disaster. As Plokhy puts it in the last sentence of his preface: 'a new Chernobyl-type dis-aster is more likely to happen if we do not learn the lessons of the one that has already occurred' (p. xvi).

There Is No Planet B: A Handbook for the Make or Break Years
Mike Berners-Lee. Cambridge: Cambridge University Press, 2019. £9.99/$12.95. 300 pp.

'Listen', concluded American poet E.E. Cummings's 1944 sonnet, 'there's a hell of a good universe next door; let's go'. Cummings was making the point that there is in fact nowhere to go to escape the 'hopeless case' of the 'comfortable disease' of progress. Mike Berners-Lee did not coin the phrase 'there is no Planet B' to express this same sentiment in the context of climate change and other environmental challenges (he attributes it to former Costa Rican president José María Figueres in 2011, and praises Ban Ki-moon and Emmanuel Macron for popularising it). But it is the perfect title for this idiosyncratic volume, which he calls 'a handbook of everything' (p. 3) from individual to international decision-making and technical details to broad questions of values and perspectives that collectively offer the chance to make a better future without breaking the planet.

Berners-Lee's holistic approach is nevertheless underpinned by the clear and present danger of climate change. He offers 14 basic climate-change points 'every politician needs to understand before they are fit for office' (pp. 51–3). These three pages neatly boil a hugely complex issue down to its bare funda-mentals in a way that cannot be summarised further without losing nuance, but basically amounts to 'it's real, it's bad, it's urgent, it's complicated, it's eve-ryone's problem and it's not too late'. These 14 points are fleshed out in an appendix (pp. 200–11), which the reader is invited to skip 'if you are sure you already know the basics', although 'even among climate policy makers [that] would put you in a small minority' (p. 200).

The book is designed to be used in multiple ways: one can read it linearly, dip in at random, look up specific topics or even browse topics alphabetically in a 'totally new order with a random logic'. The idea is that the topics interrelate so much that 'we need to hold it all in our heads at the same time' (p. v). By the same token, the endnotes contain, by design, much of substance besides references. (This postmodern structure is perhaps not unconnected with the fact that Berners-Lee's brother Tim is credited with 'inventing' the World Wide Web.) Each chapter consists of a series of questions and answers, covering food, environment, energy, travel and transport, economics, demography, organisation, values and thinking skills.

Berners-Lee writes with wit, clarity, passion and brevity – a spoonful of sugar to help us swallow the cure for our comfortable disease. *There Is No Planet B* is an executive summary of the entire climate (and broader environmental) debate, for people who want to help save the world but don't have the time.

Climate Justice: Hope, Resilience, and the Fight for a Sustainable Future
Mary Robinson. New York and London: Bloomsbury, 2018.
£16.99/$26.00. 176 pp.

Climate Justice is both the title of Mary Robinson's most recent book and the foundation she established in 2010 dedicated to leadership, education and advocacy of a people-centred approach to climate change linking human rights and sustainable development, with a focus on the poor, disempowered and marginalised across the world. Robinson was, in her own words, 'a relative latecomer to the issue of climate change' (p. 2), but her career as a legislator, president of Ireland (1990–97) and United Nations high commissioner for human rights (1997–2002), and her leadership of various non-governmental organisations, has always focused on justice and equity.

Robinson argues that dealing with climate change, both in mitigating its extent and in building resilience to its effects, requires us to 'simultaneously address the underlying injustice in our world and work to eradicate poverty, exclusion, and inequality' (p. 8). Fixing climate change on the backs of the poor is not just unconscionable, it is impossible. And fixing climate change does not just provide an opportunity to promote sustainable development, equity and justice – it requires it. While the Paris agreement provides the last best hope to fix climate change, implementing its goals requires more than nation-level or sub-nation efforts: 'the time has come to bring it to families and communities' (p. 143).

Accordingly, this is a deeply personal volume. Robinson frames it in terms of her own experience, her own family, and her hopes and aspirations for them. But more fundamentally, *Climate Justice* comprises the personal stories of women who have been fighting for climate justice from the grassroots level to international forums and organisations. We meet a Ugandan farmer, a Mississippi hairdresser, an Inupiat scientist, a Sahelian pastoralist, a Sami reindeer herder, a Vietnamese college teacher, and an Australian cosmetics executive and her union-organiser compatriot. Inspired or forced by their individual circumstances to respond to climate change by promoting resilience and policy change, through means running from community organising to international advocacy, these 'ordinary' women have shown extraordinary courage and resilience themselves.

Although there is a strong feminist undercurrent to *Climate Justice* (the subtitle on the 2019 paperback edition is *A Man-made Problem with a Feminist Solution*), Robinson does tell the stories of two men: the former president of Kiribati and a Canadian oil-sands worker. But it is ironic that this book celebrating the grassroots work of extraordinary women is bracketed by a quintessentially anti-feminist and anti-climate-justice figure: Robinson's prologue describes her dismay at the election of US President Donald Trump a few days before the 2016 UN Climate Change Conference in Marrakech, Morroco, a year after the Paris agreement, and her angst over whether to issue a formal statement critical of the president-elect's climate stance. Her final chapter covers the challenge of implementing the Paris agreement in the face of Trump's decision to abandon it. She ends with a note of optimism: Trump's action catalysed a groundswell of support for Paris internationally, sub-nationally and at the grassroots level that could scarcely have been achieved otherwise. It is in the women whose stories she tells in *Climate Justice*, and millions of men and women like them, that our hopes for a sustainable, just and equitable future now reside.

The Water Paradox: Why There Will Never Be Enough Water – and How to Avoid the Coming Crisis
Edward B. Barbier. New Haven, CT: Yale University Press, 2019.
£20.00/$30.00. 294 pp.

'If water is valuable and scarce, why is it so poorly managed?' This is the paradox of Edward Barbier's title (p. 1). The answer, of course, is that water is valuable because it is scarce, and it is scarce because it is poorly managed. There is currently enough readily accessible surface freshwater to meet demand – on average. But it is neither cheap nor easy to move water around, physically or virtually in the form of agricultural and manufactured products, and demand is rising in line with population growth. The distribution of clean freshwater is highly variable in time and space, and many regions, countries and populations have faced or are facing both short-term and sustained water shortages affecting human health and economic activity. This in turn creates a potential for transboundary disputes and 'water grabbing'.

The question of why water is so poorly managed remains. In *The Water Paradox*, Barbier explores the historical reasons for today's mismanagement regime, why it persists and how it can be fixed. He shows that 'current water institutions and innovations are largely relics of past historical eras, when development was dependent on finding and exploiting more water resources' (p. 65). Existing governance and institutional regimes are not just incapable of handling rising water scarcity, they compound it by encouraging waste and ecosystem damage. Barbier identifies the key element as the chronic underpricing of water, which creates a vicious cycle.

His solution involves changing the basis of water management from arbitrary political and administrative boundaries to watersheds or river basins; reforming the legal basis of groundwater and riparian ownership; creating water markets across sectors; pricing water and sanitation services to consumers that reflect actual cost; factoring in the costs of pollution and water quality; investing in small-scale water projects; improving water quality; and supporting the research and development of technologies for resource monitoring and desalinisation, and to improve the efficiency of water use. A series of case studies from six continents shows how these problems are being tested and worked out in practice, the issues they raise and the lessons that can be drawn.

We will, Barbier concludes, need to make drastic changes in our approach to managing global water. The question is whether we will be forced to do so abruptly and chaotically in response to declining water security, ecosystem degradation and resource conflicts, or whether we can replace the vicious cycle with a virtuous one.

Greening the Alliance: The Diplomacy of NATO's Science and Environmental Initiatives
Simone Turchetti. Chicago, IL: University of Chicago Press, 2018. £28.00/$37.50. 264 pp.

Over the last six decades NATO has been a significant sponsor of scientific research in its member states and, laterally, in its partners. One aim, according to the relatively meagre scholarship to date on the Alliance's investment in science, was to generate consensus on a North American model of knowledge production, which has certainly emerged in the post-war period. But researchers have also identified the contradictory impulses of environmental warfare and environmental protection at the heart of the Alliance's initiatives. In *Greening the Alliance*, Simone Turchetti aims to resolve this dilemma and provide a novel understanding of NATO's motives by following the money.

The primary driver was the need for surveillance and intelligence about enemy forces and capabilities, which in turn required greater understanding of the physical characteristics of the air, sea and land domains. NATO's approach was guided by the same intellectual trend of 'Cold War rationality' that informed the work of institutions such as the RAND Corporation and the IISS. But the specifics were worked out not just by military leaders or scientists, but by diplomats: 'priorities were set on the basis of what pieces of scientific knowledge the allies intended to share; what they viewed as decisive to national research; and, especially, what else they were prepared to embark on to please or appease other allies' (p. 4). Moreover, argues Turchetti, scientific research was not just the subject of extensive negotiations, it was 'a key device of NATO diplomacy' that was 'absolutely decisive in the life of this organization' (p. 5).

He traces this theme from its earliest roots in joint aeronautics work and warning, tracking systems development through the International Geophysical Year (1957–58) and the 'Sputnik moment'; the Alliance crisis of the 1960s and a parallel crisis in its Science Committee; the increased emphasis on environmental science in the 1970s (the 'greening' of the title); NATO's fraught record on climate change in the 1980s; and its post-Cold War reorientation towards the metaphorical environment of cyberspace. Along the way, Turchetti explores how the contingent personal interactions and attitudes of key players, as well as institutional imperatives and multilateral diplomacy, shaped the Alliance's approach to science and environmental research.

Meticulously researched and clearly argued, *Greening the Alliance* is a major contribution to the literature on NATO, on the history of post-war science and environmental studies in general, and on how science and diplomacy interact in multilateral institutions more broadly. A fascinating book in its own right, it is also essential background reading for the existential environmental–diplomatic challenges of the coming decades.

United States
David C. Unger

The Age of Illusions: How America Squandered Its Cold War Victory
Andrew Bacevich. New York: Metropolitan Books, 2020.
$27.00. 224 pp.

Andrew Bacevich doesn't just second-guess Washington's policy choices; he challenges the ideological premises and strategic doctrines that have guided official Washington for decades. Those same premises and doctrines, he argues, guide the government-in-waiting of temporarily out-of-power foreign-policy specialists. In ten previous books, Bacevich has questioned the militarisation of American politics, the hubris of American empire, the limits of American power and the mechanisms that have marginalised criticism of Washington's self-perpetuating foreign-policy consensus.

In *The Age of Illusions*, Bacevich serves up his most developed and wide-ranging critique yet of what he sees as the destructive ideologies driving American society to ruin, exploring these in their military, economic and cultural dimensions. Bacevich, who taught history and international relations at Boston University, is now president of the Quincy Institute for Responsible Statecraft, launched last year with initial funding from George Soros and Charles Koch. Since the Iraq War, if not earlier, elements of the human-rights left and the libertarian right have been discovering common ground over the damage inflicted on American liberties and solvency, and on the wider world, by Washington's bipartisan national-security state and its forever wars.

Bacevich's previous books won him a following among the anti-militarist, anti-neoliberal left. But Bacevich has always made clear that he considers himself a Catholic conservative. In this book, he weaves his own brand of cultural conservatism into the larger argument. These views have little in common with those of most Americans who today call themselves conservatives. Bacevich is a strong advocate for the rights of women, LGBT people, and racial and ethnic minorities. What he preaches against is what he sees as an emergent ideology of personal freedom detached from a corresponding sense of civic responsibility. That ideology, he argues, is deeply corrosive of America's democratic society.

Bacevich is a clear and lively writer. Not content to resort to the familiar charge that the Democrats and liberal media suffer from 'Trump derangement syndrome', Bacevich evokes Herman Melville's *Moby Dick*, memorably suggesting that Donald Trump has become 'the Great White Whale of the chattering classes' (p. 183). Bacevich also draws on other American literary and film classics, such as William Wyler's film *The Best Years of Our Lives*, L. Frank Baum's *The Wonderful Wizard of Oz* and John Updike's series of Rabbit Angstrom novels, to keep his narrative entertaining and original.

While devastatingly critical of Trump, Bacevich sees the president as more of a symptom than a cause of America's division and decline. At one point, he likens Trump and his 2016 opponent, Hillary Clinton, to William Shakespeare's Rosencrantz and Guildenstern, 'pawns in a drama they do not begin to comprehend' (p. 194). While advancing the plot, these 'throwaway characters do not determine its outcome' (p. 194).

To illuminate what he sees as the real plot, Bacevich points to three portents from the 1992 presidential campaign: Republican insurgent Pat Buchanan, representing a form of proto-Trumpian tribalist nationalism; third-party contender Ross Perot and his protectionist populism; and the Democratic candidate's wife, Hillary Clinton, standing for the untethered ideology of personal freedom that so disturbs Bacevich. Clear lines can be drawn from Buchanan and Perot to Trump, but Bacevich makes a less convincing case for the role he assigns to the younger Hillary Clinton. In fact, Bacevich presents two very different Hillarys in this book. While the 1992 Clinton is presented, unfairly I think, as a stealthy advance guard for what Bacevich sees as a destructive shedding of cultural constraints, the 2016 Clinton is more fairly pilloried as the embodiment of an out-of-touch elite establishment.

The Great Delusion: Liberal Dreams and International Realities
John J. Mearsheimer. New Haven, CT: Yale University Press, 2018. $30.00. 313 pp.

John Mearsheimer, who teaches political science and international relations at the University of Chicago, has earned a reputation as a provocateur by challenging conventional wisdom on a variety of sensitive and high-profile subjects: Ukraine's 1991 decision to give up its nuclear weapons (a move he thought unwise), NATO enlargement (which he saw as a costly mistake), the 2003 US invasion of Iraq (which he opposed) and, not least, his controversial 2007 book with Stephen Walt on *The Israel Lobby and U.S. Foreign Policy*.

Mearsheimer takes these positions not because he is a contrarian, but because he is a realist (more precisely, an 'offensive neorealist') who disagrees with the dominant liberal-internationalist school of international relations. *The Great Delusion* is his extended critique of that school's theories. The theoretical model on which his own reasoning is built is both the strength and the weakness of this book.

Theoretical realism is a venerable tradition reaching back through Niccolò Machiavelli to Thucydides. Those authors often illustrated their theories through the behaviour of human actors, but Mearsheimer prefers pure theory. The gains this allows in terms of theoretical clarity are offset by the appearance of reductionism, diminishing the persuasiveness of his arguments.

In Mearsheimer's model, agency resides primarily with states, not the people who constitute them or the leaders who direct them. Because the international arena is a Darwinian anarchy with no sovereign – or, as the author puts it, no 'night watchman' – states must put their survival first, since without survival, there can be nothing else. This obliges states to maximise their power, which generally compels liberal states to act on realist principles and to embrace nationalism. This is because nationalism, not liberalism, drives the actions of most states, and because nationalism can, as liberalism cannot, rally necessary domestic backing behind realist policies, up to and including the use of military force. Mearsheimer favours liberalism in domestic politics, but he finds that liberalism's core principle of pluralism only works at home because of the presence of a night watchman.

Liberal states get into trouble when 'unipolar moments' tempt them to replace the anarchy of the international arena with their own policies of liberal global hegemony. They then concern themselves with the internal arrangements of other countries, a mistake that encourages them to attempt international social engineering, also known as 'nation building'. Externally promoted nation building can never work, in part because, while some states practise liberalism some of the time, all states must practise nationalism all of the time.

George Orwell foresaw totalitarian superpowers waging forever wars against ever-shifting foes. Mearsheimer sees such dangers when liberal-internationalist superpowers operate in what they mistake for a unipolar environment. These states are also doomed to forever wars because their domestic ideologies require them to 'make the world safe for democracy' by defeating and re-engineering the rogue states that do not accept liberal rules and are seen to threaten the liberal superpowers' own survival. But as Mearsheimer argues, these wars threaten liberties and liberalism at home. This is evident, he says, from the example of United States' foreign policy in the quarter-century after the Cold War.

Does Mearsheimer's theoretical analysis hold true in practice? Mearsheimer gleefully demonstrates that for liberal-hegemonist theory to work in the real world, one must, like Lewis Carroll's Red Queen, believe six impossible things before breakfast. But one must also accept seemingly divergent assumptions for Mearsheimer's offensive-realist theory to fit the real world of American foreign policy. Liberal hegemonists, he writes, always overestimate other societies' appetite for their social engineering ('Iraqis will greet us with flowers') and thus underestimate the hazards of war. Elsewhere, he writes that liberal hegemonists are always obliged to consider the worst case that emerges from their assumptions (Iraq has weapons of mass destruction and/or is supporting international terrorist groups) and then act on it. The United States' liberal-hegemonist foreign policy of recent decades has been prone to both kinds of errors. Yet so too was the realist policy of Richard Nixon and Henry Kissinger half a century ago. Mearsheimer's central argument that liberal-hegemonist states are necessarily bound to act this or that way is, at the very least, open to question.

The Hell of Good Intentions: America's Foreign Policy Elite and the Decline of U.S. Primacy
Stephen M. Walt. New York: Farrar, Straus and Giroux, 2018.
£21.99/$28.00. 384 pp.

Like John Mearsheimer, with whom he co-wrote *The Israel Lobby and U.S. Foreign Policy* in 2007, Stephen Walt is a realist in a field dominated by liberal-internationalist idealists. But Walt's realism differs from Mearsheimer's, deriving more from his analysis of specific policies than from the dehumanised abstractions of international-relations theory. And unlike Mearsheimer, who believes military force can play a healthy role in the international system, Walt favours alternatives to direct US military interventions, reserving American force as a reluctant last resort. That makes Walt, who teaches at Harvard University, a 'defensive neorealist'.

In *The Hell of Good Intentions*, Walt argues that the track record of American foreign policy since the end of the Cold War has been appallingly bad. From Washington's unrewarding and unending interventions in Afghanistan and Iraq, through its worsening relations with Russia and China, to its misreading and mishandling of the Arab Spring, failure has succeeded failure and, as a result, an enviable period of global security has given way to a more challenging era of global insecurity. This did not happen by itself, or solely because of external malevolence. Walt traces these failures to the American foreign-policy establishment's commitment to an unwise, unattainable goal: liberal hegemony. Why, he asks, despite its almost unbroken record of failure, does this commitment to liberal hegemony go largely unchallenged? And why do its practitioners carry on from one Democratic or Republican administration to the next, 'failing upward', as he puts it?

Walt seeks answers through an extended examination of what Barack Obama's speechwriter and foreign-policy adviser Ben Rhodes once called 'the blob' – that extended constellation of current and former foreign-policy practitioners, the think tanks they perch in while their faction is temporarily out of power and their big-name journalistic acolytes. It is this blob, according to Walt, that enforces conformity to approved doctrines of liberal hegemony, marginalises dissent and dissenters, excuses failure, rigs the marketplace of ideas and pre-empts accountability. Walt names names, giving us a long bipartisan list that includes Elliott Abrams, Martin Indyk, William Kristol, Daniel Kurtzer, Aaron David Miller, Dennis Ross and Paul Wolfowitz. The overrepresentation of pro-Israel Middle East specialists on this list may have something to do with the bruising fights waged over *The Israel Lobby*. But Walt's account of the recycling of failed foreign-policy ideas often hits its mark.

Walt angrily condemns the foreign-policy establishment for putting the goal of 'improving the lives of ordinary Americans' in second place behind 'preserving America's capacity to shape events around the globe' (p. 172). He sees Trump's election in 2016 as, in part, the deserved comeuppance of a failed foreign-policy elite. But, he continues, the Trump administration's serial incompetence and incoherence in matters of foreign policy have not made things better. Walt's disgust with Trump's policies in some areas seem not so different from that of his derided 'blob'.

In place of failed liberal hegemony, Walt recommends offshore balancing as a more promising, less sacrificing way of preserving US global primacy on the cheap, restoring the strategic and fiscal solvency that has been lost through the last quarter-century's misadventures in unattainable global hegemonism. He would focus US foreign policy on specific areas of vital interest, permanently station fewer US troops abroad and send Americans into foreign combat only as a last resort. He sometimes overstates his case by too easily dismissing possible national-security trade-offs that might come with a less activist US foreign policy. Greater solvency might come at the cost of greater risks. Walt still makes a convincing case that the present course is unsustainable, but as he acknowledges, selling the American voter on this less ambitious global strategy will not be easy.

The Forgotten Americans: An Economic Agenda for a Divided Nation
Isabel Sawhill. New Haven, CT: Yale University Press, 2018.
£20.00/$28.00. 255 pp.

Isabel Sawhill has written many well-received books about unemployment, poverty and stagnant social mobility, and how government programmes can most effectively address these problems. She brings to *The Forgotten Americans* an impressive amount of fieldwork, both her own and that of her

Brookings Institution colleagues. She has also had hands-on political experience as an associate director of the Office of Management and Budget during the Clinton administration.

In this book, she seeks to digest the lessons of the 2016 US presidential election by exploring the plight of what she calls the white working class, a group that for years mostly voted for Democrats, but in 2016 gave Trump his margin of victory in the Rust Belt states of Michigan, Ohio, Pennsylvania and Wisconsin. Sawhill defines this demographic as white working-age adults without four-year college degrees whose annual family incomes are below $70,000. This definition, in common use by social scientists and journalists, comes with built-in distortions. It takes no account of what people actually do (or did) for a living, and it filters out more educated white workers. 'Working class' once meant people with manual skills and manual jobs, people who worked in factories, workshops, mines or construction sites, not office towers. They typically felt something in common with other such workers, and in many cases joined unions.

That was the old working class that regularly voted for Democrats from the New Deal through to the Great Society. It was a class that rightly or wrongly felt it had some political agency. By contrast, Sawhill's forgotten Americans are 'left behinds', with more anger than agency. They are people she believes more fortunate Americans, like her intended readers, as well as the government, must do more for, lest their rage, mobilised by demagogues, wreck the otherwise welcome prospects of globalisation, free trade and liberal democracy. The book reads like the work of a social scientist who has glimpsed pitchforks and torches, a former budget hawk who has come to see the value of entitlements as an insurance policy against populism. But not, she explains, entitlements in their present form.

Sawhill identifies today's underlying problem as the lack of well-paying jobs, a view shared by her forgotten Americans. Rather than address possible systemic causes such as automation, deregulation or neoliberal trade agreements, Sawhill devotes most of the book to advocating new government programmes to mitigate their effects. These are meant not simply to address economic needs, but to do so consistently with what she finds to be the core values of the forgotten members of the white working-class: work, family and education. In deference to those values, Sawhill is ready to set aside or dilute programmes she concedes might make more effective or efficient use of taxpayer dollars, such as direct income transfers or a guaranteed basic income. She offers potentially useful proposals such as changing income-security programmes to allow for more time off earlier in life for child-rearing and education in exchange for less later on. She also advocates education and training programmes to raise the skill levels of American workers, since the least-skilled Americans are generally the least in demand in today's labour markets.

Would reskilling yield more well-paying American jobs? Highly skilled workers in lower-wage countries would still be competing for the same work. And some of Sawhill's ideas for paying for her programmes, such as making Pell Grants for college contingent on participating in national service, recall the nanny-state liberalism forgotten American voters have repeatedly rejected. Reading this book in 2020 is like travelling by time machine to a world we are unlikely to see again, where bipartisanship is possible and the potentially helpful findings of social scientists command broad respect. The book claims to speak for what the forgotten Americans really want. But does it? And can it?

American Dialogue: The Founders and Us
Joseph J. Ellis. New York: Alfred A. Knopf, 2018. $27.95. 283 pp.

Joseph Ellis is known for his individual and group biographies of America's founding generation – the men who led the war for independence, shaped the US Constitution and guided the new nation through its formative decades. The many years he has spent in the archival company of these men has given him an easy familiarity with their political views, intellectual development and personal interactions. He is also an exceptionally graceful writer.

Ellis puts these qualities to good use in *American Dialogue*. His central idea is to mine the thoughts, writings and deeds of the founders for insights on contemporary American problems. Dialogue is technically a misnomer, since the present cannot be heard by the past. But Ellis enriches our view of past and present by examining both in the frame of problems that were with us then and are still with us today, albeit sometimes in altered forms.

The exercise works because Ellis avoids the obvious perils of hagiography and anachronism. He gives us the founders in their full, and not uniformly admirable, complexity. The book delves into Thomas Jefferson's painfully contradictory legacy on race, John Adams's deep misgivings about equality, James Madison's opportunistically shifting perspectives on law depending on which side of a controversy he was involved in, and George Washington's cold, calculating foreign-policy realism (with the notable exception of his failed attempts to steer the nation toward more honourable treatment of Native Americans). Ellis's founders are imperfect mortals, their special gifts called forth by the demanding times in which they lived.

Ellis makes good use of the extended correspondence between Adams and Jefferson in their later years. This allows him to feature a real-time dialogue within the book's larger intergenerational dialogue. Both kinds of dialogue allow Ellis to convey what he contends are opposed but essential elements of American life. The United States is not a single entity with a unitary history. Rather, Americans are a complex and contradictory people with a complex and contradictory heritage.

Summing up, Ellis points to three great achievements and two great tragedies of the founding generation that continue to define and shape today's America. These are the founding of the first nation-sized republic and of the first wholly secular state, and the demonstration, in defiance of conventional wisdom going back to Aristotle, that sovereignty could successfully be divided between states and the central government. (Today, of course, the operating definitions of American federalism derive more from the Civil War than the revolutionary era.) The two tragedies are the treatment of Native Americans and African Americans.

Other historians will question some of Ellis's contentions. While he argues, for example, that the Louisiana Purchase was Jefferson's great lost opportunity to find a geographical exit from the curse of slavery, perhaps the real lesson of subsequent decades of failed compromises over the new territories is that there was no exit to be had short of civil war. Even more questionable is Ellis's claim that the Supreme Court has until recently stayed above the partisan political fray. The partisanship that surrounded *Marbury v. Madison* and *Dred Scott*, two of the most consequential decisions of the court's first century, seems to suggest otherwise.

Letter to the Editor

Trump Unrestrained

Sir,

Georg Löfflmann's article 'America First and the Populist Impact on US Foreign Policy' in the December 2019–January 2020 issue was a constructive attempt to make sense of a maddeningly amorphous concept. Despite the challenges, I think his analysis is generally accurate. However, his suggestion that I am an 'intellectual sympathiser' (p. 127) with President Donald Trump's 'America First' vision, citing my book *The Power Problem* as evidence (p. 136, note 76), is badly misleading.

A central argument in *The Power Problem*, published nearly seven years before Trump's entry into the 2016 presidential campaign, was that US foreign-policy elites should take account of Americans' rising opposition to costly wars and unnecessary foreign entanglements, and embrace instead a vision of global engagement through peaceful means. I warned that:

> if Washington refuses to do so, or simply tinkers around the margins while largely ignoring public sentiment, then we should not be surprised if many Americans choose to throw the good engagement out with the bad, opting for genuine isolationism, with all of its nasty connotations.

> That would be tragic. It would also be dangerous … If Americans reject the peaceful coexistence, trade, and voluntary person-to-person contact that has been the touchstone of US foreign policy since the nation's founding, the gap between the United States and the rest of the world will grow only worse, with negative ramifications for US security for many years to come. (pp. 168–9)

I submit that that is precisely what has occurred on Trump's watch.

More recently, I and others have explained why Trump's approach to the world is inconsistent with a foreign-policy vision grounded in realism

Survival | vol. 62 no. 2 | April–May 2020 | pp. 191–192 DOI 10.1080/00396338.2020.1739969

and restraint, and we have outlined alternatives that don't merely take us back to the status quo ante. For example, John Glaser, A. Trevor Thrall and I published 'Towards a More Prudent American Grand Strategy' in the October–November 2019 issue of this journal. The article is derived from our book, *Fuel to the Fire: How Trump Made America's Broken Foreign Policy Even Worse (and How We Can Recover)*. Both the book and the article detail an approach that diverges radically from Trump's 'America First'. In the book, for example, we write:

> Notwithstanding sporadic and shallow likenesses … the substantive similarities between Trump's vision of US foreign policy and that prescribed under a grand strategy of restraint are scarce. Indeed, in a certain sense, Trump's foreign policy is closer to the *inverse* of restraint. Advocates of restraint tend to favor low-tariff free trade, liberal immigration policies, robust diplomacy, and a reduced military role for the United States. By contrast, Trump favors economic protectionism, restricted immigration, weakened diplomacy, and energetic militarism. (p. 66)

In his article, Löfflmann correctly notes that 'Trump's nationalist–populist attack on the US foreign-policy establishment has produced the most intense debate' about America's role in the world in over a generation, but admits that any tenuous 'overlap of ideas [has] not translated into anything like an endorsement of America First overall, or realist support for Trump's foreign policy in practice' (p. 127). That should be the key lesson from the last three years. If there is to be a new approach to US foreign policy, Donald Trump should not be its author.

Christopher Preble
Washington DC

America and Israel: The Thrill Is Gone

Steven Simon

I

Mitt Romney's signature foreign-policy line in his 2012 bid for the White House was that Barack Obama 'threw Israel under the bus' and 'disrespected' the Jewish state. It was a potent phrase. It was also a departure from the usual campaign discourse. Until that race, Israel had been largely a bipartisan issue in American politics. Both parties had lined up behind US support for Israel, perhaps with differing points of emphasis, and neither was inclined to use the US–Israel relationship as a political football. Israel's security was a sacred American cause, not the parochial concern of a particular political party. Indeed, for decades the strategy of the American Israel Public Affairs Committee (AIPAC) has been to elevate the relationship into a principle that no patriotic, responsible American could dispute. Until 2012, this strategy had worked.

It's not hard to see why. Israel appealed to the American imagination. It had all the ingredients of American exceptionalism. Israel's cultivation of a desolate wilderness and settlement of remote outposts surrounded by hostile natives looked a lot like the westward expansion of the frontier.

Steven Simon is a professor in the practice of international relations at Colby College, an analyst at the Quincy Institute for Responsible Statecraft and a contributing editor to *Survival*. He was US National Security Council senior director for the Middle East and North Africa from 2011 through 2012. His book *The Long Goodbye: The US and the Middle East from the Islamic Revolution to the Arab Spring* will be published next year. He is co-author, with Dana H. Allin, of *Our Separate Ways: The Struggle for the Future of the U.S.–Israel Alliance* (PublicAffairs, 2016).

Survival | vol. 62 no. 2 | April–May 2020 | pp. 193–204   DOI 10.1080/00396338.2020.1739971

Sabras as cowboys and Palestinians as Indians were a natural fit. Popular culture reinforced the connection. Hollywood shaped American perceptions of Israel, as exemplified by the 1960 blockbuster *Exodus*, directed by Otto Preminger. Pat Boone, a politically conservative Christian pop singer and actor, sang the title track. It summed up the Zionist case in terms to which American Christians could easily relate: 'This land is mine, God gave this land to me.' The message was that Israelis, like the European settlers of the American continent, were fleeing persecution, taming a wilderness, self-reliant and independent, and beleaguered by unruly locals. The movie emulated memes familiar to fans of westerns. In one scene, Ari Ben Canaan, played by Paul Newman, brings his *shiksa* partner, played by Eva Marie Saint, to the kibbutz where he was raised. His mother comes out of their humble prairie shack, squinting into the sun with her hand shading her eyes, her hair in a bun. It could have been a scene out of *Shane*.

The 1967 Six-Day War seemed a natural culmination of the narrative. A small army defending the frontier defeats an onslaught of angry marauders through sheer grit, iron discipline, audacity, and mastery of Western technology and organisation. The society the army defended was virtuous: a simple people working the land and sharing their meagre goods, while creating great universities and siding with the West in the global war against international communism. This image captivated liberal American anti-communists. It was immensely gratifying to US Jews as well, for obvious reasons. American (and Soviet) military power had brought the Holocaust to an end a mere 22 years earlier. US Jews were beginning to appreciate their potential as a voting bloc, and were less worried about drawing unhealthy attention to themselves in the process. As they settled into their role as normal Americans, intermarriage rates began to rise – a trend that is now weakening American–Jewish ties to Israel. But even then the community's interests were not defined in expected ways.

In response to domestic pressure to intervene diplomatically on Israel's side during the crisis preceding the 1967 war, Lyndon Johnson, on his own and through his close Jewish friends, proposed a quid pro quo. If the Jews would get behind the Vietnam War, the administration might be more forward-leaning on Israel's behalf. Leaders of the American–Jewish community could not sign up to this deal. For them, social justice at home and an ethical foreign policy were the main priorities. But American–Jewish interest in Israel grew, especially in the wake of the 1973 war, partly because it was such a close-run thing. The Syrians had nearly wiped out an Israeli armoured brigade and badly mauled another, making it all the way to the pre-June 1967 border. Had they advanced unimpeded, they would have penetrated the central valley of northern Israel and wrought considerable havoc. But Israeli forces stopped them, owing to the Nixon administration's swift airlift of armour to Israel, which was motivated less by sentiment than by a strong interest in repelling a Soviet client.

Between Jimmy Carter's presidency and Ronald Reagan's first term, decisive shifts occurred in the politics of both countries. In Israel, Likud comprehensively defeated the Labor Party, and the New Deal Democratic ascendancy ended in the United States. Although Menachem Begin, Israel's dour right-wing leader, did not share Reagan's sunny optimism, the two embodied a convergence of conservative values and projected tough certainty. As the Cold War intensified, Reagan suppressed his distaste for Begin and enlisted Israel as a military partner in anticipation of Soviet aggression in the Persian Gulf and eastern Mediterranean. A relationship rooted in shared values evolved into one also based on over-lapping strategic interests, substituting hard-headed calculation for fuzzy idealism. Some Israelis were troubled by this shift. If we ground the rela-tionship with the US in strategic terms rather than democratic values, they asked, what happens if US interests change? As the US pivots to Asia, this question has taken on an ominous cast, and not just for Israel.

Hollywood's take on the US and Israel reflected this evolving American approach. In 1977, Paramount Pictures released *Black Sunday*, a taut thriller directed by John Frankenheimer about a Palestinian plot to attack the Super Bowl using the Goodyear blimp as a gigantic bomb. The conspira-tors include an unhinged Vietnam vet (Bruce Dern), a chilling German radical (Marthe Keller) and a clutch of deceptively sensitive-looking young Palestinian men who were, in reality, stone killers. The Israelis pick up intelligence about the plot, but the FBI – earnest, sceptical of Israeli spies, afraid of being hoodwinked by Jews with an agenda, naively committed to civil liberties and due process – won't act. It falls to Robert Shaw's lugubrious Israeli agent to end-run the feckless Americans to save the Super Bowl.

Now the Israelis were to be admired not because they were righteous, but because they were prepared to do what had to be done without getting wrapped around the axle of human rights and rule of law. The US, it was implied, would do well to emulate Israel's ruthlessness. As the liberal moment in the US began to fade, Israel would become the darling of the right. There was, to be sure, a revival of the old order during the Clinton administration, when Yitzhak Rabin led the Israeli government and he and Palestinian leader Yasser Arafat signed the Oslo Accord on the south lawn of the White House. But a Jewish terrorist assassinated Rabin shortly afterward and Palestinian extremists went on a killing spree within Israel. The opponents of Oslo on both sides managed to destroy it. Thereafter the Israeli right wing advanced steadily toward its current command of the electorate. George W. Bush made an 11th-hour attempt to broker a peace agreement, but his Israeli and Palestinian counterparts were too weak to follow through.

II

Barack Obama and Benjamin Netanyahu were famously antagonistic. Netanyahu enjoyed baiting his counterpart and humiliating him in Congress. Hence Romney's reliance on Obama, Israel and the bus for his campaign mantra. He, if not his campaign, believed that Obama's alleged betrayal of Israel and Netanyahu's unmistakable contempt for Obama would split the Jewish vote and confer an edge in closely contested cities. His hope was misplaced. Obama retained 69% of the Jewish vote. This may have been nine points lower than it was in 2008, but in 2012 the president lost ten points among whites overall in any case. In the interim, Orthodox Jews had completed their shift to the Republican Party and, as Jewish identity began to weaken, Jews in general were freer to vote Republican just like other well-to-do American whites.[1] Still, the vast majority of Jewish voters either didn't believe the 'under the bus' narrative or didn't care.

Curious about these results, I met with one of the lions of the American Jewish community, who over the past 30 years had enjoyed easy access to the White House. I asked him whether Romney's politicisation of the US–Israel relationship was a fluke or a feature of future campaigns. He observed that up until the 2012 campaign, he could walk into the Oval Office and warn the occupant, regardless of party, not to cross the community on a particular issue because of the electoral consequences. In light of Obama's capture of the Jewish vote despite Romney's savaging him as a betrayer of Israel, my interlocutor predicted that no Jewish community leader would ever again be able to threaten blowback. For him, the 2012 election was clearly a watershed, and not in a good way.

He was right. The Trump campaign, replicating Romney's ploy, instrumentalised the US–Israel relationship to bludgeon Democrats. Yet despite Donald Trump's baroque praise for Israel during the campaign, his pledge to tear up the Iran nuclear deal and his affection for his Orthodox Jewish son-in-law, he did no better against Hillary Clinton than Romney had done against Obama, garnering only 24% of the Jewish vote.[2] This was unsurprising in part because Jewish ties to the Democratic Party are historically deep – Jews provide half of all contributions to the party[3] – while Trump was flirting with an extreme right that carries strains of anti-Semitism. Trump himself characterised torch-carrying neo-Nazis chanting 'Jews will not replace us' in Charlottesville as 'very fine people'.

American Jews care less about Israel than they used to. Why is a complicated question. To the extent that concern for Israel is wrapped up in religious conviction, the long-standing focus on it was bound to diminish as religious commitment weakened.[4] In an analysis of in-depth surveys by the Pew Research Center, 28% of Jewish Americans were characterised as 'solidly secular' and 17% as 'religion resistors', who think religion does more harm than good. Combining these two categories indicates that nearly half of the Americans who self-identify as Jewish are either indifferent to Judaism as a religion or hostile to it. In this respect, Jewish Americans merely typify a broader trend toward religious disaffiliation in the United States.[5] There are, of course, secular Jewish Americans who do strongly support Israel for reasons of ethnic pride – Israel is both Jewish and powerful – or because they view Israel, in a conceptual sort of way, as both a refuge from and response to the twentieth-century annihilation of European Jewry. When asked what it means to be Jewish in a 2013 Pew survey, the top response was 'remembering the Holocaust'.[6] Presumably this priority will recede as the last Holocaust survivors die and the event itself fades further into the intangible past.

At the other end of the spectrum, over 20% of Jewish Americans qualify as 'Sunday stalwarts' – that is, religiously observant synagogue-goers. This distribution is bimodal. As Steven Cohen, a leading Jewish sociologist, has pointed out, there are relatively few American Jews occupying the space between the Sunday stalwarts on the one hand, and secularists and religion resistors on the other.[7] One plausible scenario, given the alluvial effect of generations of intermarriage among secular or secular-ish Jews, is that the non-Orthodox will eventually reach a vanishing point, while the Orthodox segment of the demographic curve increases due to greater cohesiveness and higher fertility rates. This is the future that a gleeful Netanyahu forecast to his aides last year, telling them that liberal Jews would 'disappear in a generation or two', thereby strengthening the hold of Orthodox Jews and evangelicals on US policy toward Israel.[8]

Whether or not that happens, the disenchantment of a good many American Jews is going to grow. Although remembering the Holocaust is the essential ingredient of Jewish identity for 73% of Pew's respondents, leading an 'ethical/moral life' was the next most popular choice. Caring about Israel came in far lower at 43%. And that was more than five years ago. The most recent J Street poll shows that only 4% of American Jews hold Israel as one of their top two concerns.[9]

In recent years, Israeli policy has come to be seen as increasingly misaligned with the ethical and moral life that most American Jews regard as the core of Jewish meaning. Netanyahu's enthusiastic embrace of Trump – and Saudi Crown Prince Muhammad bin Salman – places the prime minister squarely at odds with the ethos of most American Jews. According to a study conducted by the American Jewish Committee in October 2018, only 34% of American Jews approved of Trump's handling of the US–Israel relationship, while 57% disapprove.[10] *The Economist* and YouGov looked more broadly in 2018 at Americans as a whole, and discovered that support for Israel was dropping sharply among women and millennials.

Only 25% of 18- to 29-year-olds see Israel as an ally, just 29% of women and only 19% of African Americans.[11] This generational, racial and gender seam appears likely to widen.

These trends are clearly reflected in the growing gap between Democratic and Republican perceptions of Israel and the bilateral relationship. Democrats at this point sympathise about equally with Israelis (27%) and Palestinians (25%). The remainder sympathise either with both parties or with neither (23%), or say they don't know (25%).[12] These numbers represent a significant drop in Israel's status in the past two years alone, coinciding with Trump's cosseting of Israel, moving the US Embassy from Tel Aviv to Jerusalem, and punitive US measures directed at Palestinians, such as cutting funding for the United Nations Relief and Works Agency for Palestine Refugees in the Near East (UNRWA), which administers Palestinian refugee camps.

The 2016 Democratic convention fight between Bernie Sanders and Hillary Clinton over platform language regarding Israel reflected these dynamics. Although Sanders's wing did not get everything it wanted, in particular a reference to Israel's occupation, it did prevail on Clinton's team to accept the first-ever reference to Palestinian rights in the party platform, stipulating that in addition to securing Israel, a two-state solution must provide the Palestinians with 'independence, sovereignty, and dignity'.[13] Older Democrats have expressed some anxiety about additional pro-Palestinian changes presaged by the revamped platform.[14] Intensifying this dynamic, in February Sanders repudiated AIPAC as supporting a bigoted president and refused to address the annual AIPAC policy conference – a major event that typically draws presidents and presidential aspirants as speakers. AIPAC had just run – and then withdrawn – a series of Facebook advertisements that savaged Obama, thereby affirming a broad perception that AIPAC had lashed itself to the Republican Party. Sanders's stance placed his rivals for the Democratic nomination in a difficult position. While Joe Biden, Michael Bloomberg and Elizabeth Warren indicated their readiness to address the massive audience that the AIPAC conference typically attracts, Pete Buttigieg and Amy Klobuchar followed Sanders's lead. A better illustration of the generational divide within the party regarding the US–Israel relationship would be hard to imagine.

The US Christian evangelical community, for its part, has not been standing still. A generational divide has opened up within it as well. Younger evangelicals are more open to lesbian, gay, bisexual, transgender and queer (LGBTQ) rights (including gay marriage), are more concerned about income inequality and its adverse effects on social cohesion and public health (especially as manifested in the opioid crisis), and are as worried about climate change as other sensible young Americans. This shift in priorities extends to Israel and its current policies. If they see video coverage of demonstrations in Gaza and ask themselves what Jesus would do, firing live ammunition probably does not leap to mind. A December 2017 poll of evangelicals that ricocheted through the media showed that younger ones are more or less indifferent to Israel. Regardless of age, 60% of the respondents thought that Christians should 'do more to love and care for Palestinians', but among younger evangelicals the proportion is higher. About one in five sees the rebirth of Israel as an injustice, and nearly half aren't sure.[15] While most evangelicals remain in Israel's camp, the influence of these emerging alternative views is only just beginning to register.

III

The election of a handful of new, left-leaning congressional representatives in the 2019 midterm elections – including Ilhan Omar, Rashida Tlaib and Alexandria Ocasio-Cortez – will not greatly affect the Democratic stance on the US–Israel relationship for the 2020 US election. The party leadership has the overriding task of containing a runaway White House. And key Democratic supporters of Israel in both chambers – senators Chuck Schumer, Jon Kyl and Bob Menendez, and representatives Steny Hoyer and Eliot Engel – have already declared that Israel remains in good hands on Capitol Hill. A real and crucial question is what happens when Trump leaves office and is replaced by a Democrat.

In the US–Israel relationship, Congress functions as a gigantic ATM. It will have dispensed $38 billion to Israel between 2016 and 2026. When US strategic interests are not seen to be at stake, the White House will generally take the politically expedient course of deferring to Congress or acceding to Israeli requests. The White House has occasionally gone its own way on a strategic issue, as Obama did in blocking Iran's path to a nuclear weapon through negotiation rather than military action, to Netanyahu's consternation. During the Gaza crisis of 2014, a senior Israel Defense Forces (IDF) officer explained to the *Wall Street Journal* that Israel's disregard for the White House was only natural; Israel had Congress, which was the real prize.[16] Serious policy differences between the American president and the Israeli prime minister might or might not be bridgeable – Israel has little control over them – but Congress could be relied upon to raise the political cost to the White House of such differences while unflaggingly appropriating large sums. Until 2017, however, neither Republican nor Democratic presidents since the Eisenhower era had materially subordinated the United States' strategic interests to Israel's. Trump, in prioritising the interests of Israel and other regional powers over those of the United States, represents a departure from the historical pattern.

Since the level of US foreign-military financing and direct funding of anti-ballistic-missile development and production is locked in through 2026, and a new administration would want to avoid steps that appeared to threaten Israeli security, a Democratic administration would find other ways to reverse Trump's excesses and distance itself from a right-wing Israeli government. Firstly, the White House would likely move quickly to re-enter the Iran nuclear deal as a state party and suspend US nuclear-related sanctions against Iran; naturally, this would depend on whether Iran were still in substantial compliance and the other states had not dropped out of the agreement. Secondly, given the overwhelming likelihood that the Palestinians will continue to reject the peace plan that the Trump administration rolled out in January 2020 – which defers statehood for years, situates the Palestinian capital outside the boundaries of Jerusalem in the town of Abu Dis and annexes a substantial portion of the West Bank – the incoming team would probably be inclined to tackle the peace process yet again, but with a difference. The White House could spell out the terms of a deal it considered fair to both sides (something no administration has done since the Reagan Plan), recognise a Palestinian state with its capital in Jerusalem, restore the post of consul general in Jerusalem (eliminated by Trump) and perhaps even redefine it as ambassador to Palestine. At the same time, the US would restore funding to the UNRWA and restart US Agency for International Development programmes that the Trump administration shut down in 2019. A right-wing Israeli government would vehemently oppose these initiatives, but a centrist or left-of-centre government might not.

This scenario is not inevitable, however. Joe Biden, for example, would likely maintain the status quo, while a Sanders White House would be more disruptive. From an Israeli perspective, the consequences of a crisis with the US would be offset by diplomatic gains that Jerusalem has made in the Persian Gulf, Asia, Southern and Eastern Europe, and Brazil. Also easing the pain would be the continuing flow of US funds into the IDF budget. From Washington's standpoint, the political consequences would be seen as manageable, given Jewish relief at the recovery of the Democratic Party after Trump and the understanding that the evangelical vote would remain a Republican preserve regardless of US policy toward Israel.

Two powerful countervailing factors could also perpetuate the status quo. Parts of the region could descend into violence as or more severe than what has erupted thus far in Yemen or Syria. If so, Israel will continue to look like the only port for the US in a Middle Eastern storm. And in the US political system, in which congressional representatives must run for office every two years, newly elected members will have to court campaign funding from an array of interest groups, including friends of Israel who command considerable resources both within an institutional framework and outside of it. New members will also have to strike deals with the old guard to secure local benefits for their districts. Thus, despite the clear direction of the survey data, the near-to-medium future might not look very different from the recent past.

As these developments play out, popular representations of Israel again illuminate changing American perceptions of Israel. The sabra imagined as the farm-boy-cum-freedom-fighter has long since faded from the imagination. The Israeli patriot, grimly determined to thwart the plans of treacherous and implacable Palestinians, still hovers in the form of Doron Kavillio, the flawed protagonist of *Fauda*, an Israeli military drama on Netflix set in the present, but he's short, bald, scruffy and miserable. Unambiguously heroic portraits of Israelis are consigned to nostalgic and somewhat jingoistic fare like Netflix's miniseries *The Spy*, in which Sacha Baron Cohen plays the suave Mossad covert operative Eli Cohen, who was executed in Syria in 1965. Baron Cohen's more celebrated character is the burlesque Mossad counter-terrorism expert Colonel Erran Morad, who has a thick Israeli accent and lats so wide he can't lower his arms. He's a hideously funny cartoon to many Americans and a hero to the witless Republicans he dupes in his outrageous, often bawdy charades in Baron Cohen's Showtime spoof series *Who Is America?* No pop-culture character could capture Israel's complexity. But Israelis should still worry when their country's image in the American mind has devolved from Ari Ben Canaan to Erran Morad.

Notes

1 See Emma Green, 'Are Democrats Losing the Jews?', *Atlantic*, 13 November 2014, https://www.theatlantic.com/politics/archive/2014/11/are-democrats-losing-the-jews/382665/.

2 Elizabeth Podrebarac Sciupac and Gregory A. Smith, 'How Religious Groups Voted in the Midterm Elections', Pew Research Center, 7 November 2018, http://www.pewresearch.org/fact-tank/2018/11/07/how-religious-groups-voted-in-the-midterm-elections/.

3 Jeremy Sharon, 'US Jews Contribute Half of All Donations to the Democratic Party', *Jerusalem Post*, 27 September 2016, https://www.jpost.com/US-Elections/US-Jews-contribute-half-of-all-donations-to-the-Democratic-party-468774.

4 See Robert Israel, 'Red Flags for American Jews', *Harvard Divinity Bulletin*, vol. 43, nos. 1 & 2, Winter/Spring 2015, https://bulletin-archive.hds.harvard.edu/articles/winterspring2015/red-flags-american-jews.

5 See Pew Research Center, 'America's Changing Religious Landscape', 12 May 2015, http://www.pewforum.org/2015/05/12/americas-changing-religious-landscape/.

6 'A Portrait of Jewish Americans', Pew Research Center, 1 October 2013, http://www.pewforum.org/2013/10/01/jewish-american-beliefs-attitudes-culture-survey/.

7   See Lauren Markoe, 'US Jewish Numbers No Longer Declining, but Demographic Worries Persist', *Washington Post*, 12 June 2015, https://www.washingtonpost.com/national/religion/us-jewish-numbers-no-longer-declining-but-demographic-worries-persist/2015/06/12/28333b6e-110d-11e5-a0fe-dccfea4653ee_story.html?utm_term=.c5a98a34f174.

8   Aiden Pink, 'Non-Orthodox Jews Will Disappear in Two Generations, Netanyahu Tells Aides', *Forward*, 3 December 2017, 'https://forward.com/fast-forward/388838/non-orthodox-jews-will-disappear-in-two-generations-netanyahu-tells-aides/.

9   Pew Research Center, 'A Portrait of Jewish Americans'; and J Street, 'Polling', https://jstreet.org/polling/#.W_b_cS2ZPvw.

10 AJC/Global Voice, 'AJC 2018 Survey of American & Israeli Jewish Opinion', 10 June 2018, https://www.ajc.org/news/ajc-comparative-surveys-of-israeli-us-jews-show-some-serious-divisions.

11 Chemi Shalev, 'New Poll Shows Support for Israel Plummeting Among U.S. Liberals, Millennials and Women', *Haaretz*, 26 October 2018, https://www.haaretz.com/israel-news/.premium-poll-shows-support-for-israel-plummeting-among-u-s-liberals-millennials-and-women-1.6594182.

12 Pew Research Center, 'Republicans and Democrats Grow Even Further Apart in Views of Israel, Palestinians', 23 January 2018, https://www.people-press.org/2018/01/23/republicans-and-democrats-grow-even-further-apart-in-views-of-israel-palestinians/.

13 National Democratic Committee, '2016 Democratic Party Platform', p. 44, https://democrats.org/where-we-stand/party-platform/.

14 See Jason Horowitz and Maggie Haberman, 'A Split over Israel Threatens the Democrats' Hopes for Unity', *New York Times*, 25 May 2016, https://www.nytimes.com/2016/05/26/us/politics/bernie-sanders-israel-democratic-convention.html.

15 Bob Smietana, 'Millennial Evangelicals on Israel: "Meh"', *Christianity Today*, 4 December 2017, https://www.christianitytoday.com/news/2017/december/us-evangelicals-support-israel-peace-survey-millennial-meh.html.

16 Adam Entous, 'Gaza Crisis: Israel Outflanks the White House on Strategy', *Wall Street Journal*, 14 August 2014, https://www.wsj.com/articles/u-s-sway-over-israel-on-gaza-at-a-low-1407979365.